Mapping Our Selves

Mapping Our Selves,

Canadian Women's Autobiography in English

HELEN M. BUSS

McGill-Queen's University Press
Montreal & Kingston • London • Buffalo

© McGill-Queen's University Press 1993
ISBN 0-7735-0975-5

Legal deposit second quarter 1993
Bibliothèque nationale du Québec

Printed in Canada on acid-free paper

This book has been published with the help of grants
from the Canadian Federation for the Humanities,
using funds provided by the Social Sciences and
Humanities Research Council of Canada, and the
University Endowment Fund of the University of
Calgary. Publication has also been supported by the
Canada Council through its block grant program.

Chapter 2 is a rewritten version of "Preserving
the Past / Rescuing the Self," which appeared in
Reflections: Autobiography and Canadian Literature,
published by the University of Ottawa Press in 1988.
An earlier and shorter version of chapter 4 appeared
in *Biography* (Spring 1990).

Canadian Cataloguing in Publication Data

Buss, Helen M. (Helen Margaret)
 Mapping our selves: Canadian women's autobiography
in English
 Includes bibliographical references and index.
 ISBN 0-7735-0975-5
 1. Autobiography – Women authors. 2. Women –
Canada – Biography. 3. Canadian prose literature
(English) – Women authors – History and criticism.
 I. Title.
 PS8089.5.W6B89 1993 C810.9'49272 C92-090724-5
 PR9188.8.B88 1993

Typeset in Palatino 10/12 by
Caractéra production graphique inc., Quebec City.

To My Family

For my husband, Richard Buss, who, when I needed courage to do my own mapping, gave me the autobiographies of Anna Jameson and Emily Carr, the seeds from which this book grew.

For my father, Harold Clarke, who by his own writing taught me to respect the need we all have for a history of family and place, with the hope that he will appreciate my search for a history and literature of my own.

For my mother, Kathleen Clarke, who once prophesied that since I liked argument so much, I would probably argue with St Peter at the gates of heaven. It is my hope that my writing will persuade her that I have learned to argue well.

For my children, Matthew, Erica, and Michael, whose growth as persons is the seedbed of all I know about identity.

Contents

Acknowledgments

This book began as a doctoral dissertation at the University of Manitoba, where my adviser, Dr Evelyn Hinz, encouraged me to pursue my interest in women's autobiography. It was only because of her generous guidance, her patient instruction, and her editorial rigour that such a project came within the scope of my abilities.

While I was still resident in Manitoba, I was grateful to receive the support of a Social Sciences and Humanities Research Council (SSHRC) doctoral fellowship. Since then, many persons and institutions have helped me, only a few of whom I can thank here. Dr Shirley Neuman, who was the external examiner of my dissertation, encouraged my efforts and shared her own works-in-progress with me. As well, Dr Marlene Kadar has become an enthusiastic co-planner as we both begin to imagine all the ways in which women's neglected autobiographical accounts can be brought to the attention of scholars and the public. I have been the recipient of a Canada Research Fellowship from SSHRC, which brought me to the University of Calgary. I am grateful to the University of Calgary and to the people who work here for the stimulating intellectual atmosphere that gave my theory and practice an invigorating growth in the years since I came here to work. I wish to thank the past and present members of the feminist reading group, Department of English, University of Calgary. In the four years since we have been meeting, they have offered me a place of challenge and adventure that has helped me understand the relationship of the personal and the theoretical, the personal and the professional, the personal and the political, and most importantly, the personal and a feminist critical practice.

Finally, I would like to thank Richard Buss, who took on most of the work of indexing this study.

Mapping Our Selves

My subject is Canadian women's autobiography, and my purpose is to ascertain whether I have in fact a subject, or instead an insoluble riddle, a violent yoking together of incompatible categories. For it is ... not immediately clear that these three elements ought to get along together, in theory at least, in an amicable or productive fashion.

...

The problem in criticism posed by Canadian women's autobiographies is both complex and compelling, and becomes more so all the time. Self-portraits by Canadian women, already numerous, are being added to every year, either through publication of archival material, or in reprint, or as part of the current literary scene. These books stand at the meeting-point of three contemporary developments in scholarship: the recent interest of literary scholars in autobiography, the explosion of feminist research and criticism, and the long-awaited maturation of Canadian writing. If literary criticism is to do justice to all branches of the writing of women in Canada, it can no longer leave autobiographical texts out of account.

Susan Jackel
"Canadian Women's Autobiography: A Problem in Criticism"
Gynocritics / La Gynocritique

Introduction: Contexts

In spite of the fact that autobiography is impossible, this in no way prevents it from existing.

Philippe LeJeune, *On Autobiography*

In closing the "notebook" that describes her 1840 journey across the Atlantic and down the river route from Hudson Bay to Red River, Isabel Finlayson speaks directly to her reader: "But should my little note book ever be perused by the dear domestic circle, for whose amusement it has been written, I feel assured that the eye of affection will regard it with indulgence and forgive its faults for the sake of the Author."[1] As a late twentieth-century feminist reader seeking a women's culture, I want to map the rich ground that lies beneath the self-deprecation of Finlayson's closure. Two markers of figurative language in the quoted text offer me sites for my revisionary reading: her mention of her readers, "the dear domestic circle," and her inscription of her identity as "Author." It is my intent to theorize that the sense of family represented by the "dear domestic circle" offers a way of reading that does not denigrate or elide the domestic, the personal, or insist on the critic's distance from the circle that encompasses writer text, and reader. As well, I want to map the subtleties of women like Finlayson, to better understand the complex subjectivity of women writing themselves into the literature and history of this place.

To do so I begin by exploring current theories of subjectivity as expressed in autobiographical writing. However, to do this is quickly to find oneself between a rock and a hard place. The two figuratively hard theoretical positions are the humanist and the poststructuralist, the first represented by critics such as Georges Gusdorf, the second by figures such as Paul de Man. Gusdorf attempts to set the "Conditions and Limits of Autobiography," finding that the autobiographer occurs only in a civilization with a concept of the unique individual, a "conscious awareness of the singularity of each individual life."[2] Such a society creates a "subject who seizes on himself for object" and heroically experiences the "agonizing sense that the encounter of a man with his image carries. The image is another 'myself,' a double of my being but more fragile and vulnerable, invested with a sacred character that makes it at once fascinating and frightening" (32). For Gusdorf, such a version of the self has only been possible in "the tradition of self-examination" (33) represented by Western Christianity and its desire for self-critical revision, in the romantic tradition of the centrality of the human subject in nature, and in modernity's emphasis on ego development, self-assertion, and individual accomplishment. Therefore, autobiography, the product of such a view of subjectivity, is only properly written by a very select group, all of whom are males shaped in the European tradition. What makes the autobiographical project so possible and necessary for such persons is the transience of the spoken word and the belief that for the self-defining individual "writing adds the virtue of permanence."[3]

Poststructuralists question both the control of the subject over his self-construction and the assumption of the referentiality of language. Paul de Man, in writing "Autobiography as De-facement," recognizes that a writer may want to represent his sense of himself but emphasizes that he must do so in language – by creating a literary figuration that disfigures as much as it figures.[4] De Man's viewpoint is based on the poststructuralist theory of language and subjectivity, which contends that the self, as Paul Jay puts it, "is not a unified psychological representation whose 'essence' or 'identity' is fixed prior to the language which gives it being, but, rather, its essence and identity is constituted in and by the language which produces it."[5] Since that language is only conditionally referential (denotative) and is subject to an infinite play of meaning (connotative), the autobiographical act describes only an illusive, unstable version of a self that did not exist before the act of writing and has little reference to the writer in his ongoing life.

For women writing autobiography, the hard nature of these two extreme versions of subjectivity and its representation in language is contained in what they have in common; that is, both versions exclude women's experience by their assumption of a history and cultural experience that is male and, by implication, a subjectivity that is gendered male. Women's historical and cultural experience has neither allowed them to be the self-actualizing individuals proposed by Gusdorf nor allowed them the illusion of power implied by the power to assume a "face" of their own that can be "de-faced" in the act of writing. In fact, entering language from an already defaced position inside men's culture and language, women and their autobiographical efforts require quite a different description, one that has become the concern of critics and theorists working with women's accounts.

Many of these recent theoretical descriptions of women's autobiography begin with revisions of humanist and poststructuralist positions and are situated around the nexus of Freudian-Lacanian psychoanalytic theory. Whereas Freud explains the development of the individual subject as one centred on the division of mental processes into the unconscious and the conscious and the consequent division of personality into id, ego, and superego, Jacques Lacan revises Freud by contending that the conscious and unconscious are not prior to language making, but rather are constructed from language and thereby exhibit all the characteristics of language.[6] Central to Lacan's thought is his metaphor of the "mirror" stage of human development. Just as a child might realize his or her separateness by seeing his or her reflection in a mirror, so we all, as human beings, begin our development when we begin to use language as a mirror of ourselves. But just as the mirror offers us not the body itself but a two-dimensional image, so language offers us a false self. Language (signs) is our only access to self-construction, and through language we are continually in the process of moving away from fusion, from our existence as an extension of our mother's body, towards separation, a state of false cohesiveness that we construct in imitation of the mirror's (the language's) seemingly cohesive image of our selves. Thus, human development is a condition of lack, of loss; for Lacan it is a castration, which the human child seeks to correct by identifying with the father, the one who commands the power of the phallus, of authority, of symbolic language and the powers it yields. Female identification with the father can, by this reading of identity, never be as full as the male's, since she cannot take on the symbolic power of the phallus. Thus, women's lack in language is greater than men's. Such a theory of human subject formation always involves loss, more for women than men, a loss as great as the loss of Eden, which is figured in a text as central to Western tradition in the past as the male texts of Freud and Lacan have been in this century.

I would like to highlight the work of three women theorists who attempt to come to terms with the consequences for female auto-biographers of Freudian/Lacanian theories of human identity. Each of them makes use of psychoanalytic models, but each tries to exhibit these models as interwoven with the forces of history and culture. This interwoven nature, the idea that psychoanalytic theory is, in fact, a description of cultural and historical situations, is an important theoretical pivot for feminist theorists of subjectivity, for whereas many psychological theorists imply that models are necessarily true in all times for all peoples, that is, essential and ahistorical, these women make explicit the idea that models are descriptive of cultural and historical conditions in different eras and therefore open to variation and change, thus allowing for different gender constructions in different times. Sidonie Smith is helpful in showing this inter-twining of psychology and history by situating the "misbegotten man" identity that Western tradition offers to women. Shari Benstock explores the site of the "seam" between the unconscious and con-scious to make it yield "fissures of female discontinuity," thus offering a view of women's possible variations from male writing styles and models. Susan Stanford Friedman extends the mirror metaphor to its cultural implications to find women's reaction to the special false-ness offered by male cultural constructions of women in language.

Smith's use of Thomas Aquinas's label for woman – the "misbe-gotten man" – helps her illustrate that all Western linguistic/philo-sophic symbol systems, from the Aristotelian through the Christian to the Lacanian, hold that "a female of the species results from a deprivation of nature, a generative process not carried to its conclu-sion."[7] Therefore, if man is fallen, as in Christian belief, or begins from a false position, as in the Lacanian mirror metaphor, then woman is doubly so, since she is not only fallen or false, but has no direct access to the symbolic power of whatever sign represents the opportunity to overcome the state of lack, be it God the father, the phallus, or the patriarchal language. In fact, Smith contends, speaking directly of females' constructions of self in the public genre of autobiography, women's stories always "resonate with privileged cultural fictions of male selfhood" (52) in a genre constructed for and by males.

Smith's work is useful in demonstrating a kind of worst-case sce-nario for women's writing of the self. Her description shows us historically and culturally how bad it can be, has often been, and still is for many women. Shari Benstock offers an imaginative revision of Lacan's mirror image by proposing that we view the place where the conscious and unconscious join as a seam between the inner "je" (I) of the unconscious and the "moi" (me) of the conscious, whose construction begins in the mirror stage. Benstock finds that the female has a very different reaction than the male to encountering the seam between the two possible selves: "Hers is not a shock of recognition in the mirror but rather a linguistic space (a 'scene') that conceals – and tries to seal itself against – the gap (the 'crack') of the unconscious ... 'Writing the self' is therefore a process of simultaneous sealing and splitting that can only trace fissures of discontinuity."[8] Benstock notes that "this division cannot be 'healed'; identity itself rests in this division, the effects of the working of the unconscious" (31). Examining Virginia Woolf's account of her childhood reaction to her mirror image, Benstock uses the sexual abuse of Woolf by her half-brother to symbolize patriarchy's injuries to women, and women's consequent shame and dread on looking into the mirror to symbolize women's subject position on entering language. By this construction of the mirror stage, the fissures of discontinuity traced by writers such as Woolf represent a writing style that has "no investment in creating a cohesive self over time," a writing style that, in fact, suggests that these women "seem to exploit difference and change over sameness and identity; their writing follows the 'seam' of the conscious/unconscious where boundaries between internal and external overlap" (15). By locating the mirror metaphor in the autobiographical work of a prominent woman writer such as Woolf, Benstock not only offers an actual alternate possibility for the critic concerned with women's texts, but also historicizes her psychological paradigm. This is an important point, for once theory is located in practice, then variation is possible, since practice is open to changes due to specific factors – personal, historical, racial, and cultural – and of course open also to changes in gender definitions.

While Smith exposes the dark side of history and culture and Benstock suggests making a stylistic virtue of a historically and culturally necessary condition, Friedman proposes that we use "psycho-political" readings of female-centred social science research in order to discover the more positive results of encountering what the cultural mirror of language reflects to women. She refers to Sheila Rowbotham's theory that women develop a dual consciousness because they do not see anything like themselves in the cultural mirror, and to Nancy Chodorow's observations on the special nature of the mother/daughter relationship and the way in which that relationship allows a female to continue the childhood "experience [of] herself as involved in issues of merging and separation."[9] According to Friedman, women have more "fluid ego boundaries" (44), caused by their different relation with the mother, who as a same-sex significant other identifies more with the female child than the male child and allows a different identification from the female child than from the male child. Because girls always have to come to terms with their similarities to their mothers, they are often led to explore their "sense of shared identity" (44) with other females, as well as their places as separate beings. Friedman proposes a theory of women's writing of the self as a group act by which "women project into history an identity that is not purely individualistic. Nor is it purely collective. Instead, this new identity merges the shared and the unique ... Writing the self shatters the cultural hall of mirrors and breaks the silence imposed by male speech" (40–1).

While helping me to arrive at a psycho-political portrait of women's experience in culture and offering me specific directions for the exploration of women's autobiographies, these women's theoretical positions are still anchored in the mirror metaphor (even when intent on breaking the mirror), and I find the metaphor of the mirror insufficient to describe the core experiences of human identity formation, especially female identity. I am not alone in my discontent with the language currently used to represent theoretical considerations concerning autobiography. Paul John Eakin has argued that the present language of theory is "inadequate to 'picture' 'the thing itself' of life history" and what is needed is a new model of autobiographical discourse to help us read changing autobiographical texts.[10] Eakin's highlighting of Paul de Man's wording (picture, the thing itself) emphasizes the problem with metaphors that are sight and mirror based. It is most important that I deal with the problem of the mirror, since as a metaphor not only is it used by Lacan and poststructuralists, but it is an embedded humanist metaphor as well, the only difference being that the humanists see the mirror as capable of revealing truth, while poststructuralists, realizing the slipperiness of linguistic mirrors, expose its falsity. Bella Brodzki and Celeste Schenck propose that since "the archetypal female prop of the mirror has been used variously in relation to woman, and always ... *against* her," we replace the mirror metaphor, as Luce Irigaray does, by appropriating the instrument used in the gynaecological examination of females, the speculum. As an instrument that "seeks both to reflect and to penetrate interiority," the speculum can be used to restore female subjectivity, but "without romanticization," by allowing us to inquire into "the distorting mirror of male-inscribed literary work."[11]

However, I find the speculum as problematic a metaphor as the mirror. Despite its practical use in feminist consciousness-raising as a method of increasing women's knowledge of their own bodies, I find that as metaphor it remains external to the subject, a penetrating instrument that relegates the female to passive object of an observing, non-subjective, male science.

I wish to use another metaphor, one that can represent not only the individual subject's psychic development in language, but also the activities of female writing of the self and the critical and theoretical acts to which that writing gives birth. I propose a very old, but hopefully reconstituted, metaphor derived from the ancient art/science of cartography.[12] One of the limitations of mirror/speculum metaphors is their dependence on the sense of sight, certainly not the only sense on which language making and identity making are dependent. Cartography, although usually producing maps dependent on sight, may also produce relief maps so accurate in their scale and subtlety that they can teach the blind the contours of the world. Map making also involves a complex of intellectual and practical skills that offer a dynamic metaphor far superior to any offered by passive mirror gazing. As well, mapping can be seen metaphorically as joining the activities of self-knowledge and knowledge of the world. Language "maps" both the self and the coexistent world. If I understand the child's activity in language as an increasingly sophisticated mapping of the embodied self and the external world and as an activity that grows in complexity in direct relationship to the language makers around the child, then I am not forced by my metaphor to propose some climactic moment or stage in which the child experiences the crisis of separation as opposed to fusion. As well, in the art of mapping, the child's language making and self-construction in language allow for both *survey maps*, actual sensory exploration of self-territory and other-territory from various vantage points, and *compilation maps*, selections made from the information contained in the surveys.

Obviously each child will survey and compile differently, depending on many factors of biological inheritance and cultural situation. Gender, like biological sex, race, class, national, and ethnic considerations, will be a great influence on the personal map each child learns to construct. For some, the mapping of the personal self, the embodied self and its possibilities, will seem an activity very different from mapping the world outside the body. This will have much to do with the conditions of the first experiences of the sense of one's separateness as a body. For example, if a child first maps separateness through the time-honoured game of peek-a-boo with a beloved parent, and what is hidden always returns laughing with shared pleasure (and if the parent chooses to "reappear" just before curiosity turns to anxiety), then the experience of separation and rejoining becomes a delightful game. If these initial experiences are enacted in the context of the touch of loving arms and the sound of a reassuring voice, then the mapping of one's separate self is always contextualized by the ways in which one is joined to the other. At the same time, the Lacanian scenario of loss is quite easily imagined as well. The metaphor of mapping does not preclude the possibility of highly traumatic experiences of self as separate; it merely contextualizes the mirror stage as one possible scenario. Thus, what I seek in the mapping metaphor is the possibility of multiplicity of identity formation within a single process. For me, the Lacanian metaphor lacks the complexity to express the multiplicity that is human personality.

As a metaphor, the activity of mapping is more useful to me than mirroring because it implies both picture making and lettering, so that development is metaphorically interdisciplinary and multisensual from its beginning. It is also profoundly culturally influenced, so that just as map making for the early Babylonians (who were very speculative in map making) was a very different activity than it was for the early Greeks (who added skills based on astronomy and mathematics), so making the maps of self and world is different for people growing up in different cultural and historical moments. It is also an activity one can professionalize by learning the special skills of astronomy, mathematics, drafting, and so on. I would compare this professionalization to the special status chosen by those who write their lives. Besides using language, as all humans do, to map the self and the world for the purposes of daily living, the autobiographer makes special surveys of personal experience, retrospective and/or ongoing, while the critic and theorist of autobiography work to compile the individual surveys in different ways so as to facilitate awareness, understanding, and future map making activities. Similarly, the historian of autobiography performs a kind of archaeological map making, marking out a territory for excavation, recording the location of each find, contextualizing it in terms of the total site, and thus unearthing the neglected, lost areas of human life, untouched by history. Mapping also recognizes that the world changes over time: waterways change their course, oceans rise and fall, erosion wears at the contours of earth, wind builds up soil around ancient cities. A mapping of autobiography recognizes both the palimpsest of layers in human subjects and the erosion of those layers; it recognizes that the contours of the world, the language people use to shape the self, to communicate the self, the ways that language assigns meaning, creates symbols, have not always been the same. Indeed, mapping itself and its technologies change constantly, shifting and readjusting our concepts of the self and the world. The word "mapping" and attendant terms such as survey, compilation, selection, drafting, reproduction, relief, contour, terrain, model, symbolization, shading, and projection can be used as analogues for the ways in which humans use language to know themselves and the world and to know also that the world as they know it and those selves *are* the language (the maps) that produces them. I wish to use these terms in mapping both the individual surveys of experience I study here and the critical activities associated with the language of autobiography and its theory.

Mapping is also a more useful metaphor than mirroring because it more closely figures what language actually does, but at the same time does not lie to us in the way the mirror pretends to be the thing that it reflects. A map does not pretend to reflect the world; certainly an archaeological site does not pretend to map the whole of human history on the earth. Problems with representing perspective, scale, size, relief, and the arts used to overcome these problems are externalized in the map itself; all the structuring devices of the archaeological site are painstakingly evident. I hope I too can externalize the particulars of the mapping I undertake here.

The history of map making has grown from pictures on cave walls of humans and their abodes, animals and their territories, to the kind of accurate mapping of the planetary system now accomplished by space vehicles that command all the arts and sciences of humans. From earliest time, when women may well have been the first drawers of ephemeral maps in the dirt of the earth, to very recently, the more professionalized and politicized and therefore more powerful map-making activities, those used for exploration, trade, warfare, and empire, have been men's activities. This is true also of language. In most cultures with a history of written language, societal and biological pressures have worked to leave women almost completely in charge of the earliest mappings a human child makes of the self and the world, and almost completely excluded from direct participation in the more power-based mappings of a culture. This means that not only have women not had direct access to whatever knowledge the "sophisticated" map makers have, but the men who make a culture's maps have had no direct access, after early childhood, to what women learn of language mapping in the world that has contained

their work. Gender must then be, historically and culturally, a powerful influence on the way we make maps, the way in which mapping
(language making) shapes our view of ourselves and the world.

   When I refer to the way in which one group or another is excluded
from certain kinds of language usages, I wish to avoid the limited
and dualistic positions implied by Lacanian theory. I do not see
language as sharply divided into presymbolic and symbolic language,
as if mothers and their infants, joined in presymbolic communication,
lived on a different planet from those that use language as symbol.
In fact, our first experiments in using language as symbol are most
likely to be shared experiences with our mothers. However, access to
particular language usages, and to the power systems that accom-
pany those usages, has varied over history according to one's sex,
one's role in life. This political fact shapes psychological development.
It is my wish to use my mapping metaphor to put psychoanalytic
models in cultural/historical contexts, showing how mapping identity
for females can partake of that world of first language mappings in
a way that culture does not encourage for men. The metaphor also
allows me to show that Lacan's theory of women's exclusion from
symbolic language is not a psychological necessity but a political fact,
and that the problem lies not with women but with the maps men
have made, that is, with the language and its usages from which
women have been excluded. As well, by implication, the psychological construction of men's identities may have less to do with the
necessary loss on entering symbolic language than with their cultural
poverty when it comes to the language of the intimate world of
relationship and child rearing, which culture encourages them to
leave early in life. Finally, at no time do I wish to imply that exclusion
is complete for either group. Language usages leak into one another,
individuals follow eccentric talents despite societal conditioning, and
subversion of dominant discourses is always a possibility.[13]

   With this in mind I return to the mappings of the women who are
concerned with the theoretical mapping of women's autobiographical
efforts. I find that although there is much that is useful from the
psychological, social, cultural, historical, and political "maps" of theorists such as Benstock, Friedman, and Smith (who themselves col-
late maps by feminist, humanist, and poststructuralist theorists), I
am especially helped in the mapping of Canadian women's autobiography, of my home territory so to speak, by two Canadian theorists, Shirley Neuman and Marlene Kadar. Neither is concerned
exclusively with Canadian women, as I am in this study, but both
offer me revisions of certain generic considerations that give me an

important meridian for my methodology. As one trained in literary perspectives more than in psychological, sociological, or historical perspectives, I am predisposed to identify the generic aspects of written works. The generic aspect establishes where a work situates itself in terms of both public and private genres and tells much of its cultural and personal contexts. Thus, as well as considering psycho-cultural aspects of women's accounts, I wish to include the insights into the works offered by locating them in a range of literary genres.   .

Neuman, in speaking of women's "life narratives," describes a kind of writing that combines aspects of manifesto, drama, novel, and poetry in order to write a selfhood that must find itself in the gap, the fissure, the slit, the lack, that exits between the dominant culture's representation of women (in every mode from the evening news to pornography, as well as literary genres) and women's perceptions of themselves. Such writing, Neuman finds, must be "consciously illusive," lyrical, utopian, erotic, to give expression to the female agency that remembers/invents the female bodies that culture has not allowed women to know.[14] While Neuman ties the psycho-political writings of other theorists to broad considerations of generic choices and actual writing styles, Kadar makes a direct call for a literary-political activism that comes from naming a new genre of life-writing that "allows the canonical, or marginally canonical, to be considered alongside the legitimately marginal" and will allow "us to get rid of both the wooly terms and the implicit value judgements" learned from our former genre education.[15] "Naming" is a powerful linguistic act, formerly reserved for patriarchal figures from Adam to the makers of modern dictionaries. Kadar is working to make us question the systems by which all of us, from the least to the most sophisticated readers, have internalized genre rankings. Public genres are ranked above private genres, print over electronic media (perhaps this is reversing), aesthetically privileged genres, such as poetry and theatre, over more accessible genres, such as the novel and film. I find that any consideration of what women in the past have written of their selves and their lives, as well as the ways in which women of the present are attempting to recuperate and reinvent their sense of female living, must be placed in the context of what forms of showing and telling, what literary mapping techniques, have been available as means of expression. How women have worked inside these genres, bridged them, undermined them, tells me much about the conscious and unconscious selves of the writers. Thus, my psycho-cultural map will be informed by a generic overlay.

GENERIC CONTEXTS

We live our lives through texts. They may be read, or chanted, or experienced electronically, or come to us like the murmurings of our mothers ... Whatever their form or medium, these stories have formed us all; they are what we must use to make new fictions, new narratives.

Carolyn G. Heilbrun, *Writing a Woman's Life*

In this study I will present only written texts, but they will range from diaries that seem naive of any literary considerations, through accounts hardly distinguishable from novels, to sophisticated and subtle texts by women who have studied the productions of postmodern literary masters. I will call them all "autobiographies." I am tempted to call them "life narratives" as Shirley Neuman does, "personal narratives" as Lenore Hoffman and Margo Culley do, "autogynographies" or "autographs" as Domna Stanton does, "lifewritings" as Marlene Kadar does; all of these terms teach me something about the way lives have been uttered.[16] My choice of the older term, autobiography, probably has a great deal to do with my own need to refresh old terms rather than invent new ones. But as well, even though "autobiography" has some unfortunate connotations of the "biographies" of public men's lives (historically, in English, the term derives from biography), and even though the history of autobiographical theory from Misch through Olney to Mehlman and Jay largely documents the erection and dismantling of an ego-centred and male-centred writing history, the term's Greek source words offer enough play of meaning to provide me with a suitable term to investigate the generic considerations important to women's works.[17] *Autos* (self), *bios* (life), and *graphie* (writing) are the three Greek terms that fortuitously describe what is involved when we set out to write autobiographically. None of the terms can be left out and none of them can be taken for granted. It is also fortuitous that they remind us always of another language, of strangeness, so that no matter how familiar "autobiography" becomes, no matter how powerful a certain kind of generic expression becomes in a certain culture, the word's very explicit foreignness each time we write it, every time we say it aloud, destabilizes it and makes it new again. The very fact that it is tied to self and life as well as to writing helps to keep it from being too long appropriated by any one generic writing form. The life-centred accounts of famous men have given way to the self-centred accounts of postmodern male writers who concern themselves with the concept that their selves may not have the firmness their fathers believed in, but rather may be merely a trace of the "graphy," the signs they scribble and gesture into the world. As James Olney points out, in our century we have moved from emphasizing the "bio" as life history, to beginning a re-examination of our sense of what "auto" or self means, to questioning the whole problematic of language as "graphy."[18] Some women theorists now want to remove the "bio" to emphasize that life accomplishment may not be true to the "auto." The word becomes further destabilized when we consider the implications of "graphy" not just as the alphabet of letters that makes writing, but "graphy" as mapping, which implies many alphabets of communication, from writing to graphs. Metaphorically, the mapping of an identity could be told through a language of oral signs or a choreography of gestures from many arts.

Before the subject of autobiography begins to seem in "great and present danger," as Olney puts it, of "slip[ping] away altogether," let me emphasize that the very unstable nature of the word is what makes it suitable for describing the writing acts featured in this study, for those acts have been found to be themselves fairly unstable. The word used by Estelle Jelinek in 1980, when she set out to describe the features of women's autobiography as opposed to men's, was "discontinuous."[19] The word presents problems because it implies that there is a continuous style in autobiography, which would be more male. In other words, women's works seem discontinuous only when we evaluate them by culturally established norms of what makes for a continuous account. What Benstock calls the "fissures" of female identity have bearing here. If, in a culture made to suit others' needs, women find identity not always located in that man-made map, but seemingly welling up from some unwritten, unspoken other map, other language, from the unconscious, then such identity would be experienced exactly as a fissure or as any of the other parallel words used by Neuman, such as slit, gap, or even lack. I have called this possibility of alternate identity "a black hole." This term works for me because it suggests the negative emotions with which many women first recognize parts of themselves not described or permitted by the dominant culture. As well, in its current scientific meaning, a black hole appears at first observation to be a negation in a universe of positive bodies, a place where matter is sucked in, made to disappear. But on our further investigation, the black hole promises to be a place where matter is so dense that none of the normal ways we have used to map the universe can give it a language. Perhaps this is what is happening in the discontinuous, fissured style of many women's accounts.[20]

Françoise Lionnet describes the efforts undertaken by many postcolonial women (women of colour, of the Third World, of ethnic marginality, etc.) as a positive expression of this phenomenon, in which such writers undertake a *métissage*, a hybridization or braiding of "cultural forms through the simultaneous revalorization of oral traditions and reevaluation of Western concepts." Lionnet feels that this practice leads to the "recovery of occulted histories." What would first seem marginal, even negative, in one's identity (by European, male cultural standards) is revalued so that "opacity and obscurity" are recognized as the "precious ingredients of all authentic communication."[21] Therefore, if mapping female identity can be enhanced by finding strategies for surveying and compiling what has previously been unused, then accounts that seemed merely discontinuous can be seen as extending the possible realms of "fictivity," as Victoria Myers has claimed for the style of an autobiographer such as Maxine Hong Kingston. Myers finds that Kingston mixes "techniques usually associated with myths and tales together with techniques more usually associated with non-fiction" to create a refreshed version of what is acceptable fictive technique. Interestingly, Myers connects this generic strategy with a psychological phenomenon in that Kingston wishes not only to locate her identity in "the perceiving self" but also to "locate ... it in her effort to extricate her voice from the many already existing voices of tradition, myth, and story in her speech community."[22]

Both Lionnet and Myers put emphasis on the speech or oral sources of these identity strands, showing how these women value language as *parole* (communication) rather than as *langue* (abstract system). The desire to communicate immediately implies a community and many theorists have commented on how women's autobiographical efforts are connected to a desire to actively engage some significant other in their past, present, or future life. This phenomenon has been called women's desire for a sense of "alterity" (Mason), of a "plural self" (Sommer), or of community whereby a woman's "I" is a "kind of connective tissue" (Watson) rather than an ego construction emphasizing separation and individuality.[23] Bella Brodzki offers an intriguing psycho-linguistic explanation for this special sense of otherness when she connects women autobiographers' relationship to language to the operation of the mother/daughter bond:

The[se] autobiographies [those of Natalie Sarraute and Christa Wolf] ... struggle with the complicitous (and not always revolutionary) relationship between displacement and language. The struggle, represented by each narrator's/protagonist's linguistic disability or instability and cultural disorientation, pivots on one figure or object: her mother. Emblematic of the way language itself obscures and reveals, withholds and endows, prohibits and sanctions, the mother in each text hovers from within and without. Still powerful and now inaccessible (literally or figuratively), she is the pre-text for the daughter's autobiographical project. Indeed, these autobiographical narratives are generated out of compelling need to enter into discourse with the absent or distant mother. As the child's first significant Other, the mother *engenders* subjectivity through language; she is the primary source of speech and love. And part of the maternal legacy is the conflation of the two. Thereafter, implicated in and overlaid with other modes of discourse, the maternal legacy of language becomes charged with ambiguity and fraught with ambivalence. In response (however deferred), the daughter's text, variously, seeks to reject, reconstruct and reclaim – to locate and recontextualize – the mother's message.[24]

Brodzki's conflation of language and maternal relationship has enormous and compelling implications for the consideration of how women relate to a culture's literary genres. If women build themselves in language, not in a continuing act of defining the separate self, as has been suggested by Freudians for male development, but in a continuing act of separation/merging, what I would call a *re-e-merging* process, then the forms they are drawn to will emphasize this desire. They will construct maps of relationship within forms that emphasize the integration (or reintegration) of the individual in the various contexts of human society. Even when some significant other has replaced or displaced the mother, one might expect issues of maternality to predominate in the new relationship, and thus in the autobiographical account. When one defines one's life on the grounds of successful separation, individual achievement, and abstract goals, one requires quite different means of expression than when one defines a *living* where all achievements, personal and communal, are interrelated. In autobiographies written before the contemporary historical moment, the sense of inner self will have much more to do with the private world informed by the mother than with the public world informed by the father. Positive and negative feelings for the mother will affect all activities, including the writing of the autobiography. However, since all women enter public generic forms burdened by the plots, images, and symbols of a male genre, as Smith would have it, "with privileged cultural fictions of male selfhood," the effect of the maternal pre-text may well be hidden by or be in contention with these privileged fictions. Thus, reading generically, a critic will need to be watchful, not only for the ways in which women situate themselves inside the genre, but also for the ways their texts transgress the generic bounds in search, consciously or unconsciously, of their maternal pre-texts.

One of the most privileged genres of the history of generic development in the last two hundred years (until very recently) has not been autobiography, but rather the novel. As Evelyn Hinz has commented, "the hegemony of the novel has misled critics [of autobiography] into using a generic analogy that is too purely literary" and drama may well provide a better touchstone for comparative purposes. Indeed, drama, with its emphasis on ritual re-enactment, may well better describe the kind of psychic scene making and the need for reintegration with the maternal pre-text noted in the theories of the female psyche presented by Benstock and Brodzki. Drama highlights aspects of "visual immediacy or quality of actual presence," as well as the contextual nature of autobiography, referential as it is to actual lived lives.[25] Dramatic analogues also work well in terms of my mapping metaphor, as actual maps are often re-enactments of voyages of discovery during which the map maker has to ritually repeat certain measurement acts under highly dramatic situations, from conditions of adverse weather to conditions of warfare. However, other critics have in the past proposed the diary as touchstone form, since it is particularly generically facilitating for women, and I have proposed that the memoir is also a serviceable genre for women's self-inscription.[26] I prefer to leave the question of genre as open as possible because of the transgressive nature of women's approaches to genre decisions and in order to preclude too swift a closure in a territory where mapping has only recently begun.

In this regard it would be well to locate the more speculative theories within a historical portrait of women's lives in culture, and in cultural genres, during the time period of concern (for this study the eighteenth to the twentieth centuries). Margo Culley, for example, points out that the history of the diary, a form that became increasingly popular with women as the nineteenth century progressed, is one of movement from the semi-public world of family and community history to the private world where the intimate diary explores the individual psyche. Culley emphasizes that the romantic movement's discovery of the secular self, the industrial revolution's splitting of life into the public and private domains, and the more recent study of individual consciousness by psychoanalysis have been the broad cultural forces shaping the generic changes in the diary.[27] Although earlier diaries will, on the surface at least, be more concerned with the social fabric of women's lives, especially in the case of emigrating women "for whom that fabric had been torn" (4), later diaries may more directly manifest the personal psychic condition previously described. But even the earlier ones will be concerned with connection and reintegration, albeit in terms of the "kin and community networks" (4) rather than in terms of individual psychology. As a genre, Culley concludes, the diary offers rich research in the "surprises, mysteries and silences" of women's lives (21).

These "surprises, mysteries and silences" may not only be a result of the increasingly private referential world of the diary genre, but also be contingent on the particular historical and cultural facts of an "oppression based on gender" that Felicity A. Nussbaum describes in her exploration of eighteenth century women's public autobiographies.[28] These writers had little access to philosophical discourse, equal wages or equality under the law, creating in them a "dichotomy between public passivity and private energy" that makes such autobiographers exist in a divided world with many psychic consequences (150–1). By the nineteenth century, as Linda Peterson points out, women are not so much excluded from public discourse as they are excluded from the ability to analyse, compare, or combine ideas by a culturally valorized version of women's psychology that limits female language-making activities.[29] Thus, even when they undertake to imitate forms such as the *res gestae* of adventurers or the spiritual confessions of religious figures, their exclusion from certain kinds of public discourse and their sophistication in some modes of private discourse, undervalued in the history of the chosen genre, affect their writing and its reception.

Patricia Meyer Spacks's series of articles and books on female identity in literature (written over two decades) has described the various shades of female oppression and opportunity during three centuries and offers a composite portrait of many of the features of women's cultural position, especially as it manifests itself in the Anglo-American tradition. She describes the ways in which women have had to establish selfhood based on their operating within assumed limitations, since, given their oppressed positions, they cannot hope to surmount societal limits as men might. They often compensate by "transform[ing] difficult reality into glamorous myth."[30] Therefore, as a way of dealing with their social situation, women tend to mythologize their lives, each autobiographer "affirming her womanhood through imagination" rather than action.[31] As well, Spacks sees women as having a great preoccupation with being good rather than exceptional. This is because being exceptional is specifically forbidden by the definitions of womanliness in the culture and because being good, that is, fitting into a carefully prescribed behaviour, is the norm expected. This situation leads to a desire on the part of the woman to examine every part of her life to see how it measures up to internalized standards of goodness, standards that may well be at war with the reasons the woman wanted to write her autobiography, that is, as a record of her achievement. This accounts for what Spacks calls the "expressiveness" of women's accounts, a style in which autobiographers need to set down, seemingly spontaneously, the textured detail of life in an effort to find the goodness, to give the impression that all demands have been met.[32] Obviously, this would lead to a very different style and content than that of a text preoccupied with how one great talent or achievement, or one very specific course in life, made the subject exceptional, outstanding, separate from his social milieu.

In *Gossip*, Spacks illustrates how this private and denigrated mode of communication, often associated with women, has had a widespread and unacknowledged presence in more public genres, thus suggesting that growing up female may actually be a linguistic advantage in certain writing situations. Spacks contends that women have often made an autobiographical advantage of a disadvantaged societal position, and in her most recent work she gives a literary formality to what she once called the "disguises" under which women wrote, by referring to the various rhetorics of female autobiographical expression.[33] And, in fact, this strategy of giving a critical naming to what has been denigrated is a useful way to point to the imaginative generic variations women have made in the past inside generic restriction and allows us to re-evaluate texts formerly marginalized because of their lack of complete adherence to generic rules.

Historical investigation tends to verify that subjectivity, language, and cultural situation are interrelated. As long as the conditions of conflicting role demands, of alienation from public genres, and of suppression of creative expression exist, women will have to don various disguises, create their own rhetorics, as Spacks puts it, in order to write their lives. Therefore, women's accounts in many ways will "lie" about the generic choices they emphasize as well as the issues and concerns they focus upon; other agendas may lie necessarily hidden beneath respectable generic choices and acceptable subjects. But lying does not necessarily mean that an autobiography does not tell the truth. The lie told may be autobiographically very telling in the context of the entire written account. As Timothy Dow Adams observes, quoting Roy Pascal: "What we choose to misrepresent is as telling as what really happened, because the shape of our lives often distorts who we really are, and because as Roy Pascal reminds us 'consistent misrepresentation of oneself is not easy,' even those autobiographers with the most problematic approach to lying should be valued for telling the truth of their lives."[34]

What Spacks would call "disguises," or more recently, "rhetorics," and what Adams might call "telling lies" are ways in which women negotiate a map of the ground of their personal psychology, their linguistic dichotomies, their cultural positions, within the generic choices offered by literary history, to create maps that select across a range of generic features, modelling and shading them to communicate the contour and terrain of their existence, while fitting that existence into the symbolization and compilations recognizable to the readers with whom they expect to communicate. The reader's influence on genre, a most important feature of life-writing, has recently been emphasized by Neuman in *Literary History of Canada:* "Biography, autobiography, memoirs, diaries, letters, travel-writing: each establishes a different relationship with the reader."[35] It is my own relationship, as reader, to the writings under consideration that I would now like to explore, thus bringing another overlay to my growing map, one that recognizes my specific literary and ideological location as a reader of texts.

REFLEXIVE CONTEXTS

I understand that the place I am now occupying will not be left out of the exhibit or withdrawn from the scene. Nor do I intend to withhold even that which I shall call, to save time, an *autobiographical* demonstration, although I must ask you to shift its sense a little and to listen to it with another ear. I wish to take a certain pleasure in this, so that *you may learn this pleasure from me.*

Jacques Derrida, *The Ear of the Other*

In 1980, James Olney pointed out that a special feature of autobiographical research was that it "requires a reader ... to participate fully in the process, so that the created self becomes, at one remove, almost as much the reader's as the author's."[36] In 1984 Domna Stanton observed that feminist research in women's autobiography seemed to suggest that "the feminist scholar's own identity depended on the referential reality of the woman in the text, as if that woman was the same and different other through whom F[eminist] S[cholar] needed to construct and relate her self."[37] Although Olney's and Stanton's statements would seem to point to a related phenomenon, they are of a different order. Olney's words recall the theory of the phenomenology of reading as proposed by Georges Poulet: "The extraordinary fact in the case of a book is the falling away of the barriers between you and it. You are inside it; it is inside you; there is no longer either outside or inside."[38] Barrett Mandel describes this merging of reader and autobiographer in lyrical terms as "sharing life," as belonging, as being mutually "embodied by language."[39]

These descriptions are versions of the kind of romance of reading, or the erotics of the text, proposed by Roland Barthes in the *Pleasure of the Text*, in which pleasure and, in more elite texts, bliss occur when the merging is one in which the text "wounds or seduces" the reader.[40]

The feminist scholar's reading implies something a measure more complicated than the surrender to a rather violent kind of romantic love. After all, most metaphors based on romantic love have the implied assumption that someone gives up identity, consciousness, in the merging. Traditionally that figure has been the woman, or the more yielding partner (and therefore more womanly) in the couple formation. Poulet, Mandel, and Barthes would seem to indicate the reader is "woman" in a reader/writer context. However, a feminist reading for identity, referentiality, and otherness implies a very complex activity involving active and sophisticated operations of both the emotions and intellect, rather than a simple surrender to a very gendered pleasure.

Patrocinio Schweickart explores the various recent theories of reader response in order to suggest differences in the way both women and women who are feminists read texts. In order to do this she explores a passage by Adrienne Rich in which Rich figures herself as reading Emily Dickinson. Schweickart summarizes Rich's inter-subjective reading as a dialectic in three parts: "The first moment of the dialectic reading is marked by the recognition of the necessary duality of subjects; the second, by the realization that this duality is threatened by the author's absence. In the third moment the duality of subjects is referred to the duality of contexts. Reading becomes a mediation between author and reader, between the context of writing and the context of reading."[41] Schweickart's exploration of reading is useful to me in that she emphasizes the recognition, not of subject/object relationships as do most reader-response theories (even when expressed in the language of eroticism), but rather the subject/subject nature of reading: I as a person am in conversation with the voice of another person. This gives urgency to the second part of the dialectic of reading, that I recognize that the text represents an absent subjectivity, one different from my own, that cannot reply to me, interrupt me, as in a real conversation. I need to make a special effort to allow this subjectivity to speak to me in a voice different from my own. Thus, "reading induces a doubling of the reader's subjectivity, so that one can be placed at the disposal of the text while the other remains with the reader" (135). I do this through the third part of the dialectic whereby I recognize the circumstances of the writer and the contexts of my own reading in a very personal way, and I indicate that to *my* reader by my rhetoric of the personal voice. The "personal voice serves as a gesture warding off any inclination to appropriate the authority of the text as a warrant for the validity of the interpretation" (136).

This kind of reading is very active. A reader must explore her own perspectives in terms of gender, class, culture, and disciplinary orientation. An active search for self-knowledge precedes and accompanies the exploration of the other. As well, the reader must undertake to know all that she reasonably can about the personal, cultural, historical, and literary contexts that informed the writer. This contextual reading, when undertaken systematically by professional readers, is what Barbara Myerhoff and Jay Ruby call "reflexivity," and it creates a style of scholarly writing in which "we are not allowed to slip back into the everyday attitude that claims we can naively trust our senses. We are brought into a different reality because the interplay between illusion and reality continues. The frame is repeatedly violated, and the two stories [researcher's and subject's], commenting on each other, travel alongside, simultaneously commanding our attention and creating a different world than either represents by itself."[42] Such an interplay is sometimes experienced as intrusive by readers accustomed to having a researcher assume objectivity or address special biases outside the body of the work. But for the kind of reading I intend to undertake, the intrusion is absolutely necessary. For me, a particularly important aspect of this kind of reading, one not commented on by the theorists I have quoted, is the need to emphasize the names of the critics and theorists who shape my reading strategies. They are subjects also, and I wish to acknowledge that and refer my readers to their utterances through the use of their names in the text as well as in the notes, bibliography, and index. If one undertakes this kind of very active, personal reading, a reading that in Barbara Godard's words is "dynamic, empathetic,"[43] of both autobiographers and critics, the reader accustomed to the defacement of the personal in scholarly writing will perhaps be led to consider the investigation unscholarly.

The risk must be taken, for the more personal reading is essential to my mapping. For one thing, the works I read are often very personal in nature, only minimally constructed for public readers. In diaries we are engaged in a task of decoding encoded materials; that is, we use historical knowledge unavailable to the diarist to decode significances in her writing, whereas she had personal knowledge she has not shared with us, but which led her to encode certain presences as silences in her text. As Margo Culley puts it, paraphrasing a poem by Adrienne Rich, we identify the "technology, ritual, etiquette, plan, history and form" of these silent presences (23). For example, one of the most consistent silent presences in women's accounts in the past has been caused by the absence of any language of conception, pregnancy, labour, and delivery. Babies are announced after the reader has worked through many seemingly unpregnant months with a diarist. But reading for encoding allows the researcher to mitigate the silence that male-centred language imposed on women's real lives. Undertaking such activities is a great responsibility for the reader and requires that the researcher confess "the underlying epistemological assumptions that have caused the formulation of a set of questions in a particular way, the seeking of answers to those questions in a particular way, and finally the presentation of the findings in a particular way."[44]

As well, a woman autobiographer may be engaged in an attempt to differentiate identity strands that are her own and those assumed by her community, identification that will allow her a sense of herself more in keeping with her experience of her self. She may also be attempting to do this within the restrictions of a certain genre tradition not easily turned to new purposes. Such a writer, Victoria Myers suggests, will "construct a complex interaction of implications"[45] demanding an understanding by the researcher of the "system of implicature" in the given community, and an ability to "distinguish between the implicature of the literary conversation and the implicatures of the discourse as a whole" (117).

These considerations turn the time-honoured activity of reading between the lines into a complex operation, but a necessary one. For example, cultural definitions of a "good" woman as one always sacrificing the self for the other has meant that while it is possible for a woman to write a memoir (a recounting of one's place as a member of a group) without too much censure, autobiography (the account of one's self-development) is a risky activity for women. A researcher must expect that a woman's memoir will often be more than it purports to be. For example, Lynn Bloom points out that in the accounts of women pioneers we must always consider the "figure-ground" relationship and see that although the woman may emphasize the pioneer "ground," she may be also involved in representing the special nature of her "figure" in that ground.[46]

In fact, we are, in reading any woman's accounts, as Helen Carr observes regarding native women's accounts, engaged in "interpreting a text in which a marginalized subject speaks a dominant discourse" that requires a Ricoeurian "hermeneutics of suspicion" by which the reader recognizes that women are always inscribed as other in patriarchal language and "texts give no direct access to an 'author' or to 'true' women's experience."[47] If that is true, what happens to the feminist scholar's need for the referential reality of the account under consideration? Carr suggests that we see these accounts as examples of Freud's talking cure, which offers these women the chance to become subjects (137). Therefore, although we may not completely accept the literal reality of the figure the autobiographer presents, we believe in the power it gave her and we believe in the power of language to liberate her desires, her deeply felt selfhood. Like Domna Stanton, we can see women's accounts as having "a global and essential therapeutic purpose: to constitute the female subject" (14).

Lionnet's braiding metaphor is useful here. For not only does the writer braid an identity, but as reader I may "allow my self to be interwoven with the discursive strands of the text, to engage in a form of intercourse wherein I take my interpretive cues from the patterns that emerge as a result of this encounter" (28). I hold that in such an intercourse something of the merging of erotic reading is implied, but something of a conversation is also suggested: that is, if there is love making here it is a learned love making, not a surrender guided only by an (impossibly) unconditioned instinct. It demands equality, active initiation and response, and a non-coercive interweaving of self and other.

For me, the metaphor of lovers is not a sufficient one, but the metaphor of reading I am offered by Schweickart, that of poets Adrienne Rich and Emily Dickinson in intimate but polite conversation, is also not fully sufficient to figure the complex of responsibilities and pleasures that my reading embraces. Although I want to retain some of the erotics of ecstasy that physical love making between lovers connotes, I seek a metaphor that maps relationships that male-centred discourses have muted, distorted, and ignored in favour of the privileging of those more obviously based on physical erotic desire. I seek a metaphor that maps subtleties which the plots of traditional genres cannot encompass. I seek "(m)othering." By this bracketed version of mothering, I mean to imply the configuration of three relationships with significant others that I know in actual life. I wish to be mother, sister, and daughter to the text I read, and I wish my reading to contain all the dynamics of those three relationships.

I want to be very certain that my readers do not immediately assume that I am sentimentalizing my reading strategies with motherhood statements. I choose my metaphor very deliberately. All reading is institutionalized. Certainly the accounts of reader-response critics indicate theirs is institutionalized in the framework of the academy and its disciplines. The institution I know best, the one where my initial responses to language were formed, where I was first read to and learned the rudiments of reading, the institution in which I gave others their first "readings," is the family. Since this is the context in which my subjectivity as reader was first formed, it is a suitable metaphor for my reading.

If I am to be the mother of the text, I will hold more responsibility in reading than if I were in intimate conversation with an equal other. Mothering is the most profoundly radical intersubjectivity. It demands a consciousness that understands it is in intercourse with a subject that is not absent, but not yet formed, that needs the most enabling, nurturing, and delicate of intercourses possible, one that at every moment is open in every way to nuance, to feeling, to possibility. It is an excitingly contingent situation. It is terrifyingly open to failure, breathtakingly open through its healing affective activities to retrieving success from failure. Like the reading of a text, its conditions of existence change with every moment. Mothering demands every reader ability, from patience through tolerance to imagination. But the most radical demand of mothering is the necessity of knowing that although one's nurturing love seems to have given the text its very being, the text is finally and profoundly the other. It is not an extension of myself. If I am to fully read it, I must recognize its separateness, its own life.

In doing so I can become the sister of the text, and since my text is a woman's text, there will be many parallels between my subjectivity and the subject it expresses. One of the startling reading phenomena of reading women's autobiographical accounts is the way the reality represented in the text, despite the differences in time, cultures, and personal histories, suddenly touches my own reality and wakens me to the conditions of female life in language that have existed throughout the patriarchal ascendancy. I make common cause with the text, we may weep in grief together, we come to know our common wounds, our startling differences, we laugh together in the pleasure of our subversive language.

While realizing the ways in which the text represents my sister, my own subjectivity is in the process of change. I am becoming the daughter of the text, shaped, enabled, nurtured in my own growth by another woman's utterance. The kind of daughter I am becoming is always in the future. For the purposes of this text I am writing, it lies in the chapters ahead of me. I hope my reader can enter into this future with me. I promise that the strategies I will use to earn your reading will take its cues from each text as my relationships with real or surrogate mothers, real sisters (genetic or feminist), and real or surrogate daughters take their cues from all the past and future possibilities of communication, and the growth of self and other, that exist between us.

My (m)othering will thus be a gendered reading. I will not present, as do some mappers of autobiographical discourse, as Nancy Miller notes, a "theoretical model *indifferent to* a problematics of genre as inflected by gender."[48] I will assume, like Miller, a "practice of the text that would recognize the status of the reader as a differentiated subject, a reading subject named by gender and committed in a dialectics of identification to deciphering the inscription of the female subject" (56). In other words, I will know that in mapping the auto-biographical accounts of my countrywomen, I am tracing the pattern of the life of my own arteries of action, my own veins of response, searching for correspondence and difference, delighting in discovery of the self and the other. I am surveying myself to interweave that survey to the compilation I make of these others. I will speak openly of my pleasure so that *"you may learn this pleasure from me."*

CONTEXTUAL TRUTHS

Lies will fall from my lips, but there may perhaps be some truth mixed up with them; it is for you to seek out this truth and to decide whether any part of it is worth keeping.

Virginia Woolf, *A Room of One's Own*

The relationship of reader to autobiographer in feminist research of women's accounts is then different from the kind of pact between equals, equals sure of the cultural privileges they share, sure of their readership. Such is the pact that is understood by Philippe LeJeune in which an agreement between writer and reader is "sealed by the proper name" on the title page of the text.[49] Some of the women I have studied wrote under their husband's name with the Mrs tag added. Pioneer women often denied autobiographical intention, claiming their accounts were merely to inform, or warn, the folks back home. Many of them certainly believed that claim. Present-day sophisticated postmodern women writers, aware of the unfortunate connections made between amateurism and women's autobiography, aware also of the impossibility of autobiography by postmodern stan-dards, give their accounts quite imaginative namings to avoid the stigma of autobiography. They may also believe these namings. But for my purposes, these texts are capable of revealing autobiographical truths that help me construct an alternate view of the female subject to the one presented by my culture and history. Therefore, for my purposes, these texts are autobiographies.

In speaking of truth I wish to take a position somewhere between the rock and hard place of humanism and poststructuralism. I do not seek truths that are true in all times and places and that generalize the female condition. This would make me guilty of the same kind of stereotyping of women that has been the case inside a humanist mind-set. At the same time I need the academic skills of structuralist approaches and the broad working hypotheses that have allowed academic humanism to exist and succeed. However, the truths I seek are not true because of their ability to hypothesize female experience into an academic mythology or because of their ability to rise above individual experience. As the women of the Personal Narratives Group assert: "It is precisely because of their subjectivity – their rootedness in time, place and personal experience and their per-spective-ridden character – that we value them."[50] Like the oral stories of elders in pre-history, these women's stories help me map the world, help me test the reality value of the cultural constructs that surround me, and they confirm the reality of "difference and complexity and stress the centrality of gender to human life and thought" (263).

At the same time, I do not seek a critical position that will force me to reduce everything to relativism, nor do I preserve an attitude concerning the illusiveness or playfulness of language that keeps me naive of language's ability to construct real personal and political power in the world. I cannot afford the luxury of declaring the author dead, the individual signature a chimera, for that would "spell a return to female anonymity."[51] The contemporary male subject may well feel burdened with too much identity, too much fixedness inside the discourses of power. He may indeed need to cast off the weight of ego definition. But as Nancy Miller has observed, women have not been burdened with too much ego. At the same time as I reject some of the more extreme scenarios of poststructuralism, I need a post-structuralist theory of language that will allow for freely connotative interpretations that recognize the possibility of many texts in one text. I need to understand the human female subject as historically and culturally situated. Most of all, I need the poststructuralist belief that language is composed of various powerful discourses and that membership in a particular discourse community bestows special privileges. Because of the political importance of this fact, I need a poststructuralist understanding of language that recognizes that a linguistic community is "in fact a *heterogeneous* society composed of many conflicting interests" where the signs that are language are the powerful point of contention where "conflicting social groups, classes, individuals and discourses [seek] to appropriate it and imbue [language] with their own meanings."[52] Terry Eagleton's images of conflict and appropriation do not represent the methodologies I seek. However, he does figure accurately the emergency quality of the situation. Women's need from language and the maps of experience we make in language is politically and personally imperative. As Bella Brodzki and Celeste Schenck observe: "At this felicitous juncture of feminism, psychoanalysis and modern critical theory, the case of [women's] autobiography raises the essential problem in contemporary feminist theory and praxis: the imperative situating of the female subject in spite of the postmodernist campaign against the sovereign self."[53]

When Virginia Woolf set out to figure the female condition in *A Room of One's Own*, she understood the problematic nature of language and subjectivity. She knew that every assertion could easily further reify women, that every cultural myth she wished to contend was also a part of her own identity in culture, in language. She understood, in the way that fiction writers come to know, how fully we must make fictions to make truth, how often, given the tenacity of cultural myth, we must make a new myth to undermine an older, less useful myth. So she alerted her reader as I alert you: I must construct frameworks, name priorities, assume particular readings. I use methodologies that a fiction writer would call "lies," lies that serve the same function as the fiction writer's fictions. What I call my "contexts" may seem to you strange and awkward, given the culturally inscribed contexts of patriarchal hegemony. I do this to attract (win) (construct) (create) a certain kind of reader, one who will use the lies that fall from my lips to construct her/his own truth. For this book "is meant to stand as a testimony: to become a feminist reader of autobiography is to become a new kind of subject."[54]

PART ONE

Reading for
an Alternate Tradition

When I began to read the autobiographical accounts of women who visited or settled in pioneer Canada, my repeated reaction was one of sudden recognition of figures from my own childhood. These women were like my Newfoundland grandmothers and their peers, the women who, to my childhood's eyes, seemed busily in charge of the village communities in which they ran small mixed farms, worked as midwives, supervised the activities of large extended families, and acted as moral arbiters and spiritual guides in the lives of their contemporaries, both male and female, and as beloved but unchallengeable authorities shaping the lives of their grandchildren. Like the world of my rural grandmothers, where men were largely absent, off at sea or on the railroad, these early women revealed to me a world of female solidarity, of respect and common purpose between sisters, of genuine understanding and affection between mothers and daughters.

When I first began to consider these accounts in the light of current theories of women's autobiography and feminist thought, I found little published support for my positive viewpoints regarding the lives of these women and for the cultural situation I remembered from my experience of the matriarchs of my Newfoundland childhood. Instead, I found the theories that characterized women's place in culture as that of the "misbegotten man," of the damaged individual who does not recognize herself in culture's mirror. In theoretical characterizations, I found, in Julia Kristeva's words, a figure of woman as "estranged from language ... visionaries, dancers who suffer as they speak."[1] How was I to reconcile the very real disadvantages that culture imposes on women, a situation I experienced in my own life as well as learned through the stories and theories of feminists, with my memories of my grandmothers' power and the testimony of these pioneer accounts? The next three chapters document that reconciliation and its continuing ambiguous nature as I map the diaries, journals, and memoirs of early Canadian women.

In compiling a map that included the full contours of my foremothers experience, I found that to assume that written language is only masculine or patriarchal is too simplistic. Some language usages have indeed been the domain of men, but I must, as Patricia Yaeger advises, assume that "the discourse of our foremothers was also in process – was also a discourse of inscriptive social change."[2] Just as Yaeger found the nineteenth-century novelist to be her ancestress, I too could read the diary of an early Canadian woman as that of "an explorer who gives us a map for defining a counter-tradition within women's writing, a tradition in which the woman writer appropriates the language 'racked up' in her own body and starts to sing" (28).

In my search for this alternate tradition, the texts of three theorists, besides Yaeger, have been particularly helpful. Margaret Homans examines the works of nineteenth-century women writers who lived inside the romantic cultural myth that demanded women's absence, their silence, to show how these writers nevertheless inscribe a female presence. Homans argues that by being especially alert to traces of another language through several recurrent literary situations, we may map this presence.[3] Homans discovers that this presence is particularly traceable when a woman writer literalizes normally figurative language and calls our attention to the literal (and female) underpinnings of symbolic (and masculine) language. She also finds that female figures who act in certain maternal roles, especially a mother who gives birth to a child who in some way represents language, or women who carry on some activity of translation copying or transmission, are traces of this inscription of an alternate cultural myth, inscribed within the patriarchal cultural myth.

It is my own reading experience that this alternate world is especially present when women write of mother/daughter relationships. But as Marianne Hirsch proposes, these "mother/daughter plots" are "submerged in traditional plot structures,"[4] exist in a tradition that "insists on the incompatibility of creativity and procreativity" (8), and often emerge only as interruptions, aberrations, disturbances, in the male "family romance" that dominates the plot structures in the history of the novel. These reshapings all depend on the "heroines' refusal of conventional heterosexual romance and marriage plots and ... on their disidentification from conventional constructions of femininity" (10–11). The unconventional "constructions of femininity" include an emphasis on mother/daughter relationships, which are absent from patriarchal plots. Quoting Adrienne Rich, who in *Of Woman Born* writes of the "cathexis between mother and daughter" as the "great unwritten story" (17) of our tradition, Hirsch argues that a "feminist family romance" is emerging in women's writing "which highlight[s] mother-daughter bonding as a basis for a vision of gender difference and female specificity" (15).

In addition to learning to read women's accounts as marked by the figures Homans points out and by the female plot variations Hirsch explores, I have found the reading strategies outlined by Nancy Miller in *Subject to Change* to be particularly instructive in helping me heed the alternate surveys of identity and experience, marking a changed subjectivity, that are women's maps of self-hood. Briefly summarized they include attention to the special emphases that women add to their writing ("diachronic reoccur-rences") which appear as a kind of metaphorical "italics" in their accounts. These "italics" may seem to be as inconsequential activi-ties and opinions, ones that are even contradicted by the narrative voice, or they may seem to be implausibilities, oversentimental expressions, extraordinary or out-of-place figures (by traditional aesthetic standards), but they are, by a feminist reading, the inscription of women's attempts to cure their lives of certain pre-scribed patriarchal conventions. When speaking directly of women's autobiography, Miller advises that an appropriate strategy for revealing female subjectivity, given that women must veil their rev-elations because of "a culturally devalued femininity," is the "double reading" of a writer's autobiography with her other writings, a reading that "would provide a more sensitive measure for deci-phering the female self."[5] In the case of the women I study, whose autobiographical writing often constitutes their only published writing, I would argue that the research of the biographer, other documents related to the autobiographer's life, the records of women in similar circumstances, as well as the information gleaned from unpublished correspondence, can help provide a similar inter-textual reading for female subjectivity, a reading I would call a "contextual" reading.

But even more useful to me than her reading strategies of emphasis added and double reading is Miller's description of "arachnologies" of female writing and reading. In seeking "to con-struct a poetics that could account for the problem of signature posed by 'underread,' works excluded from the library of general culture" (as the works I examine are often excluded), Miller evokes the mythical figure of Arachne, whose tapestry weaving tells the story of the oppression of women in patriarchy. Arachne's text is "first discredited, then detached from the cultural record and finally ignored" (77–8). For Miller, Arachne's tapestry represents a female "textuality hopelessly entangled with questions of material" (77) that requires a "critical positioning which reads *against* the weave of indifferentiation to discover the embodiment in writing of a gendered subjectivity" (80).

A strategy that helps me find the female subject in the "hope-lessly entangled" materials of early Canadian accounts is essential to my task. Most of the stories of selfhood that I have read not only are interwoven with the fact of the new world and the lives of significant others (both those on the journey and those left behind), but are entangled with the generic expectations of a variety of formats: the public genres of the novel, poetry, travel literature, memoirs, and contemporary historical and geographic discourses, as well as the conventions of the private genres of the letter, the diary, and the personal travel journal. Reading for women's embedded arachnologies reveals to me features of the landscape, shadings of experience, formerly left out of our map of pioneer literature, and offers me an opportunity to theorize generic locations for Canadian women's autobiography.

1 Pioneer Women's Diaries and Journals: Letters Home / Letters to the Future

> The study of history is useful to the historian by teaching him
> his ignorance of women; and the mass of this ignorance
> crushes one who is familiar enough with what are called his-
> torical sources to realize how few women have ever been
> known. The woman who is known only through a man is
> known wrong.
>
> Henry Adams, *The Education of Henry Adams*, as quoted in
> Elizabeth Hampsten's *Read This Only to Yourself*

In describing the history and characteristics of the diary's development as a genre in English, Harriet Blodgett notes four focuses: the
diary as record of daily travel and business, a sixteenth-century
development; the public diary focused on public events and persons,
a popular seventeenth-century use; the appearance in the seven-
teenth and eighteenth century of the formulaic diary of conscience;
and the continuing presence during this time of the "diary consisting
of brief entries of personal memorabilia and family records," the form
that became the "germ of the diary proper" as we understand it
today. Blodgett also notes the influence after 1740 of the novel of
sensibility on diaries (many diaries became "passionate explorations
of consciousness") and the increase in the "letter diary" as a means
of personal recording and communication with a significant other.[1]
By the late eighteenth century the diary was already a healthily
eclectic genre, a form that would be extended and enriched by many
English-speaking women coming to Canada.

For these women, the diary would become a public record of travel
and settlement, a private record of their own development in the
course of the new experiences offered them in the new land, a letter
home to family and friends in the old country, and, fortuitously, a
history and literature of women's pioneer Canadian experience.
Indeed, women's unwillingness to let go of the old life and old
connections is the chief reason we have these accounts. Frances
Stewart, for example, whose letters of half a century of settlement in
the Peterborough area (1822–72) were published as *Our Forest Home*,

was still writing home to England, after forty-seven years, to her one remaining correspondent who knew her in the old life: "In a few days we shall have the memorable anniversary of our last parting and our departure from country and dearly beloved friends."[2] Anne Leveridge found time out from the back-breaking labour of life in a one-room shanty in the early 1880s on a backwoods Ontario farm to write to her mother in one of the letters of *Your Loving Anna*: "Come and stay awhile in these backwoods. There you will see the wild beauties of nature to perfection."[3] In her *Letters from a Lady Rancher*, Monica Hopkins, a turn-of-the-century settler in Alberta, marvels at the change her immigration made in her life and herself: "The new life that I had taken on so cheerfully was so entirely different from anything I had ever experienced before ... nothing had prepared me for the difference in every way that I am finding out here."[4]

These women's accounts are part of a rich archive and express three principal characteristics of the form of the diary/letter as developed by Canadian women: a deep and abiding attachment to relationships, both those severed by the move to Canada and those that facilitate entry into the new land, a desire to represent the experience of the new land in accuracy and detail, especially when there is a wish to convince the other to immigrate or when the account is meant for the woman's personal posterity, and a keen and growing interest (as each account covers a number of years) in showing the unanticipated personal changes in abilities and consciousness that the new world has afforded. In this chapter I will offer some initial mappings of three women's diaries, those of Elizabeth Simcoe, Mary O'Brien, and Sarah Ellen Roberts, which in their variety represent the wide-ranging possibilities of this early Canadian autobiographical form.

Elizabeth Simcoe, the wife of Upper Canada's first lieutenant-governor, was hardly the type of hardy woman pioneer whose days were filled with domestic labour. As heiress to a large estate and fortune in England, she was trained in the responsibilities and privileges of rank. She expected to perform as her husband's chatelaine, to entertain and be entertained, and to carry on the polite activities of a lady, even in the wilds of Ontario in 1791. Since she was raised in the arts of a lady and was a careful letter writer and a trained landscape painter, we might expect simply an intelligent and detailed account rich in resources for the social historian. But in addition to this, we also receive an account rich in documentation of a female subjectivity that reveals both the limitations and possibilities of female life in the late eighteenth century. The reason the account is so rich is because it is addressed particularly to Simcoe's beloved woman friend, Mary Anne Burges, her companion since childhood, and through her to Simcoe's four young daughters who remained behind in England. In contrast to the private genre we often think of as "diary" in the twentieth century, a spontaneous record of thoughts and feelings recorded almost in the moment of occurrence, the *journal intime*, Simcoe's diary was carefully shaped in moments of leisure from detailed notes recorded on the scene earlier in the day or week; Robert Fothergill calls such diaries a "digested relevance," prepared for the reassurance, instruction, and pleasure of those left behind.[5]

To make what Nancy Miller calls an "overreading" and what I call a "contextual" reading of Simcoe's diary, we must realize the special grounds of its composition. In her biography of Simcoe, Mary Beacock Fryer outlines the contours of the life of a woman who understood the importance of family in all its meanings. Elizabeth Gwillim never knew either parent, for she was born months after her father's death and her mother died when she was only hours old. Raised by relatives in the knowledge that she represented the entire posterity of both sides of her genteel Welsh and English families, the young heiress had both a profound sense of her duties to family and a tenacious attachment to all of her close friends and relatives. She married John Graves Simcoe in 1782, and by the time he was to take up his post in Canada in 1791, they had six children. Because of their very close companionship (Simcoe often acted as her husband's personal secretary and used her artistic skills in drawing maps and sketches of settlements and garrisons), Colonel Simcoe wanted his wife with him in Canada. Her sense of duty as a wife and her sense of duty as a mother came into collision for the first time. As Fryer observes, because he had fought against the Americans in the revolution and felt it his duty to help shape the new British North America, John Simcoe was willing "to spend five years in the backwoods of Canada, obliging his wife to travel and to live in ways she could not have foreseen. He who so loved his children was willing to be parted from them for much of their formative years because he felt himself a true patriot. As Elizabeth points out, if a child died, they might not hear of it for six months or more."[6]

Over the summer before they left, Elizabeth Simcoe worked out an ingenious caretaking and communications system for her family. A senior female relative, Mrs Graves, was left as chatelaine of her home, Wolford Lodge. A mother and daughter manager/governess team, Ann and Mary Hunt, were left in charge of the running of Wolford Hall and the education of the children, and Mary Anne Burges was to act as special adviser, aunt, and correspondent, informing Elizabeth in the form of journal/letters: "She begged Mary Anne to tell her everything, the bad as well as the good, and to spare her nothing that would cause her to worry. A mother had the right to worry about her own children" (32). As Fryer's biography reveals, Mary Anne Burges was as good as her word, and a constant stream of communication crossed the Atlantic over the five years of the Simcoes' stay in Canada. Therefore, it is in the context of this correspondence and its purpose that we must read Simcoe's diary. As well, during her last preparations for departure, Simcoe decided that she could not go without at least two of her children. She chose to take her baby son, Francis, and two-year-old Sophia with her, since neither would need the benefits of an English education for a number of years. Thus, her diary takes on an additional dimension in the form of reports to the older girls on the younger children in an effort to keep a strong sense of family ties alive in the older siblings.

When I first read Simcoe's diary, I was aware of the daughters as readers and of many of the facts of Simcoe's life before and after her Canadian years. However, I was unaware of the special personal, cultural, and communal imperatives that the Fryer biography introduces through the careful documentation of Burges's complementary correspondence. Thus, in my first reading, I saw a Simcoe similar to the one the critic Marian Fowler sees, an adventurous, picturesque artist developing a taste for wilderness scenes and an increased confidence in her own abilities, the special combination of "embroidery" and "tent" that Fowler posits for the "androgynous" early heroine in Canada.[7] This Simcoe certainly exists in the diary, and my own earlier view was perhaps only more conservative than Fowler's concerning the amount of development that occurred as the result of the Canadian experience. I was concerned, as well, with a broader range of significant others. However, like Fowler, I was largely interested in a heroine and her singular life history. But seeing Simcoe more fully in the contexts I have described here, as correspondent with her best friend, and with the two of them in a mother/daughter relationship with Simcoe's daughters, I began to realize the special emphasis that certain parts of her account have, the metaphorical italics she places around certain versions of herself; I began to understand certain maternal stances – her emphasis on her role as visual translator and as copier of her husband's plans and purposes, the attention (or silence) she gives to certain maternal moments. In short, I began to understand the balancing act that was female subjectivity for Elizabeth Simcoe.

Even in the opening pages of *Mrs Simcoe's Diary*, Elizabeth Simcoe begins to create the special versions of herself she wishes Mary Anne

Burges and the four Simcoe daughters to know.[8] She is, first of all, always the correct wife to the girls' father, describing herself being charming and diplomatic to French and English alike in Quebec City (coincidentally illustrating to her daughters the value of a training in manners and the French language). She is always hospitable as chatelaine at Niagara and later at York (Toronto), and lets her daughters know that even when feeling ill she seeks to fill her role as hostess to her husband's associates and their wives. Her travels with John Simcoe and the maps and drawings she makes for him are frequently mentioned, and there are no overt complaints about a man who, we learn from other letters and the biography, is frequently ill, demanding, and absent from her at crucial moments.

But Simcoe also wants the admiration of her beloved female readers, and so her stances as female adventurer begin early in the account: "I quite enjoy the thoughts of the long journey we have before us & the perpetual change of scene it will afford, but the people here [in Lower Canada] think it as arduous & adventurous an undertaking as it was looked upon to be by my friends in England. It is surprising that those who are so much nearer to a Country should esteem it as impracticable as those who are so many thousand miles distant" (55). But as well as portraying herself as above the mundane opinions of less adventurous souls on both sides of the Atlantic, Simcoe is careful to undercut the fearful details of her journey at the very moment she describes them. One can imagine the mixed thrill of fear and relief four little girls would feel reading this discourse on snakes: "Capt. Shaw also advises me not to believe the formidable accounts I have heard of Rattle Snakes ... He affirms they never bite but when trod upon or attacked, & the wound they make is cured by well-known herbs, as horehound & plantain Juice" (55).

But the sensitive maternal correspondent was also a very serious artist. Simcoe's training, as well as the years she and Burges spent in their girlhood companionship comparing and improving their sketching and painting techniques and the attention she gave to her daughters' instruction in the visual arts, verifies the importance she put on this aspect of her life. Indeed, the amount and quality of her Canadian production affirm that her art was equivalent to that of a present-day professional artist in seriousness and scope. For my reading to give the same emphasis to this part of her life as she did, it is necessary to point out Simcoe's devotion to the picturesque school of art articulated by William Gilpin and advocated by Sir Joshua Reynolds, a movement that reached its height in the last decades of the eighteenth century. The style emphasized the

harmonious bringing together of opposites: light and shade, rough-
ness and smoothness, irregularities of shape and colour. But as well
as being trained to see the world in these formal terms, the picturesque artist learned that "feeling is fundamental to the intuitive
perception impelled by the visual stimuli of picturesque travel and
is complemented by another subjective operation of the viewer – the
exercise of the imagination."[9] Simcoe's Canadian experience, in terms
of the new artistic challenges of the Precambrian Shield lakes and
rivers, of untouched wilderness and colonial outpost, and in terms
of her personal experiences as friend, wife, and mother, offered her
a range of female experiences that certainly allowed for the intense
feeling that her lively imagination brought to bear on her art, enabling
her to make her changed self literal through the art she created.

Throughout the diary we can trace a maturing of her artistic ideas
as her observations change from the conventional (she describes the
appearance of burning woods along the St Laurence as a "very picturesque appearance, a little like Tasso's enchanted wood" [72]) to
the more complex (when viewing Niagara Falls, she observes that it
is difficult to find just the right view of this "grandest sight" [76]
and hopes that "after the eye becomes more familiar to the objects I
think the pleasure will be greater in dwelling upon them" [77]). Fryer
records what must have been an additional spur to her artistry:
Burges writes to Simcoe that the receipt of a packet of art and diary
entries from her "equals a shock of electricity" to those waiting impa-
tiently for news of her adventures (95). Simcoe's treatments of the
Canadian subject matter show a growing attempt not to impose
herself and her ideas on the landscape, but to experience its impact
on her through her feelings and imagination, as expressed in her
painting.

But this desire to let the country make its effect on her is illustrated
in other ways as well: in her decision to spend as little time as possible
in comparatively civilized Quebec City and to stay in Upper Canada
even during the difficult winter; in her decision to leave the comparative security of the military post at Niagara and to take up residence
in the wilds of York; and even in the delightful details of tenting life
she sends home to her children – "A wet day ... is very dismal in a
Tent but to see the light again & feel the air dry is such a pleasure
that none can judge of but those who have felt the reverse" (99). In
fact, Simcoe was beginning the experience of great pleasure and its
reverse that marked her stay in Canada.

She took great pleasure in the company of Lieutenant (later
Colonel) Talbot, her husband's young aide, and is able to relate their
carefree adventures at York. Together, she and Talbot went on jaunts,

sighted bald eagles (78), and gathered birch-bark for sketches (120). They skated (115) and rode on her favourite peninsula (now Toronto's Centre Island), and when writing of one of these incidents, she brags to her girls: "My horse has spirit enough to wish to get before others. I rode a race with Mr. Talbot to keep myself warm" (107). The four daughters back home could take as much envious pleasure in the account of their mother's victories as they must have taken in her adventure of building and visiting "Castle Frank," named after their little brother, Francis, and erected on the heights above the Don River valley. Here, in an atmosphere typical of Simcoe's ability to combine opposites, in a Parthenon-type structure built of Canadian logs and inhabited by a tent in which Francis and Elizabeth slept, she came to know the new land first hand, without the hindrances of mosquitoes and disapproving settlers. Her painting of this structure is a very literal expression of the contrasting tastes that she brought together in her experience in Canada.

But the inevitable illnesses, danger, and discomforts – the reverse of the pleasure of her adventure – are more difficult to write home about; they appear in a certain disguise, a female rhetoric, letting Mary Anne know the other side of her adventure while keeping the girls from too much concern for the safety of the family. When she wishes to relate the story of a rather dangerous passage of Lake Ontario, she manages to offer the truth of the danger while defusing it: "My servant came several times to tell me we were going to the bottom. I told her to shut the door & leave me quiet, for the motion of the Vessel made me sick" (157). The mother portrays herself as concerned with practical details of sleep and motion sickness; fear and danger are neatly displaced onto the servant. This displacement into another's experience, both of her pleasurable adventures (as seen in the emphasis she often gives the activities of Talbot or Francis in her account) and of her pain and fear (as seen in this example), is a strategy that while seeming to de-emphasize herself and her feelings, draws attention to them. In fact, for the reader reading Simcoe's account in the contexts I have outlined, contexts encouraged by Simcoe's own diplomatic but detailed descriptions, a special emphasis – a metaphorical italics – is added, one that cues us to the alternate text of her account. This was to prove a useful strategy for many writing women, wishing to speak fully of their lives yet aware of the special concerns of their intimate readers.

Yet there is a part of her female experience for which Elizabeth Simcoe's diary cannot find a discourse. There are no entries in her diary between 31 December 1792 and 3 February 1793 and, again, between 18 April and 2 May 1794, uncharacteristic gaps for Simcoe.

These silences enclose the birth and death of her daughter Katherine, who was born at Niagara on 16 January 1793 and died at York on 19 April 1794. Simcoe's only comments on her pregnancy are contained in a letter to Mrs Hunt, when in describing the dances in Upper Canada, she remarks, parenthetically, that she has not attended them for the greater part of the winter because she was expecting to be "confined." When describing her "apartments," a canvas house boarded outside for insulation, she says, "The comfort I derived from these apartments was extremely great when I lay in, because, being in a manner separate from the rest of the house, it was so very quiet."[10] Katherine's death does not appear in the diary either, but once again, like the birth, in a private letter to Mrs Hunt, who as the girls' governess will have the duty of telling them the bad news. Elizabeth writes:

It is with pain that I take up my pen to inform you of the loss we have sustained & the melancholy event of our losing poor little Katherine, one of the strongest healthiest children you ever saw ... She had been feverish one or two days cutting teeth, which not being an unusual case with children I was not much alarmed. On good Friday she was playing in my room in the morning, in the afternoon was seized with fits. I sat up the whole night the greatest part of which she continued to have spasms & before seven in the morning she was no more ... She was the sweetest tempered pretty child imaginable, just beginning to talk & walk & the suddenness of the event you may be sure shocked me inexpressibly.[11]

The expression "inexpressibly" is both a conventional idiom and a literalization of Simcoe's situation in language. In patriarchal cultures the subjects of pregnancy and labour are not fit subjects for the public discourses that are centred on men's activities. It is not that a woman like Simcoe would consciously hide such subjects. Rather, she has never been given permission, or even an idiom in public language, to express emotions and thoughts that centre on this important female activity. In this regard the language is insufficient to her needs.

It is insufficient as well in its ability to express maternal feelings. Suzanne Bunkers has observed concerning women's diaries written a century later than Simcoe's that such a writer needed "an outlet for emotions such as intense grief and anger, which her culture did not deem appropriate for public expression by a woman."[12] Bunkers feels that for the women she studies, the diary does become that kind of personal document, at least for the expression of grief. However, Simcoe's diary is caught in the double bind of needing to deal with the intimate on occasion while being intended for eyes other than the diarist's. As a public document and as mother/daughter connection, Simcoe's diary is not open to the full expression of her experience in Canada. The more detailed report of Simcoe's daughter's death in the letter indicates that Simcoe's language was somewhat open to such descriptions. Perhaps because death is no respecter of gender, the patriarchal language has some idiom for its description. What it does not have is an idiom for the maternal guilt implied by Simcoe's reference to not taking the fever seriously because she thought the child was teething, and for the complex of emotions that move through a mother in the hours spent at a child's deathbed. That these emotions are intense and continuing is shown in Fryer's recording that Simcoe's further correspondence indicates she was "panic-stricken" when her son became sick a few days later.

I find that early women's diaries displace their unexpressed emotions in subtle ways. For example, often when a beloved child or parent dies, the diarist hardly notes the passing, but later a detailed description of the grave or a sentimental rendering of a pet's death will indicate the continuing "inexpressible" grief (one young woman mourned her favourite calf in great detail months after her mother's death had made her prematurely responsible for a large family). Mrs Simcoe's uncharacteristic recording of her day of tears two years later, as she was about to take leave of Toronto to return home, indicates a similar displaced mourning of her daughter. She records: "Took leave of Mrs. McGill and Miss Crookshank. I was so much out of spirits I was unable to dine with them. She [Mrs McGill] sent me some dinner, but I could not eat; cried all the day" (189). Mrs McGill, the wife of the commissary captain, and her sister, Miss Crookshank, had been two of Simcoe's companions in the place where her daughter was buried. Women encode, both in conscious and unconscious ways, what cannot be openly expressed, given the rational nature of patriarchal language. Only by decoding – or, as Miller calls it, by "overreading" and "double reading" in reference to a broad intertext of documents – can such lives be disclosed. Through reading related private and public documents, examining other contemporaneous women's accounts, and understanding the special cultural situation of each woman, the critic may begin to map the female subjectivity of these autobiographical accounts.

This is a task greater than the normal literary reading that assumes a certain set of principles of reading, be they thematic, formalist, or deconstructive. A contextual reading is interdisciplinary, relying on information from a broad range of cultural documents, and theoretically eclectic. For example, even my limited reading of Elizabeth

Simcoe's diary involves several steps. The 1911 book compiled by her earliest editor and biographer, J. Ross Robertson, gives a great deal of background on John Simcoe and the Canadian historical and military situation but is sparse on details of Mrs Simcoe's personal situation. Mary Quale Ennis provides the most useful version of the diary, and her notes help establish the audience of the diary. Critics like Marian Fowler point to special motifs such as the wilderness/self exploration. However, it is not until Fryer's 1989 exploration of Burges's role in Simcoe's life and letters that the fuller intertext becomes known. This contextual reading of Simcoe is necessary, for as Henry Adams observes, if we depend on men's histories to know women, no woman will be known. If we depended on the report of men for our opinion of Elizabeth Simcoe, we might find someone as bland and meek as the lady described by a French duke (quoted by Fryer) who met her in Canada: "Mrs Simcoe, a lady of thirty-six [she was thirty-two], is bashful, has wit, is obliging and kind-hearted, speaks little, is occupied with her duties as mother and wife which she carries so far as to be her husband's confidential secretary; her talent for drawing, which she applies to tracing maps, gives her also the ability to be useful to him." Of course, in all fairness to the duke it needs to be said that Mrs Simcoe's comment on him and his American companions as recorded by Fryer was that they looked "democratic and dirty" (143). Perhaps this explains her "bashful" silence.

Simcoe is a good candidate for a fuller, contextual reading, since there are so many documents pertaining to her life, as is sometimes the case with the female relatives of important men. Gathering an intertext for the diaries of women less well known in the patriarchal world is a more difficult and speculative task, but no less rewarding, as is indicated by an exploration of the diary of Mary O'Brien. Finding appropriate intertexts for a woman's diary involves what Elizabeth Hampsten calls "a special inventive patience"[13] on the part of the critic, an attention to repetition and reoccurrence and to the incremental changes these undergo over time. In that way we may distinguish the special preoccupations of a diarist, and through surveying others in her cultural situation, the special preoccupations of a group of women. In this regard, Julie Jeffrey suggests that we need to moderate our views of the frontier period when speaking of women. Far from desiring adventure and a loosening of society's hold, women sought to replicate as quickly as possible what they had left behind: "The reality of the frontier, far from rejecting the civilizing mission, reaffirmed it."[14] Jeffrey is referring to the American frontier, but this "civilizing mission" was especially true of early Ontario settlement, since the women who came were often consciously genteel and middle class. Hampsten points out that this makes it necessary to change our view of the effect of place on the writing that comes out of this experience. Our viewpoints, shaped by male history and artistic production, tell us to distinguish regionalism and strict time periods in the literature of settlement. We look for "prairie realism" and separate the time of the earlier trader world from the first waves of farm settlement. Under this rule the literary production of early Upper Canada should not be placed with that of twentieth-century Alberta. Interestingly, the diary of an Alberta farm woman in the twentieth century on first reading could be confused with that of a woman in early Ontario. In fact, the last early diarist I consider in this chapter is a twentieth-century Alberta settler. As Hampsten points out, place is not geography and time period for women: "Women ... locate themselves in their immediate circumstances and not in the kinds of unifying myths based on time and place that ... legitimize the work of [male] artists ... 'Place' in these writings has other boundaries than topography: dangers ... fire, flood, cold, drought, disease, madness and death" (40). She might have added that for more fortunate and/ or resilient women, place also involved supportive female relationships, self-reliance, learning new skills, adapting old ones, and establishing a civilization for their children.

Anne Langton, an early settler in the Peterborough area, expresses succinctly the new place the gentlewoman might find in the pioneer Canadian economy: "As long as the lady is necessarily the most active member of her household she keeps her *ground* from her utility; but when the *state* of semi-civilization arrives ... then she must fall, and must be contented to be looked upon as belonging merely to the decorative department of the establishment and *valued* accordingly [emphasis mine]."[15] Langton seems to be quite consciously literalizing her political situation as woman as if she understands that place has political, cultural, psychological, and economic locations for women.

To read Mary O'Brien's diary is to watch a woman engaged in finding her place in Canadian life. This is an ambiguous activity, since as the bringer of civilization she must first learn to adapt to the pioneer conditions and once this is accomplished she must also welcome being dislodged by "civilization" from important aspects of the value she had achieved in the pioneer economy. *The Journals of Mary O'Brien 1828–1838*, an edited version of a larger collection of journal entries, supplemented by letters that O'Brien (née Gapper) sent to her sister, brother-in-law, and brother during the years in which she changed from a genteel English maiden lady of thirty to a Canadian pioneer mother of several children, had the practical purpose of informing the family back home of the nature of life in the new land and the health and progress of family members in Canada. The primary readers of the journals were her sister, Lucy Sharpe, and Lucy's husband, and the journal seems at first to be for their amusement. For example, O'Brien's typical observations on frontier society have the tone of a witty outsider, superior and external to the action: "They are making such rapid strides in civilization as to have had two murderers tried and condemned at the same assizes."[16]

Once O'Brien and her mother begin to decide that their visit to Upper Canada is becoming an immigration, O'Brien's purpose seems to shift to an effort to persuade Lucy to come to Canada. But her point of view also shifts, so that although she remains the humorous tour guide, she is becoming a narrator within the scene of action as well: "When I settle here I mean to have a maple sugar farm, both for the sake of encouraging a very valuable source of wealth, which the natives are prone to neglect from improvidence and prejudice, and because it will give me no trouble for eleven months of the year. Besides, it will ensure me plenty of wood" (24). As the years go by and Mary marries Edward O'Brien, her sense of humour is more and more directed towards her own efforts to achieve a domestic efficiency equal to her blue-stocking intellectual talents: "I ... stirred a bowl of cream into butter, in which I succeeded much to my heart's content, sitting under the verandah and reading Milton all the time. Only I found to my sorrow when my work was finished that I had ground off one of my nails" (118). The move from educated lady to housewife involves a subjectivity move from witty intellectual observer to engaged participant. O'Brien neatly makes her old self part of the new through the witty style of her diary.

It is when she makes her first trip from the more settled Thornhill area to Lake Simcoe, which will become her home when she marries, that we see an interesting shift in style that indicates the way in which O'Brien seeks to place herself: "Now Mr. O'Brien has got into our canoe and paddled out to get a water lily which is spreading its beauty to be admired by the frogs. Now we get into the lake and make way. The Indians' canoes cast off and I, casting my eyes on the water, see the whole verdant carpeting of its bed – every leaf and insect distinct. Now I am attracted by the Indians on the bows who are singing in a rich soft voice a common psalm tune in Indian words ... Mr. O'Brien sits at the end with his paddle, Bill is in the bottom leaning over on one side with another. This allows me to lean over and dabble on the opposite side. Thus we glide along with a motion soothing though hardly perceptible" (60). O'Brien begins with her usual observer's humour: "a water lily … spreading its beauty to be admired by the frogs." But then the place, the place she is exploring with her future husband, captures her and it is she who is the admirer of the "whole verdant carpeting." She does not put her own development at the centre of the account, but rather represents herself as perceiver of the natural world and its human inhabitants. By way of this passage I wish to point out the literary and stylistic results of Hampsten's point concerning women locating themselves in their "immediate circumstances." In this way O'Brien begins to create a writing style that does not centre narration on the omniscient narrator or on the first-person narrator, but rather creates a more inclusive awareness based on an autobiographical narrator who perceives her own and others' realities and uses her feelings and imagination to re-create that perception in words in the same way that Elizabeth Simcoe wedded her art and her experience in Canada. This kind of narrator I see as an extension of the translator figure that Homans speaks of vis-à-vis nineteenth-century fiction, except in these autobiographical Canadian accounts the translator has the task of translating a whole new world through the translation of the self. "Translation" as a description of writing purpose and style is used by Barbara Godard to describe recent feminist writing, but the term applies equally well to nineteenth-century women's accounts. Godard observes that "feminist translation is a signifying of difference despite similarity".[17] Many of the features identified by Godard as typical of contemporary feminist discourse, such as parody (especially self-parody), pastiche, and palimpsistic and polyphonic texts, are also typical of earlier women.

The diary can be seen as centring more and more on O'Brien's own development as a person and on her place in the evolving pioneer world, but this emphasis on ego development does not fully describe what is happening in her text. For her, self-development *is* the development of other persons and of the place in which she settles. O'Brien places family, rather than self, at the centre of her concerns: first her mother and then her brothers and sister and their families. Her purpose in visiting Ontario was to help her sister-in-law with a new baby as well as to spend time with her beloved brothers. Her family loyalty is indicated by the fact that when she and her mother begin to want to stay in Canada, she writes a great deal about ways to arrange for her sister and family to emigrate so that she will be able to fulfil her promise to tutor her niece without leaving Canada. This duty is so important to her that she actually delays accepting Edward O'Brien's marriage proposal until Lucy releases her from her promise. As well, Edward O'Brien must confirm that his future mother-in-law wishes to stay in Canada because no marriage can take place, according to the bride, if she cannot carry out the duties of a youngest daughter to an aging mother.

Thus, O'Brien's sense of her place revolves around her family relationships. With new loves and duties emerging, the purpose of the diary becomes one of integrating the new with the old, of creating a version of the self located in a constellation of others. When her attention does, of necessity, seem to centre on the ego self, she typically uses the strategies of indirection, humour, and self-parody to present this self. For example, she advises an old friend about to immigrate to Canada that "an active wife will be worth more to him than anything else except his own industry and honesty" (138). When describing her own second labour and delivery, she breezily observes: "After dinner I went into Mama's room to get out of their way and from thence I did not immediately return, for a few minutes made me the mother of another son. The nurse had not arrived, but Mama was so completely taken by surprise that she had no time to be alarmed. With Edward's assistance and Flora's ministrations she did all that was requisite for me and the baby." The next day she adds: "I was glad to find that my nurse had patients requiring assistance more imperiously than myself, so having got rid of all useless hands, we had nothing to do but enjoy ourselves, look at the baby which is tolerable ugly, write my journal and await the return of the boat. Such is the way we manage things in the bush" (197). This newly confident account is from the young woman who once described her sister's confinement with great circumspection and who wrote of her own first pregnancy that on one occasion she was so "sick and faint" that she "was obliged to lie down and go into hysterics" (125). The understatement of "this is how we manage things in the bush" covers years of struggle and hard work in learning how to manage in the new place, how to make that new place part of one's own self; the passage describing the delivery, despite its necessary (given the nature of public language) understatement, fairly bursts with pride in the new confidence she and her mother and husband gain from the experience.

Not all is victory in the bush, but when O'Brien comes to describe the darker side, it is often displaced into others' experience. At one point she chooses to relate the story of a Mrs Monck, and the detail and serious intensity with which she does so indicates that it contains a special emphasis that points out the precarious nature of female selfhood in the wilderness. When acting as midwife to Mrs Monck, O'Brien discovers the lady to be in a state of nervous and physical exhaustion. O'Brien takes her to her home, nurses her, delivers her baby, cares for her. Later she visits her in her own home, and when the unfortunate woman suffers a mental derangement and runs away into the woods, it is O'Brien the rescuers bring to her for her comfort. O'Brien relates that "she was in a state of quiet but decided insanity, refusing to see her husband. She treated me as usual and told me that she had left home with the view to coming to Shanty Bay [O'Brien's home]. Towards morning, she began to talk a good deal of the supposed causes of her miseries and her wanderings in the woods. These appear to have left a comparatively comfortable impression on her mind. She promised to come to me as soon as she could be moved" (244). The woman and her children spend some time with the O'Brien family and O'Brien later visits her where she is being cared for in Toronto.

The incident emphasizes that achieving a balanced sense of self is not the breezy and humorous task that O'Brien's often self-deprecating text would indicate. We have to be aware of different levels of discourse in nineteenth century women's personal writing and the systems of implicature they represent. As a woman writing in patriarchal language, O'Brien must make less of her own achievement by self-directed humour, since by any other style it would appear to be heroic, a stance only permitted to male writers of the self. But when Mrs Monck's story is told in this more serious tone and careful choice of words, another level of implicature becomes available. Not only does the incident imply that our narrator's ability to cope in the wilderness is not necessarily the rule, we are also made aware that the reasons women collapse may not be due to the wilderness itself, since Mrs Monck's wandering "left a comparatively comfortable impression on her mind." (I assume the wanderings are what is meant by the indefinite article "these," since it would be hard to believe the word refers to her "miseries." Interestingly, the normally specific O'Brien leaves the reference ambiguous.) Since the woman refuses to see her husband and has been fleeing to the comfort of O'Brien (the person she must remember as a maternal and sisterly presence at her delivery), the phrase "a good deal of the supposed causes of her miseries" takes on a new implication, suggesting that it is her relationship with her husband and not the wilderness that has made her insane. In fact, both the husband and the wilderness are elements of the place this woman must come to terms with.

From the moment this passage begins, with the ambiguous observations that Mrs Monck is "quiet" yet "decidedly insane" and that despite her insanity she treats O'Brien "as usual" yet refuses to see her husband, the account is typical of the doubled discourse of women's writing of the self in which a correct patriarchal stance is taken on the surface of the text, but is undermined by the word choice, sentence construction, and the unremarked presence of conflicting evidence. I do not draw these inferences concerning the negative references to the husband in this passage from O'Brien's account alone; rather I see the passage in the context of other accounts where I learn that a woman's survival in the wilderness has a great deal to do with the quality of relationship she has with her husband, so that husbands, although incapable alone of maintaining a woman's sanity, are often held responsible for her insanity. The Mrs Monck incident also suggests new implications of the many references to Edward O'Brien's frequent absences from home for political meetings and his frequent illness when home. Although O'Brien never complains about the load of farm work this leaves for her organization and execution, she does let us know that the farm work continues while he is away.

Nevertheless, she remains as optimistic at the end of her ten years of diary keeping as at the beginning. She writes enthusiastically in a late entry: "This has been a *great day* [italics hers]. The mud wall is finished and the bear which has for some time been prowling about is shot, after having terrified the pigs ... A magnificent animal the bear is or, rather, was. Even when dead there was a spirit about him" (256–7). Her sense of a life located in the activities of her pioneer wilderness farm is so great that she no longer actually identifies who has built the mud wall or who has shot the bear. These are not the activities of any individual – the hired hand, the husband, herself – but part of her place, the italicized "great day" she is living, in the way that the bear's spirit is a part of her place.

We can only speculate on why O'Brien's journals ended in 1838. By the time they did she was superintending a large household of children, hired hands, and an aging mother, while her husband spent more time in political activities. She boarded several young neighbourhood girls, whom she tutored at her home, and they paid their board by doing household duties, showing that O'Brien kept the educated old self alive as a teacher while accommodating her farm existence. Perhaps she was too busy with motherhood (she eventually had six children) or perhaps, as her editor speculates, Lucy immigrated and the intimate audience for the account was missing. I would like to believe the diary had served its purpose in terms of building the figure of the ideal pioneer woman who created "a perfect gem of civilization set in the wildest of natural surroundings" (292), as her editor tells us Samuel Thompson observed of her farm in 1833. It is also possible that the years that followed were not recorded because O'Brien saw that with the arrival of civilization there was less need for that special useful place a "lady" could serve in the pioneer economy. I suspect not, however, since the editor remarks in her endnotes that even after taking up residence in Toronto after 1845, O'Brien moved every spring to spend the summer at her Lake Simcoe home (offering us an opportunity to speculate on why Canadian women have often been such enthusiastic summer cottagers). Her granddaughter Kathleen recalls that even as an old woman her grand-mother spent her summer holidays teaching her Italian, an Italian good enough to pass in Italy years later when Kathleen visited there (284).

Despite their laudable achievements, I must note that both O'Brien and Simcoe were advantaged in special ways. O'Brien was a young healthy woman when she came to Canada. Her husband, through his political connections, was able to obtain a generous land grant for a modest sum. Elizabeth Simcoe was insulated by her wealth from many of the hardships of her extended stay in Canada. With servants in tow she was able to enjoy the virgin land without very much suffering its dangers. These advantages of class have much to do with the successful figures these women map for themselves in their diaries: Simcoe's version of the multifaceted mother/wife/artist/traveller and O'Brien's version of the pioneer woman, strong in body and mind. If we change the cultural, economic, and historical status of the pioneer woman to a great degree, does our reading of her figure of selfhood change as well?

If my first reading of Sarah Ellen Roberts in her *Alberta Homestead: The Chronicle of a Pioneer Family* is any example, the figure of selfhood would seem to change drastically to the negative when certain dis-advantages of an economic, historical, and cultural nature come into play. Roberts came to Canada from the United States in 1906 with her husband and sons, to settle near Talbot, Alberta, on some of the last of the free homestead land available in the Old West. As her son, the editor of the book, explains, she had spent her life as the college-educated daughter of an academic family and the wife of a medical doctor in Illinois, a background that was not ideal preparation for Alberta homesteading at the turn of this century. At age fifty-four, plagued with migraines, timidity, and what amounted at times to a phobia of open spaces and a near obsession with cleanliness, she made an unlikely pioneer. She came, as did many, out of des-peration because her husband had lost his practice during a long illness and they had no means to send their three grown sons to college. The homestead and the hard work of the five of them were intended to provide that lack, and for six years they slaved at it, in the end having to leave no wealthier than they came and with Roberts's always fragile health broken. But the boys did get to college, financed by the homestead's crops and the labour of the entire family, and Roberts is able to sum up her experience in these positive words: "As we look back over the years we spent on the homestead, we remember hardships, of course. But even more vividly, we remember the love we bore each other, we remember the sweet companionship of working together at daily tasks, and of sharing with each other hardship and heartbreak and trial and triumph and sorrow and joy."[18]

The arrangement of the list of words in the second half of her sentence and the careful way in which Roberts allows each to strike the reader separately by the repetition of the word "and" give some indication of the special nature of her account. Roberts's own triumph is not the figure she erects of herself, for she remains unequal to the pioneer task, unable to offer the multifacetedness of a Simcoe or the good-humoured strength of an O'Brien; her accomplishment is in her splendid use of language, a use I can only call playful in the sense that Patricia Yaeger speaks of women being playful with patriarchal language, a serious playfulness that offers "the woman writer a way of making the 'weight' of the tradition lighter ... allow[ing] the player to formulate a dialectic that may look 'finished' to the critic's eye, but is actually an adventure of shreds and patches, a way of taking risks ..." (238).

I would propose that the tradition that weighs down Sarah Roberts and that she subverts through her playfulness is heavier than the patriarchal definitions that affect the language of Simcoe and O'Brien. It is heavier because of her historical place, growing up later in the Victorian period, and her place of origin, the United States. Certain truisms of our patriarchal culture are being contended here, one being that the advance of women has been a steady one since the Age of Reason, progressing towards our present state where all has been achieved and women, if not too mired in the assumptions of feminism, may safely move to a post-feminist position. I propose that each major advance of feminist thought and practice has been met with a profoundly reactionary shift on the part of patriarchy. The various cultural definitions of woman of the Victorian period were part of one of those shifts. These manifested themselves in terms of cultural phenomena such as the "cult of true womanhood" and the belief in the "angel in the home."

In my first chapter I summarized texts by Spacks, Nussbaum, and Peterson to show that although women in pre-Victorian times suffered from exclusion from public participation, women growing up in the Victorian age suffered from a more profound psychological exclusion in that they were excluded from the ability to analyse, compare, or combine ideas. Marion Fowler's exploration of the behaviour manuals, the courtesy or copy books used to educate "genteel" women, confirms this. Earlier women, while expected to keep their private places, were also expected to be well educated in a wide variety of ways, to be energetic and witty, and to use language as well as a Simcoe or an O'Brien. The courtesy books changed in Victorian times; women were encouraged to be frail in order to be feminine, to be weak of mind and body, to express themselves in terms of their loving, not in terms of their thinking, and to doubt their abilities in a number of areas, including their ability to shape language. Barbara Welter's research on the "cult of true womanhood" in America confirms Fowler's exploration of English sources. In fact, the new ideal of a frail womanhood took a stronger hold on the American than on the British middle class in the mid-nineteenth century (the class and era in which Roberts grew up), so that many women grew up trying to imitate the four cardinal virtues that "distinguished a true woman form a false one: piety, purity, submissiveness, and domesticity," virtues that are all achieved by limiting the action of a life, rather than expanding it as the pioneer activity demanded.[19] Sarah Roberts certainly seems to be imbued with these later Victorian ideals, as her frailties would indicate: migraines, fear of open spaces, a cleanliness obsession, and an almost slavish worship of her husband's and sons' abilities combined with a downgrading of her own.

It is at first hard to imagine the playful Roberts I propose, especially given her first reaction to the Alberta prairie: "How shall I describe the feeling that then settled down upon me? I had never had it before ... It wasn't exactly homesickness or fear or loneliness or awe, although I think that all of these may have entered into it ... I felt as though I were absolutely alone in the world, and my sense of littleness and helplessness overwhelmed me" (21–2). One grits one's teeth to work through an account in which the narrator assures us that she is as weak and useless at the end of her homesteading experience as at the beginning: "I ... had the same dreadful headaches that I had had all my life, but I think they were even more severe than they had previously been and lasted longer, for they usually kept me in bed for two days and unfitted me for any work for at least one more" (253).

However, Roberts is typical of the pioneer women diarists John Mack Faragher studied, who although devastated by the breakdown of all the social "contexts" that their old place offered, nevertheless, or perhaps because of this devastation, "frequently employed a range of stylistic elaborations" to digest and communicate the experience of their western resettlement.[20] My first clue that this account was not what its surface suggests was in Roberts's frequent repetition of phrases such as "impossible to describe" or "no words can express" or "how can I say." My initial annoyance at this conventionalized self-doubt in language of middle-class women (caused by my preconceptions gained from my own orally authoritative working-class foremothers) eventually changed to an admiration of how well Roberts expresses whatever it is she has just prefaced with "how can I describe." Eventually, the repetition of the words become an ironic code to introduce moments when Roberts would describe a particular phenomenon with detailed erudition and imaginative figures. For example, here is her version of the northern lights: "How I wish that I could describe them or give some faint idea of their beauty. There has been hardly a night this winter that the northern horizon has not been aglow. Much of the time it is a steady, soft light, resembling somewhat the light thrown on the sky by a large city when viewed from a distance at night. Frequently the light mounts to the zenith and descends to the southern horizon in swiftly moving streamers of ever-changing color. These streamers play back and forth, fade away, and then grow again in intensity in a way that defies any description" (83). But the northern lights do not defy Roberts's description; she smoothly enlivens them in language first by making a comparison that urban and rural dwellers will recognize, then by suggesting the scope through the word "zenith." "Streamers" exactly represents both the brightness and buoyancy of the shapes, and the verbs "play," "fade," and "grow" amply and economically describe the action of northern lights. Here we begin to see the dialectic between articulate description and disclaimer of ability to make such use of language that is part of Roberts's play, for the effect of the disclaimer is that it not only casts the narrator in the role of the modest, awe-inspired observer, thus giving us the mood of watching the lights, but also calls out for the reader to bring her own imagination to bear on the site of language. The "how can I describe" tag is one way a writer can ask for help from the reader, thus demanding a more active reading in which the reader is a part of the dialectic of her play.

But in any concept of play, there must be an element of the consciousness of that play, a sense that the particular language usage has become deliberate, a rhetoric. I believe that the dialectic I point out is not just the knee-jerk reaction of a woman trained in deference, but a conscious crafting, a sophisticated, albeit disguised, language making. An important aspect of the special difficulty of Roberts's position, a woman's position, in the homestead economy is the absolute isolation of her place as home-maker. While the men are often at work in pairs or groups, she is alone at her work. She figures her isolation in this literary manner: "I think that during the first few weeks of our stay here I never went to the door of the tent without scanning the horizon, as they say in novels, to see if I could discover anywhere upon the seemingly boundless prairie any living, moving thing; for there were times when the loneliness was so oppressive that to see even a herd of cattle moving toward a little meadow where the grass looked greener gave me a distinct sense of relief and companionship" (34). After reading many diaries, I was brought up short by the words "as they say in novels" in the middle of this diary. These words suddenly emphasized all the ways in which this and similar accounts are different from novels, all the ways in which they do not fulfil the novelistic assumptions of the reader, all the ways in which they demand a different relationship with the reader. In the case of Roberts, we see the beginning of her experimentation with finding a voice that does not speak in the tones of the novelistic narrator who advances the complex interaction of character and event. Nor does it speak in the persona of lyric poetry in which the sudden epiphany of human consciousness joined to the natural world creates the drama and beauty of the form. Rather it speaks quietly, almost laconically, of an experience that is not an epiphany, that is not a rising action seeking a place where character and event converge, but is more like the weaving and embroidering of a musical theme that, through incremental repetition, builds its effect. It is what Yaeger characterizes as the bringing together of "shreds and patches," the risk taking in language that will build a new mapping of self and other. Thus, when the college-educated Roberts, a woman who would certainly know the form of the novel, calls humorous attention to the stereotype of the hero(ine) "scanning the horizon," creating in the reader a novelistic expectation that s(he) will see something (danger, rescue, or at least the pony express!), I must attend to her added emphasis. At this point the novelistic sensibility would move the plot along to something like "one day a figure appeared," not reward the reader instead with the unlikely effect of the "companionship" of cattle. I must assume that she is pointing my expectation away from novelistic reality and towards another reality.

In fact, Roberts is quite consciously and craftily creating (for the reader with an "inventive patience") an autobiographical narrative style that will somehow figure the experience of radical othering that was hers on the Canadian prairie at the beginning of this century. I use the phrase "radical othering" to speak of the way in which Roberts's physical, emotional, and mental integrity, built over a lifetime in non-rural environments, is assailed by her experience on the Alberta prairie, almost to the point where she sometimes seems to be in grave psychological danger, leading, through the agency of language making, not to a recoil from the new place, not to the "garrison mentality" that is said to be characteristic of Canadian literature, but to a fullness of voice that contains the experience, the relationships and work and suffering of the experience, as well as the effect of the place on that experience.[21] One of Roberts's best expressions of that voice is contained in her description of the coming of spring to the prairie:

The first winter was by far the most severe of any we experienced in Alberta, and we were more poorly prepared for it than we were for the later ones. Of course, the spring did come, as springs always do. The snow disappeared, the crocuses challenged the frost with their purple blossoms all over the prairie, and the ice melted in the ponds, which were once more alive with water fowl. It was like greeting old friends to hear the "honk, honk" of the geese as they flew northward, or to hear the musical note of the meadow lark. The men say that the best of all days is that day when the frost has left the ground and the work in the fields has begun. And I am sure that only one who has plowed early in the spring, when it seems so good to be out of doors, can know how it feels to walk out over the great breezy field, down the long, black, straight furrows. Lathrop says that when he first plows in the spring he rests under a sort of illusion, for it seems that it is he and not the team ahead that is forcing the plowshares through the stubborn soil. The grasp of the plow seems to give him a sense of power.

I used to go out to where the men were plowing. It fascinated me to watch the moist earth roll up on the moldboard and turn over, black and cool and sweetsmelling. There is nothing quite like that odor. It has in it all the essence of the spring, all the promise of the summer. It is as though the very clods had language and spoke to us of the wealth that lay latent in them. (102–3)

This passage illustrates Roberts's ability to create a personal voice (without establishing a dominant ego self) that allows her to figure the miracle of an active spring – the spring experienced by the men who plant the soil – within, but not dominated by, her own experience. Beginning with the general statement about winter, she inserts her "we," which here means her own family, thus localizing and personalizing her account. Her image of the crocuses that "challenged" the frost indicates not only her literary mindedness but also her desire to re-create the active rather than passive nature of spring. Her reference to her "old friends" the water fowl includes them in the gestalt of others she is creating. Her seemingly unsophisticated inclusion of "honk, honk" (unseemly by the standards of romantic nature description) in actuality creates a humorous, domestic mood in keeping with her low-key, family-oriented experience of spring. It also evokes the sound of spring, keeping her description from becoming too sight-bound. Her inclusionary efforts extend to the men's, especially her son Lathrop's, feelings about spring, and I note that the men are, as usual, the active characters in her re-creation. But, Roberts is not the minor character that her highlighting of the men's reality would seem to make her. In fact, her very emphasis on them makes us aware of her difference from the men; for example, her son Lathrop "rests under the illusion" that he is breaking into the "stubborn" soil, and she allows us to compare this attitude to her own more connected sense of self and soil.

In the quoted passage, she is most powerfully the perceiving and enclosing consciousness of the writing, open through all her senses and language-making ability to the moment that is spring, when, at the beginning of her second paragraph, she finally uses the word "I." The "I" position is one of "a connective tissue," a felt connection with all the elements of the scene and her own emotions as she speaks of being "fascinated" with the moment and the intimacy of the "moist" earth (the sense of touch broadens the range of perception), gathering all those connections – with the day, the birds, the men, the plowing – into her culminating place. That place is figured as a literal voice that speaks to "us," the us that is now diffuse enough to be family, self, reader – a voice that reaches us through the radical sense of finding her *self* in the *other* that is Sarah Ellen Roberts's experience of the prairie. Since I have suggested that mothering is the most radical form of othering, here we have a woman who, in making language, mothers her stronger self into being through the agency that a new language of the self gives her.

It is important to note that, as her editor (her son Lathrop) informs us, Roberts's account is both a diary and a retrospective account, as the first one hundred pages are the result of an "almost daily record" she kept in 1906–1907. The rest of the text was written in 1915 three years after the experience of homesteading had ended. Thus, the passage quoted is from the later writing time. The second half of the text maintains a remarkable degree of the immediacy of the first half, mostly due to Roberts's excellent recall of detail, especially the detail of feelings. Lathrop Roberts suggests that this is because the homestead years remained "very vivid" for the family members. The combination of diary and retrospective account, although fortuitous in this instance, creates much of the power of text, for Roberts is able to combine a convincing immediacy and the selectivity that comes with retrospection.

However, by keeping many attributes of the diary style, Roberts allows for an autobiographical form that breaks novelistic conventions and replaces them with a pattern of diachronic reoccurrence, thus building the special intimate and inclusive voice that allows this woman to express her experience of self and world. Roberts's combination of this with a retrospective stance allows her to map an identity that is a special kind of autobiographical voice, a radical othering, a gestalt of person, place, and relationships, a female arach-nology that our reading can trace. When women write, not diaries, but retrospective autobiographical accounts, what different arachnologies emerge from them for the reader who reads, as Miller would put it, "against the weave of indifferentiation to discover the embodiment in writing of a gendered subjectivity?"[22] What is the effect on the pioneer ground entangled in the weave of these accounts? And what generic markers do we require to help establish the intertext of our reading?

2 Pioneer Women's Memoirs: Preserving the Past / Rescuing the Self

> The memoir as genre is closely associated with periods of
> crisis: both historical crises ... and intellectual crisis ... In
> times of crisis, the memoir-writer understands that [her] past
> and [her] very present are stepping stones to an unknown
> future. [S]he experiences life more intensely, because the very
> foundations of life as [s]he has known them are threatened.
>
> Marcus Billson, in "The Memoir:
> New Perspectives on a Forgotten Genre."

For some pioneer women, the sense that they were living in a once-in-history conjunction of event, place, and self was extremely strong. The need to write of such a conjunction, to rescue the old self that existed before the pioneer enterprise, to re-create the structure and depth of the unparalleled settlement of the new place, as well as the changes it wrought in themselves, and to project into the future the view of life that such an experience had given them, led them to the most accommodating form for the expression of their lives – the memoir. It is the form for those who are "convinced that man's ontology derives from his historical context[.] [T]he memoir writer thinks it is his duty to fix in form and imbue with significance the random, haphazard, and accidental that once existed but would be forgotten without his narrative."[1] In contrast to my epigraph for this chapter, I leave Marcus Billson's use of "man" and "he" in this quoted passage to emphasize that although the memoir form offered the best available literary format for these women, it was still a form shaped for and by the needs of men. To tell their own stories, pioneer women, consciously or unconsciously, had to use the form differently from the way men had used it. Perhaps the very fact that critics have always considered the form to be in a no man's land between traditional autobiography and history has made it particularly suitable for women's needs. A genre that is least established in the patriarchal order is one open to the task of rescuing, through various female arachnologies, the inscription of a female selfhood.

But unlike the early Canadian diarist, who could claim the relative privacy of her genre as a shield against public criticism, the memoir writer assumes a public form and confronts immediately the problem of women's place in nineteenth-century society as the embodiment of "altruism, selflessness and reticence,"[2] especially reticence about revealing the private world in the public format. Thus, as Joanne Dobson notes concerning the poet Emily Dickinson, a woman's "art mediates in complex, nuanced, and often highly conflicted ways between individual experience and cultural imperatives" (xi). By tracing this mediation, I wish to draw the contours of the special emphasis that these early Canadian women give to the memoir form. In doing so, I hope to enlarge in detail and scope the generic map I am drafting of the inscription of female subjectivity.

When I survey the first of the texts that I have chosen to examine, Elizabeth Lichtenstein Johnston's *Recollections of a Georgia Loyalist*, I am immediately confronted with the conflicting cultural and personal agendas pressing on this woman.[3] The thirty-six–page editor's introduction would seem to indicate that the book was written to provide historical information on the background of her distinguished United Empire Loyalist family, which had fled Georgia during the upheavals of the American Revolution, but the introduction must itself supply this information, since it is not part of Johnston's account. In fact, if what we learn about that great historical event from her writing were the test of the success of her memoirs, they would be a failure. Only three of the eleven chapters feature the revolution, and they describe it only as a menacing offstage event threatening the communal life of the family. Unlike the male memoir writer who wishes to document his place in public events among the public personalities of his time, Johnston wishes to document her place in the private world of family as this basic unit of society's organization grows and changes in the vicissitudes of history. In contouring the format of the memoir to accommodate this more private world, as well as facing the problem of the necessary female reticence, Johnston also gains an advantage from the point of view of autobiographical writing: the need to write of the private, the personal, increases the need to appraise her private self as that self relates to the family as daughter, wife, and mother. Billson's argument for the memoir as autobiography is that it narrates the process of "being-in-the-world," whereas "becoming-in-the-world" is the task of spiritual or ego-centred autobiography (261). The memoir writer who wishes to establish a human subjectivity based on the historicity of lived experience, a historicity "imbue[d] with significance" (268) by the memorialist's moral vision, is more concerned with being than becoming (262). I agree with Billson's analysis of how the memoir works through its preoccupation with historicity, with being in the world, but would add that for the women I am concerned with, Elizabeth Johnston in particular, the special preoccupation with the private world allows them to bridge memoir and spiritual autobiography to write an account of their becoming women in the world, as well as the history of their being in the world.

This happens in Johnston's account because like that of many women concerned with family and personal relationships, her sense of history is different from men's. As the American historian Gerda Lerner points out, women's "history has been a special kind." When not using "the lens of men's records and observations,"[4] women have not necessarily seen the time periods considered significant by men as significant to their own development. In fact, in this familial and personal world, history is always interwoven with a woman's own development so that the memoir writer is also an autobiographer. The form of Johnston's book reveals this by its organization around three periods in her life, each with its own special approach and tone. The first section, chapters one and two (37–63), tells the story of her life up to the time of her marriage in 1779, at age fifteen, to a Loyalist soldier, Captain William Martin Johnston. The second section, chapters three through ten (64–121), covers most of her adult life until age forty-six (1810), at which time and mostly through her efforts the family settles permanently in Nova Scotia. The third section (122–64), takes the reader into Johnston's old age, to the time of writing in 1838, when she is seventy-four. The style of the first section is a chronologically based narrative, with a tone of nostalgia for a seemingly fairy-tale past, as Johnston re-creates her secure childhood as the obedient only child of doting, well-to-do parents, a childhood security shattered by her mother's death when Johnston was ten and further destroyed two years later by the events of the revolution in which her father barely escaped the fate of other Loyalists – being tarred and feathered. The notable thing about the emphasis in the section is that both of these events – mother's death and father's flight – are treated as equal parts of the same story, that of the growth to maturity of the young woman, a growth she characterizes as making her strong in adversity.

The second section, although still a chronological account, is much less narrative bound in its strategies. It tends to pinpoint certain moments of emergency in her adulthood, in the family's life together – their various moves, the sending of children away for education, a family member's illness – making the account more discursive and focusing attention on ethical problems consequent upon being the mother of a family. While the first section inscribes a female character shaped by experience, the second inscribes a female morality shaped by the ethical problems of middle life. However, the third section, whose matter is made up largely of brief memorial passages for beloved others, has a more reflective tone, as Johnston sums up the meaning she gives her life and contemplates her relationship to her conception of deity.

Interestingly, this structure corresponds with the three basic types of autobiography identified by William C. Spengemann, the historical, the philosophical, and the poetical.[5] In this Canadian woman's memoirs we see a writer bridging all three forms: her early life told as a series of historically linked cause-and-effect factors; her middle life, a philosophical problem in ethical behaviour; and her old age, a more poetic phase in which she achieves a reflective acceptance of self and other. For critics concerned with purity of form and accustomed to traditional male autobiographies, which tend to take up one form or another, Johnston's use of the three forms in a memoir format would seem to be an awkward and unfortunate mixture of styles. But Spengemann points out that the first great autobiographer, Augustine, was unusual in his use of all three forms. I would compare Johnston's stylistic blend to Augustine's, but emphasize that her account creates an emphasis added, an italicized version of the Augustinian form, to construct what Miller terms an "arachnology," or in Hirsch's term a "romance" of origins that maps the terrain of a female life cycle.

Although Augustine is concerned with the dramatization of the act of conversion and the concomitant new relationship with the deity, while Johnston's concern is a more domestic one, that of correct behaviour as mother of a family, both autobiographers present an ethical vision of life. Thus, they choose similar threefold strategies. However, Augustine's moral vision rests on the importance of the gift of faith, as opposed to reason, in creating the Christian life. Johnston's moral vision rests on the performance of the deeds that duty dictates, no matter what the personal desire may be. In a sense this has as much to do with faith as does Augustine's conversion, except that his threefold account emphasizes the coming to faith, the gift of faith, and the special relationship with God that follows; Johnston's divisions emphasize the kind of life that leads the individual to seek moral conduct, the various difficult choices made and constrictions on those decisions, and the eventual achievement of self-acceptance through self-examination.

There are other important differences in the two uses of the threefold form. Augustine's is a retrospective account that condemns and rejects his former life in order to emphasize the act of conversion and transcendence over sinful ways. Johnston's is a retrospective account, but one that attempts neither conversion nor transcendence over the past, but rather attempts to understand, accept, and modify her past self and actions in the light of discoveries of later life. The reason for this difference is inextricably a part of the kind of life emphasized by each writer. Augustine is concerned with a life that is to enter the alternative "family" of the patriarchal Christian church organization. He must cleanse himself of past ways and separate himself from past attachments to enter that alternate arrangement. As Lionnet observes regarding Augustine, his need to transcend the past life leads him to "a denial of the self, of the embodied self born of an earthly mother."[6] Johnston's past, her mother, father, in-laws, husband, children, are, in the historical writing time, also her future. Although the mother, father, in-laws, and husband are now dead, they live through the children and grandchildren of whom and for whom she writes. They cannot be rejected, transcended, left behind. Her need for a female romance of origins rather than an Augustinian or male romance of origins must shape them so that they are both the beloved others of the past and the acceptable ancestors of her posterity.

This is not always an easy task, as these figures, especially the husband and in-laws, often offer the most difficult opposition to her behaviour as a morally correct mother, the image of herself she wishes to construct. Again and again, Johnston's account becomes a balancing act between exposing some perceived flaw in herself and/or others and nevertheless continuing to hold the guilty party in an esteem suitable to a memoir dedicated to the future progeny of the family. Of her own mother's death she writes: "We may see in almost every event that befalls us the hand of our merciful Heavenly Father directing the various events of our lives for our good. Perhaps had my beloved and tender mother lived she might not have kept as strict a hand over me as my volatile nature required. My aunt was kind, but was at the same time decided in her conduct toward me, and I was made industrious at my needle" (50-1). A wealth of implicature lies in these lines. The mother is both blamed for not being strict enough in raising her and memorialized for her "tender" qualities. This is an important point for Johnston, as her whole account emphasizes that for the type of exiled and tragedy-ridden life she eventually would lead, a strict upbringing, emphasizing duty over personal preference, was a necessary prerequisite. The feminist implications of the figure of the child being "made industrious at my needle" go beyond the referential meaning of the phrase that implies that hard work builds character, and reminds us that needlework was literally and symbolically the very essence of femininity for the eighteenth- and nineteenth-century leisured classes. Thus, Johnston inscribes herself within a patriarchal economy, one especially evoked by the summoning up of "our merciful Heavenly Father" as the force responsible for the direction of our lives. This appeal to patriarchal authority would seem to be a diachronic reoccurrence of a not very subversive sort, since Johnston makes a point of informing her readers that when William Johnston, as he is about to leave to fight against the rebels, confessed his love for her, she answered him "by silence only ... then I got upstairs into my own room in the dark, and wept most abundantly, not at the thought of parting from him, but to think I should have listened to such a thing without my father's knowledge" (54).

How can such a thoroughly male-defined sensibility be capable of the "discourse inscriptive of social change" that Yaeger finds "racked up" in our foremothers' accounts? And yet it is in such an account that we can watch the process of such a development, one especially powerful because of the very limitations placed on it by the loyalties demanded of a woman who is the maternal centre of a patriarchal family in exile. In order to shade in this subtly contoured area of my map, I will ask my reader to assume that special "inventive patience" that Elizabeth Hampsten advises for the readers of personal accounts, while I explore what at first may seem to be rather insignificant details of phrasing in Johnston's account. Her narration of the events around the deaths of two of her children reveals the conflicting demands she negotiates.

As the result of her husband's taking up a medical practice in Jamaica after training in Scotland, it is deemed necessary that the older children must go to Scotland to receive a proper education. In this situation it is Johnston's duty to stay with her husband, but she does not part very willingly with her son and daughter. By implication, this parting is seen as the grounds for later tragedy. She says of her son Andrew's misspent youth, which ended in an early death from fever: "That want of firmness had been a marked feature of the child's character from very early infancy, and it proved ruinous to him in his subsequent life. In his early education many traits of character and little faults were kept by his too fond widowed aunt and her maiden sisters from his worthy Grandfather Johnston's knowledge which had he known he might have nipped in the bud" (92). Johnston would seem to be blaming the "too fond" aunt, rather than the "worthy" grandfather charged with the boy's care in Scotland, for the later debauch of his life. Blaming other women while

excusing men is typical of the male-defined woman. But her judgment wavers as the process of the reappraisal of the past goes on in
the writing of the confessional sixth and seventh chapters of the
memoir.

At times she blames Andrew's own too-easy nature, at other times
the indulgent female relatives, and then her husband's insistence on
the son's taking up the medical profession. She concludes with this
warning: "Let this sad history ... be a warning to all my grandchildren to avoid idleness and dissolute companions, and to study in
youth, the seed-time of knowledge, that they may reap the fruits of
honest industry in after life and be an honor and credit to their
parents" (99). By abandoning her exploration of past responsibility
and displacing it into the future through her progeny, she makes an
interesting swerve, which shows her hesitation in coming down too
fully in favour of a single judgment which would transcend the past
by assigning blame and thus dismissing it from further consideration.
Rather, the past and its tragedy is imbricated and implicated with the
future and its moral imperatives through the writing moment of the
present.

Johnston makes this effort at balancing loyalties even more exten-
sive when she adds that "even while at college his weak aunts rather
took part against me, judging me too severe in wishing him to devote
more of his time to study. I have had severe trials in this life, yet I
am conscious that I deserved many, and none, I believe, have been
more than was good for me. This is a long, sad history of my
lamented first-born; let it be a warning to youth, and to parents to
allow their sons to choose that profession their hearts most incline
them to" (100). This statement revises and complicates her former
conclusion, as now, while still blaming the "weak aunts" she introduces the possibility, albeit submerged in the indirection of "judging
me too severe," that she herself may be partially responsible for
Andrew's problems. This possibility is increased by her warning,
which is now not only to youth, but to parents (not just fathers), to
let young people make their own choice of profession.

At this point in her text Johnston introduces a seemingly unrelated
narrative concerning her youngest child, Laleah, who at thirteen is
so devoted a daughter that she writes a poem in praise of her mother
while they are on a dangerous sea voyage. But the digression serves
a purpose, as it allows the writer a "soft" entry into the tragic story
of her daughter Catherine. In the light of this tragedy, the unstated
point of the digression is to show that a child who remains directly
under Johnston's protection does not develop the unfortunate ten-
dencies that afflicted Andrew or Catherine. The hesitant broaching

of this new material seems justified when we learn of Catherine's life. This time Grandfather Johnston is not called "worthy," but is simply the figure who has "taken her [Catherine] from me, thinking to benefit her by the advantages she would gain in Edinburgh" (105). But as well as hinting at the helplessness of women in the face of patriarchal authority, Johnston is now ready to assume her portion of the blame, for she admits: "Perhaps I was too anxious to counteract the faults that had been fostered so long, and may have tried to check them too suddenly" (106). A typical strategy of a self-justifying memoir, when one is confronted with the possibility of personal guilt, is to turn away from the narration of the events that would expose that guilt, as Ben Franklin does in not detailing his "errata" in his autobiography. Johnston does not avoid the full narration of Catherine's unstable temperament, her descent into madness, and her eventual consignment, after the family's move to Nova Scotia, to a hospital for the insane in the United States, where the disturbed girl died just before her mother was due to visit her.

Much of the implicature that I find important to Johnston's account is in the tone of its writing, a tone that cannot be conveyed through the partial quotation allowed in my exploration. But her tone is nevertheless an important element in the special female arachnology that is being inscribed inside the more foregrounded patriarchally defined inscription of femininity of the surface of the text. Richard Hoggart has observed in his article "A Question of Tone" that nineteenth-century autobiographers speak with a tone of "splendid assurance" unlike more recent autobiographers, who display a twentieth-century uneasiness with self-justification and special pleading.[7] I would observe that Hoggart's examples are all males and that I have not found a "splendid assurance" in female accounts. Indeed, as with Johnston, any assumption of assurance is eroded as the writing continues, and gives way to another tone, one of mourning and expiation of the past, in which the self being inscribed is one who wishes to hold on to what is worthy in her past self, in this case her insistence on the centrality of the mother/child relationship, but also wishes to admit to her own implication in the failure of this maternal ethic.

Johnston observes as she ends the confessions of chapters six and seven that "at this moment, though more than seventeen years have passed since she was consigned to an early grave, I feel all the tenderness of grief as though it were very recent" (114). This moment of the autobiographer commenting on the effect of her own text is an important one in terms of the inscription of female subjectivity. The effect of the retelling has not been an act of distancing the past to keep the ego-self intact, but rather the recollection has conflated past and present so that past is reinternalized to produce the "tenderness" of grief. This tenderness, this lack of ego barriers, this vulnerability to one's own past, is an important part of the tone of the women's memoirs I have read. It would seem to indicate the desire to inscribe a subjectivity that seeks to embrace the fullness of its experience rather than to peel away portions of experience in constructing a more boundary-defined and coherent selfhood. This implies that the compilation map of women's accounts I am shaping involves a layering of personal maps that are already a palimpsest, in which the adult female sketches her subjectivity inside, over, and around the already inscribed maps of the histories of her significant others.

Such a consciousness cannot represent herself in a moment of conversion as in the Augustinian model, but rather seeks a stylistic map that allows for a position that results from a gradually moderating sense of the interaction of persons and history, a map that needs the conflation of the form of the memoir and the non-traditional use of the autobiographical form represented by Augustine. This is nowhere more obvious than in the last section of Johnston's account in which, through her individual poetic cameo portraits in words of the members of her family who have died, she composes a version of her own best self as a kind of "connective tissue" weaving itself like a thread between the beads of memory, each bead an exposure of some special quality of the mourned individual. In recounting her daughter Eliza's death in childbed, she observes: "If I were called upon to bear testimony whose individual character I had ever known most free from selfishness, I could with truth and boldness say it was my beloved Eliza's"(132). True to her moral vision of the interconnectedness of family members, she takes on the raising of her daughter's children. However, of her daughter-in-law's death in a fire caused by the young woman's careless moment with a candle, a fire in which panic overcame sense, she observes: "Hers was a strong mind in matters that concerned her spiritual welfare, but in temporal things her diffidence led her to lean on others" (152). This double inscription is always part of Johnston's account, the praising of what is virtuous in an individual while keeping clearly before her reader the values she advocates: a strength of purpose and practicality that her own life had taught her was vital to survival.

Johnston's maternal ethic is always interwoven with her place in a patriarchal economy. However, that ethic emerges more strongly when she recounts the events after her husband's death, a death which, tellingly, is not memorialized in the positive way others are.

Although the death of the husband often offers such women more of a leadership role in the family (and this emerges in their written accounts), what promotes the sense of an alternate ethic, an alternate story, in such accounts is the memoir form itself. Because it is so firmly tied to the whole life experience of the writer, a form defined by historicity, it is less easily bound by the literary genres of patriarchy. When Homans, Miller, and Hirsch speak of women developing alternate strategies inside patriarchal literary production, they are referring to the novel and poetry. In this tradition the figure of woman must keep her place in traditional plot structures, as subordinate and limited in action, and must retain her limited figuration as ornamental and additional to a male-centred creativity. As Hirsch points out, in these genres women can only reshape the form when their heroines refuse "conventional heterosexual romance and marriage plots." But an autobiographical form based on the historicity of the actual life lived is already a refusal, by very definition, of the traditional plot structures of novels and the imagery patterns of poetry. Thus, the very assumption that she must write of her life beyond love and marriage in order to fulfil the mandate of the memoir allows, indeed encourages, a writer like Johnston to inscribe an alternate subjectivity to the one offered in more tradition-bound formats such as the novel.

Ironically, we especially see the assertion of the truth of this genre imperative when a woman refuses its possibilities and insists on reinscribing her limited patriarchal role, and thus denying, silencing, the facts of her own life. Susan Sibbald is such a case in point. In *The Memoirs of Susan Sibbald*, we see, once again, an introduction at odds with its text. But instead of a male editor attempting to impose a patriarchal historical agenda on the female memorialist, we find Sibbald's great grandson, Francis Paget Hett, trying to compensate for the fact that Sibbald leaves out what he obviously considers the most admirable and exceptional part of her life, her years in Canada in the 1830s in which she establishes herself as farmer in the Lake Simcoe area and, with the aid of her sons, builds a secure and comfortable future for her family. Such an adventure on the part of a determined widow should, by our present-day standards, make for a rich memoir. But Sibbald does not choose to write about any years past her youth and early marriage. Hett speculates that "possibly she desired that an account of her happy youth and early married life only should survive, and the story of subsequent years, with their sorrows and vicissitudes, should be forgotten."[8]

But in leaving these years out Sibbald abandons the promise of the opening pages of her text in which she refers to the fact that "in my native town of Fowey, there had been many courageous females," including one who led an effort to protect Charles II in 1644, when the women of the town "shouldered their broomsticks, and mounting the hill above the entrance to the harbor, so terrified the Rebels who were approaching in ships, that they tacked about and put out to sea again" (3). We are not to learn any more of the courage of women from Fowey, who in the past spent their courage defending their male monarch. The Fowey woman writing spends her text on a closely detailed account of her life as the daughter of an English country gentleman, as a Regency era debutante in London and Bath, ending with a shorter account of the first years of her marriage to an army officer and ignoring entirely her more than thirty years in Canada, thereby staying well within the patriarchal tradition of the novel plot in which the heroine moves only between male economies. Passed from the father to the husband, she marries and disappears.

Her editor tells us that Sibbald came to Canada because of economic problems caused by her husband's death and perhaps attributable to his prior mismanagement of family estates (xvi). Thus, her Canadian life lies outside the heroic male romance in which her early life places her. When one looks at the portrait of the strong but dour middle-aged woman that appears opposite page 314, one has difficulty connecting her to the girl described in the text. To a reader seeking a feminist romance rather than a patriarchal romance of female life, one that leaves in all the female life that does not appear in male plots, Sibbald's account in unsatisfying. Yet it illustrates the strength of male romances in that many women are so thoroughly imbricated in their roles inside patriarchy that no other identity can offer them pleasure in remembrance, even, or perhaps especially, the actual lived events of their own life histories of achievement, hard work, and courage.

Sibbald's text is illustrative of Lennard J. Davis's thesis in *Resisting Novels*, in which he describes the way in which the form of the novel, throughout its history, has reinforced the dominant ideology. Davis is not optimistic about the ability of literary pursuits to resist or change ideological positions. He sums up the theoretical investigations of Foucault, whom he sees as preoccupied with the "level of effect" of ideology, and of Raymond Williams, whom he finds useful in explaining the ideological force of literature through sociological methodology, but who is nevertheless "focused on the past."[9] In fact, even though Davis also admires theorists like Frederic Jameson who perform the critical act of "unmasking" ideology and those like Terry Eagleton who extend the "definition of literature to include popular culture," he finds that these theoreticians remain in a "limited field" of the "campus walk" (49). Davis holds that the real work that needs to be done if we are to resist conservative novelistic ideological practices is to explore "the way literary works ... use specific techniques for ideological purposes" (51). I have chosen, in mapping my area of interest, to replace the work of theorists such as Jameson, Eagleton, Foucault, and Williams with the work of women-centred theorists such as Miller, Homans, Hirsch, and Yaeger, partially because I find other theorists, unknowingly caught in male-centred subjectivity assumptions, are not able to offer me the specific explorations I need. But as well, Miller, Homans, Hirsch, and Yaeger are useful because they offer me politicized texts, proactive in their sponsorship of women's texts, giving an optimistic view of women's ability to counter the dominant ideologies of patriarchy in their writing, and thus pointing to what Davis calls the "specific techniques" we need if we are to "resist" novelistic plots. Their declaration of their feminist positions does not make them less scholarly, only more honest than those theorists who are male-centred but do not declare the gendered nature of their theories. However, neither this group of women theorists nor Davis offers me an exploration outside the dominant cultural genres of the novel and poetry. I feel that if theorists concerned with the interrelationships between dominant ideologies and literary production (or more broadly in Eagleton's mandate, cultural production) turned to the ways in which women have always used marginalized, "sub-literary" genres, they would find paradigms of the resistant subject (such as Johnston) and paradigms of the subjected subject (such as Sibbald), which would enrich their theoretical explorations. I find a recent exploration of resistant and subjected subjectivity, Paul Smith's *Discerning the Subject*, useful in this regard. Smith shares Davis's and my concern that contemporary theory "shows itself unable to approach political dilemmas left open by its consistent and elaborate privileging of a view of difference which can best be described as *indifference*."[10] To solve the problem of indifference, one must turn sometimes to the seemingly most modest and ordinary cultural productions to find a *difference* that speaks to the politics of our lived life in culture.

No text illustrates this better than the very modest memoir of Mary Hiemstra, *Gully Farm*, an account of one year that Hiemstra spent as a child with her pioneer parents who came to Canada from an English farming background to settle near Battleford, Saskatchewan, with the ill-prepared Barr colony immigrants in 1903. I describe this text as modest because it does not appear stylistically adventurous, using a realistic novel format, dependent on traditional set pieces of description for its settings, and achieving character delineation through dialogue, action, and location of individuals inside easily recognized character stereotypes evoked through physical descriptions. For example, the father's pleasant face is described in realistic detail and shows signs that indicate "humour was there, and understanding, and never-failing zest." The mother is "trim," with "tiny hands and feet and a quick energetic way of walking that gave her tiny figure a look of eager importance."[11] Neither is Hiemstra's format of the type that would be called experimental, since it is a largely straightforward chronological narration of the experiences of their settlement year.

However, the text falls in that category of memoir Billson describes as "covering a limited amount of time, two years or less, [where] there is the possibility, contrary to past critical assumptions, for a great deal of introspection, which can detail many inner psychic changes" (266). Billson's example of such a dramatically revealing memoir is Norman Mailer's *Armies of the Night*. Mailer is able to locate himself in psychic and societal contexts through narrating his part in the 1967 march against the Pentagon, which "catalyze[s] Mailer's awareness of his real abilities and limitations as an active political being" (266). What Mary Hiemstra is able to do is dramatize her own formation as a subject, its ambivalences, its certainties, and its variety, through her characterizations of her beloved, but always disagreeing parents, as they lived though the first four seasons of the life-threatening, traumatic adventure which they continued to disagree about for the rest of their lives. In fact, Hiemstra literalizes herself as a figure in the way Homans describes, and that figure is one of the narrator/translator, translating her parents' differences into some version of herself that gives her certainty, translating the terror of the new country into home, and translating the realistic novel's plot into a form that can accommodate her own experience of life. As a writer, Hiemstra has two advantages that aid her in this translation: she handles her materials with considerable sophistication, at her best writing very much like Sinclair Ross in his short stories, and she has a sense of humour which she brings to bear on the relationship of her parents, facilitating her positive re-creation of their lives. In fact, her humour allows her a way out of the double bind of women's writing, the need to reveal the personal life in order to inscribe subjectivity and the need to be reticent to conform to cultural stereotypes.

The key to this is finding the right part of the private life that will re-create symbolically the whole life, and the right tone for its presentation that will hold together all the female loyalties and the subjectivity agendas of the autobiographer. Hiemstra finds it in her genre blend of novel, memoir, autobiography, and history of settlement. Since her father is buoyantly optimistic about the opportunities of the new land and her mother is at all times ready to see the drawbacks, since the Barr colony had such an extraordinary "hype" in its recruitment drive and such a devastatingly bad on-the-scene record, Hiemstra's tale is a revision of the pioneer myth, both at a societal and familial level. But as well she makes it her autobiography, as she dramatizes the effect of the parents' disagreements – and their ultimate unity in the face of the danger and adversity of one winter – on her own psyche. This is highlighted in Hiemstra's account of her father's attempt to rescue a lost settler during a blizzard. She evokes her mother's reaction while waiting at the window for her husband's return: "Mother didn't seem to notice that the fire was almost out, and that the cold was coming in. She didn't even notice the shadows. She stood by the window and looked at the flying snow, and tears ran down her young cheeks, but she did not notice the tears, either. I spoke in a low voice, but she did not answer, she simply stood there holding the light, and after a little while I became afraid. I seemed to be alone in the storm" (224). Hiemstra is memoir writer, autobiographer, and novelist at once, memorializing the incident in which her mother makes her solidarity with the husband clear, despite their differences, re-creating her own sense of separateness as the emergency leaves her outside the circle of her mother's care, and evoking these through the chronologically based and descriptively rich style of the realistic novel.

As well, Hiemstra's account of settlement gains a great deal of its power from her ability to place the narrative's centre of consciousness in others, not only her mother and father, but other settlers who shared that desperate first winter of the Barr colony. For example, her account of the lost settler incident moves from her mother's point of view to the settler's: "The wind pushed from first one side then the other, and the snow hissed as it whirled like a shroud around him. He stumbled on, but he had no idea where he was going. He was lost, and cold dark arms of the blizzard were closing around him. He fell and got up and fell again. His feet were numb and his hands like ice, and even his body in his too-thin coat felt stiff and half frozen. Soon he knew he would fall and not get up again. It was then that he began to shout" (227). As well as re-creating the reality of the unprepared settler in the severe Canadian environment, the incident re-creates the familial situation and the personal psychic complex. It is the unity that the mother and father become capable of that rescues the man, and the event becomes a literalization of the child's psychic situation as she is brought, by the united efforts of mother and father, though a winter that killed others, and is able to re-create in the writing situation, a subjectivity balanced always between the figures of her two very opposite parents.

That she does so in a form that presents itself as a traditional realistic novel speaks to Davis's point about the need to resist conservative novelistic practices. Hiemstra's specific techniques are not the overstated deconstructive strategies of the postmodernists, but rather the subtle interweaving of the historicity of the memoir format with the techniques of the realist novel. The mandate of the memoir form, with its emphasis on the fullness of the lived life's detail, deconstructs the totalizing nature of novelistic plots.

The autobiographical accounts of the daughters of pioneer parents frequently portray the relationship between the parents as the backbone of the venture. In Jessie Browne Raber's *Pioneering in Alberta*,[12] family solidarity through the efforts of the hardworking and loving parents is often the only strength of the family. In Edith Leona Van Kleek's *Our Trail North*, it is the energy and devotion of her older brother, who is her father surrogate, and the care of her widowed mother that Van Kleek figures as giving her the ability to be strong in her own adulthood.[13] But in this mythologization of the parent figures in the pioneer memoir, one aspect is rarely directly commented upon, and that is that it is often necessary for one partner in a marriage to surrender his or her views before such a unity can be achieved. This is more often than not the woman. Even when husband and wife are equally enthusiastic about the new life, the woman sees herself as making key compromises at important moments that preserve this necessary unity. This is demonstrated more clearly when we examine a pioneer memoir written by a woman who was the mother rather than the child of such a family.

In summing up her study of mother/daughter plots, Marianne Hirsch emphasizes that, in her study of women's novels in two centuries, a maternal discourse, as distinct from a daughter's discourse, is just beginning to be developed. She asks: "What model or definition of subjectivity might be derived from a theory that begins with mothers rather than with children? Can we conceive of development as other than a process of separation from a neutral, either nurturing or hostile, but ultimately self-effacing 'holding' background? I would suggest that if we start our study of the subject with *mothers* rather than *children* a different conception of subjectivity might emerge. Although it might be difficult to define, we might try to envision a culturally variable, mutually affirming form of interconnection between one body and another, one person and another, existing as social, legal, and psychological subjects" (197). Again, I would suggest that theorists interested in maternal discourses would not find their subject as "difficult to define" if they turn to the autobiographical accounts of women who speak from the subject position of mother. I turn to Susan Allison, whose life as a pioneer in the British Columbia interior earned her the accolade "The Mother of the Similkameen" and whose memoirs have been the inspiration of an opera. She wrote *A Pioneer Gentlewoman in British Columbia: The Recollections of Susan Allison* in the form of thirteen contributions to the 1931 editions of the *Vancouver Sunday Province*.[14] Allison was eighty-five at the time, and as the editor of her memoir points out, although she may have had occasional lapses of memory for dates and names, her account of her adventures as a pioneer in the 1860s, 1870s, and 1880s remains vivid and readable.

This is partially due to the fact that Allison was a published author of essays on the Indians of the Similkameen, and in her long life had also written poetry and stories, which she could draw on as source material for her memoir. As well, this position as writer and historian, poet and fiction writer, allows Allison to more easily adopt the three positions Billson sees as part of a full memorialist stance, that of eyewitness, participant, and "histor" of her own and her society's story. The eyewitness "explains the past ... by means of an interpretive strategy, characteristic of historical analysis, that allows him to focus on the thisness, the specificity of past time" (273). The participant "concentrates on himself and relates the course of his own role, however major or ancillary ... [and] acting as participant in his narrative, the memoir-writer reinforces the authority of the eyewitness stance" (275). As histor the author "narrates events he has not seen with his own eyes" (278), which allows the memorialist to "adopt a 'contextualist' strategy of explanation which is different from that of the eyewitness or participant." In addition, this stance allows for the "great digressions of the memoir genre – the editorializing and the generalizing" (279) that permits the writer to tie the personal history to the history of place and society. Once again, I leave the "he" pronoun in Billson's definition, since Allison does not practise these three roles in the rather separate, or at least easily distinguishable, way indicated by Billson's description, in which we might easily see when she is acting as eyewitness, or participant, or histor. Her place as woman in the pioneer enterprise means that the three roles are often intertwined, inseparable. For example, which role should you emphasize when describing the devastation of a forest fire when you are also fighting your way through it with your newborn child in order to get to your mother, who has never seen the child? Or, which role is performed when you describe the stoic nature of

Indians if you are also describing your panic during your first child-birth labour, which is attended by an Indian woman whose expectations you cannot meet? Should you emphasize your role as labouring participant, as disinterested eyewitness, or as histor of Indian culture?

For Allison the solution is her efficient, compressed writing style, a kind of shorthand of salient detail, with very little explanation or editorializing, a style she must have developed in the days when she was both writer and mother of fourteen children, but one which makes the contemporary reader grateful for Margaret Ormsby's extensively researched editorial introduction, notes, and index. For example, in six short opening pages Allison covers her early life, creating for us a compelling picture of sea travel in the mid-nineteenth century as she describes her family's journey from England to the West Coast of Canada, quickly moving to the place of herself and her family as middle-class people in the broad social range represented in the colony's scant but varied population, as well as presenting their personal situation (i.e., a spendthrift stepfather, a timid mother, a risky venture), while adding a cameo portrait of early Victoria. She outlines the situation, purpose, and daily lives of the inhabitants of Hope, British Columbia, where the stepfather intended to settle as a gentleman farmer, and gives us as well a portrait of her demure and genteel self at fifteen, one which will help us measure the changes about to occur in her. This breathless writing style is to be her strategy throughout the memoir, and she leaves it to us (and her editor) to create the facilitating textual aids that will help us read a subjectivity that does not define its roles separately, but rather expresses, in Hirsch's words, a "mutually affirming interconnection between one [role] and another, one [self] and another existing simultaneously as social, legal, and psychological subjects."[15]

Her straightforward, non-heroic manner of narration demands that the reader assess her own reading strategy, since Allison rarely indicates the point of view she might wish us to take in reading her account. For readers accustomed to the highly literary shaping of narrative viewpoints in more "sophisticated" texts, this can be quite confusing. It is through texts such as Allison's that I became aware of the need to read in a special relationship to the text, the relationship I have characterized as threefold, as mother, sister, daughter. As mother, I read the small signals in the text that indicate the tone with which I must understand the unmediated detail I am being given. For example, Allison explains how she and her mother earned their living after the stepfather deserted them in Hope: "My mother and I started quite a nice little school. Mr. Yates sent his little boy, Mr.

Hunter sent his girls, and Bill Bristol, who was then the Similkameen mail carrier, sent his daughter, and some children were sent from Yale. I did not like teaching but it helped out my small income" (20–1). Below the understatement of "quite a nice little school" and the seemingly random list of those attending, Allison is informing the reader that she and her mother ran a top-rated school, since the people who mattered, including those from another town, trusted and respected it. She lets us know as well that despite having to work at something she did not enjoy, she remained financially independent. This last is to remain important to Allison, as throughout her marriage she is also a working partner in money-making enterprises with her husband, from running a trading post to supplying the needs of miners.

I work at my reading as well as a sister of the text, especially when Allison narrates details of female life experiences that are shared by women across a wide cultural and historical range of patriarchy. Her statements about her personal feelings are rare and usually come as tags at the end of one of her compressed recollections. Their comparative rarity and their culminating positions give them a weight of meaning when I embrace the text as sister, reading it through similar experiences in my own life, reading it with the knowledge that I have of the power relations inside patriarchal institutions in her time and my own. In recounting the events leading up to her marriage to John Fall Allison, twenty years her senior, she offers no insight into her intimate feelings regarding the man, but concludes the account with a separate paragraph that states: "Then began my camping days and the wild, free life I ever loved till age and infirmity put an end to it" (21). Given the necessary reticence of her cultural and historical place, the unusual descriptive diction (for Allison) of "wild" and "free" reveals her attitude as one in which the husband, though perhaps seen originally as possessing these two qualities, is in retrospect seen more as the means of her introduction to her unusual life; the wild and the free aspects of her life are not always associated with his personal qualities, or indeed as dependent on him, since it is, after all, "age and infirmity" that ends her independent existence.

That Allison has this sense of herself as a separate person, with her own predispositions and talents, her own mind, is verified by her selection of detail to describe her arrival at the isolated ranch that John Allison's skill has carved out of the wilderness. She is faced with the fact of having to deal with not one man, but two, as she meets her husband's partner: "Mr Hayes had a good supper ready for us the day I first saw Princeton, though he did not approve my dressing for dinner, a habit I was drilled in as a child and has always stuck with me to some extent. As I did not object to his coming to table in shirt sleeves I did not see why he objected to my habits, but I think he half forgave me when he found I could milk cows and was not afraid to go into a corral full of cattle" (23). This short passage speaks sisterly volumes for any woman who has had to create her own place inside more powerful patriarchal arrangements. The partner feels he has the right to comment on her habit of dress, an act that could easily lead to further rudeness, and we can assume from the text's silence that John Allison made no reprimand to the partner. Allison's situation is obvious to any who have been caught in a similar power play: she realizes she has to make a kind of peace with this man if she is to make her new home her own, if she is to have her own space in the economy of the ranching venture. At the same time, it is essential in the nineteenth century for such a woman to claim status as a lady by such acts as dressing for dinner, for ladies receive the privilege of respect and protection not always offered other women. Allison manages the neat trick of telling us in a few sentences that she claimed a measure of that respect through insisting on her custom, allowing his own habits, and proving her usefulness in the pioneer venture through her skill with cattle.

I find that I must simultaneously become the text's mother, sister, and daughter at the point where Allison begins to make her many observations about Indians, their plight at the beginning of the arrival of white culture, and her own relationship to them. From her other work on Indian culture included in the book, I see that she is fascinated by the Indians, she respects them, and, to a large degree, she wishes to emulate their best qualities. Acting to elucidate the text maternally, I see that the Indian is in many ways the significant other that is most important to Allison. Their self-reliance, their adaptability, their philosophy of live and let live, their love and respect for nature, and their sense of the spiritual embodied in all life are qualities she wishes to cultivate in herself. But she draws me into her text as sister as she relates her own very personal feelings when, unable to go to her own mother during her first delivery, she is attended at the premature birth by an Indian woman. She breaks the silence imposed on women regarding child bearing for this brief telling observation: "Suzanne was very good to me in her way – though I thought her rather unfeeling at the time. She thought that I ought to be strong as an Indian woman but I was not" (28). The fear that must have been a part of the situation of delivering without the planned assistance of mother and midwife, in the company of a woman used to other customs, whose language is indecipherable, is muted – but present – below the "though I thought her rather unfeeling at the time" and the admission that she herself was not as "strong as an Indian woman." But as well, her retrospective knowledge and respect for Indian women are contained in "Suzanne was very good to me in her way." This incident becomes emblematic for the rest of Allison's text, as it allows me to read in the position of the daughter of the text; my own world view is educated and enlarged, the possibilities of resistant subjectivity enhanced for me in my own time, as I watch how this woman, through her independent study of the Indians, her variety of scholarly and creative writing activities (sometimes confined to the margins of her store's account books as Ormsby informs me), and her continuing imaginative negotiation of her place in patriarchy, is revealed to me as paradigm and inspiration for my own subjectivity.

In this position as the text's reader I read closely, rhetorically, and with the interpretive intimacy of a daughter reading her mother's censured discourse. For example, only once in her text does Allison come close to considering the kind of negative power that husbands inside patriarchy wield. It is her life in the Okanagan that occasions the recounting of a serious disagreement with her husband, whose presence in the memoir increasingly changes from one of admired, competent mate to the rather muted presence referred to as "Mr. Allison" or "my husband." He decides to move back to the Similkameen from the Okanagan in order to help promote his cattle business. She has been very happy as the mother of a growing family in the Okanagan's pleasant climate, for once not burdened by too many extra duties as store manager. In the Similkameen she will once more have to run the store, as well as look after the household – its rural economy of garden, and so forth – and mother her children: "I begged him to keep our little home and argued the long, long winters at the Similkameen and the scarcity of winter feed, but his mind was made up and that was that" (55). Later, when she argues for a return to the Okanagan, she finishes up the subject in one short paragraph: "I longed more than ever to go back to Okanagan in the fall of '81 when the cattle started back. I hated store-keeping. The poor little children, I felt, were neglected but it had to be" (60). There is no outright censure of her husband, nor any overt defence or praise of her own position, and she never refers to this disagreement again in the memoir, but worlds of feeling seem just barely disguised in the uncharacteristic words "begged," "hated," "longed," and "neglected." It is interesting that in this argument Allison accepts defeat and puts the husband's venture first, a position so much admired by Hiemstra as the daughter of such a mother in *Gully Farm*. However, in the first-person account of such a mother, she portrays her acceptance ("it had to be" and "his mind was made up and that was that") more as a necessary defeat, one sustained unwillingly in the effort to do the best thing given her place of intersubjectivity in her family, than as an admirable or desirable stance. Certainly, it is presented with none of the humour that Hiemstra's daughter position allows her. But ironically, reading from my own daughter position, a position informed by many foremothers' texts, the oblique and indirect account of marital strife given by Allison speaks powerfully of the female condition.

Allison's account is, to the end, a mélange of subject matter, at one point emphasizing the husband's business, at another the changing nature of the West, at another the plight of the Indians. Floods, disasters, railways, mining, settlement all figure in this memoir and all are informed by Allison's personal story, which gathers these fragments; through registering her own feelings and judgments, succinctly, briefly, but confidently, she acts as participant, eyewitness, and histor, at the same time. Francis Russell Hart has described the personal memoirs of many recent memoir writers as a "strange hybridization of the autobiographical genre."[16] The women referred to are writers like Lillian Hellman and Maxine Hong Kingston, accomplished twentieth-century professional writers. Yet many of the characteristics associated with these women's styles and those of twentieth-century males, which show them "seeking an intimacy with history that will give public meaning to personal identity" (209), are shared by the pioneer women memorialists whom I have discussed. After exploring their accounts I would conclude that through their autobiographical acts, they give history a personal, more nuanced face by enlivening it with their own stories.

Marcus Billson points out that the most important difference between the traditional autobiographer and the memorialist is that the latter leaves the subject-object division unresolved whereas "the autobiographer sees himself as psychic totality, and therefore he can be independent from the social matrix" (277). I would revise this observation for the women's memoirs I have mapped. For these women there is no subject-object division. Rather, there is a subject-subject relationship that is not left unresolved, but is seen as a subjectivity situation where a balance of interests, conflicting and complementary, must be actualized in the life and the written account, so that the interdependence of self and social matrix is explicated and facilitated. In fact, the memoir form is a fortuitous one for such women, since it allows women to deal with their real existence, the personal life of family, relationships, child rearing, as well as their accomplishments as individuals, in a context that gives meaning to a life. Not a subjectivity defining its difference from the world, seeking a transcendence of that world, but a complex "connective tissue" living and elaborating itself in the world and with the world. In creating their personal myths from the difficult realities of the pioneer experience, such women use the memoir as an autobiographical form, one that will hold the worlds of the spirit and the flesh, not in a hierarchy as in the Augustinian format, but in balance with one another.

3 Two Exemplary Early Texts: Moodie's *Roughing It* and Jameson's *Studies and Rambles*

But the subject should not be entirely abandoned. It should be reconsidered, not to restore the theme of an originating subject, but to seize its functions, its intervention in discourse, and its system of dependencies.

Michel Foucault, "What Is an Author?"

I have tried to imagine authorship as a more complexly contextual activity than I had dreamed ... as a matter of writing that includes the problem of agency – the marks of a producing subject; and as a question of reading that includes the gendered effects of critical and institutional ideologies.

Nancy K. Miller, *Subject to Change*

I want to explore how narrative and narrativity, because of their capacity to inscribe desire and to direct, sustain, or undercut identification ... are mechanisms to be employed strategically and tactically in the effort to construct other forms of coherence, to shift the terms of representation, to produce the conditions of representability of another – gendered – social subject. Obviously, therefore, much is at stake in narrative, in a poetics of narrative. Our suspicion is more than justified, but so is our attraction.

Teresa de Lauretis, "Strategies of Coherence,"
Technologies of Gender

I begin this chapter with these three quotations in order to lay the framework on which I can trace my model of the generic map of early Canadian women's autobiography. To even use the word "model" in these poststructuralist times is suspect. But in terms of discovering the terrain of female subjectivity, I believe it is necessary to take risks, to enter the labour as de Lauretis advises feminists enter the master narratives of our culture, with suspicion, but also with a need to understand our attraction to them and thereby begin to "shift the terms of representation."[1] In order to do that, I want to keep in mind Foucault's advice not to abandon the exploration of subjectivity, but to shift the ground of the search.[2] I wish to make that new ground the "complexly contextual" one of which Miller speaks.[3]

Perhaps the complexity of my reading problem in this regard will be understood if I dramatize the various possibilities that attract me, as they were made dramatically clear to me when I attended the symposium on nineteenth-century Canadian women writers at the University of Ottawa in 1988 and heard the three stimulating presentations on Susanna Moodie's *Roughing It in the Bush*.[4] Alec Lucas confirmed my own conviction in considering "The Function of the Sketches" in *Roughing*, which was that the work "has seldom received the credit it merits as a work in which themes, characters and narrative form a coherent whole."[5] Reviewing the critical reception of the text from Klink to Thurston, Lucas illustrated the ways in which it has been unsatisfactorily read as "'roughly-hewn' social history" (147), as "novel manque" (147), as "romantic" fiction, as a proto-postmodern text of "loose ends" (148), and as bad autobiography that fails because the heroine does not show herself in the "good light" (148) as autobiographers should. For Lucas, Moodie's project in *Roughing* is one in which she surveys her life in the bush "as it relates to community, the natural world and her own development" (153). In these interwoven surveys he finds the coherence of the text. I am on Lucas's side. I want to find coherence in this text, and perhaps would only point out that his view of autobiography assumes a patriarchal definition of the form, whereas a woman often seeks the very memoir style that shows the interpenetration of "community, the natural world and her own development." But like the critics he paraphrases, Lucas leaves something out. For him Moodie is a developing subjectivity, but a rather genderless one. For him Moodie has "learned her lesson" (153) of character building in much the same way as a nineteenth-century man would, whereas for me the engendering of her femaleness (not an easy lesson by any means) as well as her pioneer selfhood is present on every page of the text.

Therefore, when Bina Freiwald offers a paper entitled "'The Tongue of Woman,'" I expect that the missing elements that will render the fullest possible reading of Moodie will be supplied. And in important ways they are. Seeking "a new thematization of motherhood" that shifts the "theorizations of the relationship between female experience and female expression,"[6] Freiwald carefully explores Moodie's maternal language and in so doing reveals "a woman's tongue, nature's voice, native idiom, mother tongue, the mother's tongue: these are the coordinates, the discursive interventions and dependencies that constitute the language of the self in *Roughing It in the Bush*" (160). This is the gendered subject I need for my reading, a narrator who uses her mother tongue to dramatize the "co-presence of self and other" (165), the "narrator's double vision of herself as both mother and child" (167). Freiwald frees Moodie's text from its ungendered or male-gendered readings and offers us a much more positive view of a woman's ability to inscribe herself in language than is found in other recent poststructuralist considerations in which Moodie is seen as a failed narrator, "who is invaded by the voices of others."[7] But inside Freiwald's positive exploration of maternal language there is also exposed a problematic area, one that is left as a silence at the heart of all considerations of *Roughing*. Freiwald observes that "Moodie's predicament as female narrator-autobiographer ... parallel[s] that of her feminist reader, for in both instances what is at stake is a reclamation of a range of historically specific female experiences and expressions which have been appropriated to serve the ends of androcentric culture that denigrates them" (164).

Freiwald certainly shows me how Moodie makes her reclamation of maternal language, but it is not until I have heard Carl Ballstadt's exploration of "The Embryo Blossom: Moodie's Letters to Her Husband in Relation to *Roughing It in the Bush*" that I realize just how great a discursive predicament was Moodie's, why even Freiwald's maternal exploration has necessarily left something vital out of my reading.[8] For Moodie's letters perform the same function as other extra-textual documents I have referred to in regard to other early women: they allow me a more completely contextual reading. They tell me that although Moodie was able to shape the patriarchal language to allow the utterance of a maternal tongue, she could not include the body that informed that tongue. And since the experience of that female body informs every part of her subjectivity, much of her still remains hidden from me. Here are the insufficiencies of all readings. The desiring, suffering, yearning, nurturing, loving body of a woman, a body Moodie spoke of to her husband in their private letters, has always been left out of all of our readings of *Roughing*. For those of us in that conference room in the spring of 1988, hearing portions of those letters read aloud, the challenge was to return to the text and find that woman's body, and find too the subjectivity that had been radicalized, the agency that had been created, by the suffering and loving of that body.

Ballstadt's paper emphasizes how "remarkably restrained" (140) on several subjects Moodie's *Roughing* is compared to her letters, written during what were her "darkest days" (138), the time she was left alone to manage a backwoods farm and her young children while

Dunbar Moodie played his part in putting down the Rebellion of 1837. These subjects include the importance of her writing and artistic pursuits as a means of securing the family's future. The chapter "A Walk to Dummer," for example, not only outlines the truth of many women's predicaments in the bush and the sisterly strength these women showed in dealing with them, but also maps Moodie's own predicament as a nearly destitute wife and often sole support of her children. The private letters offer us access to the feelings she must have had of being neglected and deserted by the man who had brought her to these straits, feelings that cannot be expressed directly in the public format of *Roughing*. But as well Moodie exhibits strong erotic and emotional feelings for her husband, the erotic ties being ones that even in the private letter can only be touched on by a joke. The letters also show that Susanna Moodie took a much more active hand in shaping the future of her family than the public text indicates.

Moodie's restraint in her public text in contrast to the letters is especially evident with respect matters of health. Only her letters describe in detail the terrible ill health she and the children suffered, culminating in her description of her operation for mastitis (a severe breast infection): "You may imagine what I suffered when I tell you that more than half a pint of matter must have followed the cut of the lancet and the wound has continued to discharge ever since … Dr. H. seemed greatly concerned for my situation. When he looked round the forlorn, cold, dirty room feebly lighted by the wretched lamp he said with great emphasis, 'In the name of God! Mrs Moodie get out of this – ' Well, I have got through it, and am once more able to crawl about the house, but I am very weak" (quoted in Ballstadt 1988, 140). Not only Dunbar Moodie, but we twentieth-century readers, now privy to his wife's letters, can begin to imagine Moodie's predicament. In fact, for me, these private letters become the decoding device that will help me read the public text for the encoded messages which are restrained by patriarchal language and genres, but which through the reading strategies recommended by feminists well up and rupture the surface of language.

I cannot offer in this space the kind of detailed close reading that would survey all the stategies that need to be brought to bear on Moodie's text. In this mapping I wish to sketch only the scale of the model, mapping the general terrain to be covered, and to supply a few preliminary shadings and contours of the compilation that needs to be done. I find special attention should be given to aspects of narrative strategy to discover how the "mechanisms" of narrativity, to use de Lauretis's term, are used by Moodie to construct alternate forms of "coherence, to shift the terms of representation, to produce ... the gendered social subject." I wish to pay close attention to the subversive possibilities of Moodie's stance as narrator, the subtle purposes of her use of the othering strategy of women's subjectivity, and the doubled narrative purpose that inhabits her text. In regard to stance, Lucas points me to the importance of the sketches. In considering the othering of Moodie's subjectivity, I am informed by Freiwald's exploration of maternal language, and Ballstadt's exploration of the letters especially points me to the double story that Moodie's text tells.

The functions of the narrator, Susanna, are set out for us in the first chapter, "A Visit to Grosse Isle." She adopts the position of the informed traveller, offering us careful sketches of geography, demography, and social history. In fact, it was a well-worn narrative path, that of the travelling English lady, who offers the reader not only the informed view of the new place, but the entertainment of a humorous, ironic, sophisticated wit, always closely observant, even participating at times, but nevertheless the cultural emissary of the English world, which felt itself superior to the colonial.[9] But Moodie's stance is complicated, undermined, interfered with by the fact that this is the land she must settle in; much as she would like to go back to that more genteel home, economics and her husband's ambitions forbid it. This gives her a reluctant investment, a "system of dependencies" in the new place that makes the witty voice of the travel-writer stance at times more shrill, more fearful, at times more enchanted than the urbane sophistication the surface of the narration tries to present. It is a voice that, if not always attractive, is always fascinating, perhaps because a voice on the edge of hysteria casts a spell on the listener. The narrative stance is thus always pregnant with an "intervention in discourse" caused by Moodie's adoption of a voice she cannot maintain. But as well, the discourse is interlaced with another system of dependence, that of the vulnerable ego boundaries of the young first-time mother, the babe always close to her breast, her maternal body actively alive to the nuances of the needs of the child, a vulnerability that leaves her open to that "invasion of voices" that might seem to some a narrative disadvantage, but is in actuality a great boon for the reader. Each sketch is infused in a process I would call "vivification," literally made alive with the hopes, terrors, disgusts, the nervous laughter, the exclamatory wonder, the culture shock, the tears, fears, and frivolities, the tenderness and gentleness of Susanna, the new mother, psychologically very childlike herself, especially now that her protected intellectual and cultured upbringing must face the "bush."

And so she cannot sketch the practical joke the "Scotchman" plays on the French Canadian official with the travel writer's measured, cultured wit, limiting how much of their vernacular dialogue the reader need hear to catch the flavour of the occasion without being rudely shocked; Susanna gives us all of it, even to the earthy observation on the pups: "They do credit to the nursing of the brindled slut" (14). It is this inability to hold back, or to keep aloof, that makes the sketch of the pandemonium that is Grosse Île so vivid. The disgusted Susanna, who assures her reader that "we were literally stunned by the strife of tongues" and like any genteel lady "shrank, with feelings almost akin to fear," still cannot help herself from describing in detail the "hard-featured, sun-burnt harpies, as they elbowed rudely past me" (20). Narratively speaking, this is not a hypocritical stance (as it might be if we were assessing Moodie as a character in her work), it is rather the narrative stance of a gendered subjectivity, a woman who is herself physically performing a very gendered nursing function, a woman who is quite literally a connective tissue, a plural self that cannot help but find identity in "alterity," and who cannot help feeling intensely the challenge that a new place and its strange inhabitants offer to her vulnerable ego boundaries.

Our narrating Susanna, who can be "blinded with tears – blinded with the excess of beauty" (17) of the Canadian landscape – as easily as she can turn in "disgust from the revolting scene" (21) of the half-naked immigrants, never lets up in intensity. Her viewpoints moderate, her convictions and beliefs are shaken and reworked, her body is driven close to exhaustion, her psyche is paralyzed with fear of change, her will is tested and strengthened, her mothering is matured – much changes for Moodie – but her narrative stance is always completely permeable to the rich stimuli of the Canadian place.

As she moves away from the narrative stance and towards the inscription of female subjectivity that is represented by the "character" Susanna, I find the same merging of eyewitness, participant, and histor that I found in the women memoir writers. She grows and matures through infusing her consciousness with the stories of others, in the complexly contextual way Miller speaks of. Her agency as a human subject is a function of her discourse on the lives of others. Early in the text, three figures stand out as subjects of her othering: Tom Wilson, the amusing but failing settler; Phoebe, the neglected and dying maiden; and Brian, the still-hunter, who makes the largest impact on Susanna's development. Tom Wilson announces one of his functions in Moodie's narrative othering when he tells Dunbar that "as to our qualifications, Moodie, I think them pretty

equal" (63) and proceeds to explain how his (Dunbar's) "unfortunate
literary propensities" are equivalent to his (Tom's) "laziness" and "will
end in the same thing" except that he has "neither wife nor child to
involve in my failure" (64). Moodie's narrative of Tom's story becomes
a strategy by which she may say things, realize things about her
husband that cannot be said, cannot even be thought, inside the
wife's discourse. This displacement becomes a typical narrative
strategy of the text, as all unladylike observations, in many cases the
most incisive observations, are put into the mouths of servants, ruf-
fians, and clowns. While being put to use as a double for Dunbar,
Tom also functions as instructor in survivership to Susanna; in "Old
Satan and Tom Wilson's Nose," for example, Tom teaches Moodie to
discourage borrowers by borrowing from them and to get the better
of her tormentors by means of the practical joke. His figure allows
her to affirm to her readers that it is her superior wit and the sophistication of her old-world gentility that afford her this small but important first triumph in the bush.

If ladies cannot openly acknowledge that they enjoy the power to
chastise ignorance and rudeness, they also cannot acknowledge many
of their fears and weaknesses. However, they can make a vivid
identification with those vulnerabilities when they come embodied
in a needful girl. Phoebe, the daughter of a local Yankee farmer, Old
Joe, is one of a series of disadvantaged or self-sacrificing, sensitive
females (who include Jeanie Burns and later Moodie's servant Jenny)
who allow Moodie to both express and to some degree exorcise her
always present fear that the very qualities that most represent her
subjectivity as a woman – her self-effacing ethic, her fragile sensibility, her gentility – will be the source of her failure, even her death.
But as well, Phoebe represents all the vulnerable children Susanna
will have to mother in the bush, and mothering has already proved
a heavy responsibility without the aid of servants and support systems that women of Moodie's class would expect. Phoebe's story is
interwoven with Moodie's narrative of the growth of her beautiful
Katie, and her death occurs at the birth of Moodie's daughter Agnes,
and Moodie's feelings about her contain the fears of her mothering.
The choice of poem that she places at the end of the chapter containing Phoebe's story is perhaps the most revealing of the girl's
function in Moodie's psychic development. "The Faithful Heart That
Loves Thee Still" does not name its subject, except as the "dearest,"
"the ardent heart," the "love" that is mourned, but always "within my
breast enshrined" (183–4). The poem would seem badly chosen, since
its intensity would be more suitably devoted to someone closer than
the neighbour's daughter, perhaps one's lifetime mate or one's own

child. But I do not think Moodie's choice is a sentimentalization of the Phoebe figure. From the ways in which the narrative of Phoebe's life winds around the narrative of Moodie's own growth as a mother and as a survivor among rude neighbours and severe pioneer conditions we see that the girl becomes the other who represents the fragility and sensitivity, the fearfulness, the gentle passivity that Moodie has had to put reluctantly aside. But one does not put aside a quality that has seemed integral to identification without mourning it, without promising to "hold sweet concourse" with that gentler self, to acknowledge that "thy tender love survives thee still" (184).

Perhaps most illustrative of Moodie's tendency to "blur the boundaries between 'I' and 'you' and obliterate the distinction between inner and outer"[10] is Moodie's chapter "Brian, The Still-Hunter," the section of *Roughing* most often reproduced in anthologies as exemplary of her art. Brian is said to haunt the neighbourhood of Moodie's first home in Canada. He certainly haunts her text. He is both the means through which she accepts Canada as her place and establishes her agency as a person able to function in Canada and the figure that embodies all her fears of that acceptance. It is in this chapter that Moodie narrates herself into competence as she learns new skills, calms her fears of the wild, and matures as a mother and a settler. All of these are contextualized by her relationship with Brian.

The way in which she chooses to introduce him to the reader alerts us to his mythic, larger than life, allegorical function in the text. He enters her house and her life without knocking, without warning, without permission, and yet his silent presence does not frighten her, but intrigues her. His presence also highlights her maternal function, as he likes to stare at her holding the child and brings gifts of milk for her each time he comes. Through her conversations with Brian, Moodie comes to know the forest as he does, as a place where "tis fine to be alone with God in the great woods ... to know that all is bright and shiny above you, in spite of the gloom that surrounds you" (191). In fact, his story shapes the changing Susanna, for through him she comes to contemplate the paradox of the nobility of the forest life and the need man has to survive through killing that life. Brian himself represents that natural world, its mysterious presence threatening an invasion of disorder into Moodie's tightly structured reality, yet like his bountiful generosity, his simplicity, it is a compelling attraction. Like Brian, that world will feed and sustain her and her children, offer beauty and peace of a new kind, if she learns the necessary skills and allows herself the peace of mind to "know that all is bright and shiny above you, in spite of the gloom that surrounds you."

Yet Brian also represents the terror of being "bushed." He has attempted suicide, degraded himself and his family, is even now not far from madness, a madness that will overtake him once the Moodies leave the neighbourhood. In many ways the reason Brian is the figure the older Susanna will always most readily see in later years when she looks into "memory's glass" (185) is because he is the materialization of much of her own experience in the intervening years. After all, who could be more like the half-mad Brian than the figure that she describes late in the text: "For seven years I had lived out of the world entirely; my person had been rendered coarse by hard work and exposure to the weather. I looked double the age I really was, and my hair was already sprinkled with grey. I clung to my solitude ... I was contented to live and die in obscurity" (501). In fact she has lived the difficulties that Brian predicted she would when he tried to persuade the Moodies to "give up this ruinous scheme" (203). The Susanna who could not understand why Brian would not cross the ocean to England to collect an inheritance now has to be torn from her own solitude to return to town life. In her chapter on Brian, Moodie continually interrupts the narrative to contrast her subject position in the past to her subject position at the writing moment. In this way Brian and his story function to measure her own adjustment to the new land.

But Moodie's identification with Brian is not a one-to-one formula. One of her principal narrative strategies works to "undercut identi-fication," to "construct other forms of coherence," to "inscribe" a "desire" other than that of a male sensibility. That strategy is the doubled discourse of this text, which genders Moodie female and thus ultimately very different from Brian. From the beginning, Susanna Moodie is telling the story of two subjectivities, that of herself as her husband's wife and that of herself as subject of her own story. This double story becomes most obvious as her narrative separates from her husband's when he physically leaves her to help put down the outbreak of 1837. The devoted-wife image that she has been building tells one story: of the woman so devastated that she collapses in tears on her bed after taking leave of him, a devotion so great that she depicts herself as writing him letters to bring him closer, then burning them rather than worry him with her problems. The other story tells of the strong woman operating in a difficult world where only female solidarity saves her.

Central to this doubled discourse is the chapter "The Walk to Dummer," which Ballstadt points out is taken out of its actual chrono-logical context in Moodie's own life and conflated with the events of her terrible winter when both she and her children came close to death. As Ballstadt observes: "By placing the account where she does

... Susanna makes it a projection of her own experience and even of her own attitudes" (140), a strategy by which she overcomes the "remarkably restrained" discourse which patriarchy imposes on women's public expression. Reading the story of Louisa Lloyd, the brave and proud mother deserted by her husband and rescued by the combined efforts of women, through the facts and events of the letters of that terrible winter, I read a narrative which, as de Lauretis proposes women's rewriting of master narratives should, "shifts the terms of representation" to a "gendered social subject." I find it ironic that this chapter, so central to the gendered subject of Moodie's other story, has until very recently been censured out of editions of the text used in Canadian classrooms, almost as if patriarchal discourse and patriarchal editing conspired to silence Moodie's other voice.[11]

To restore that voice, the subjectivity of the suffering, loving body of Susanna Moodie, it is necessary to undertake the kind of reading Miller advises, an intertextual reading of autobiography and fiction. In Moodie's case it is a matter of allowing the letters to inform the chapter "The Walk to Dummer." The chapter is framed with references, at the end of the previous chapter and in the opening of the following chapter, to the very illness so explicitly described in the letter to her husband. Before beginning the "Dummer" chapter, she writes: "Though I escaped the fever, mental anxiety and fatigue brought on other illness, which for nearly ten weeks rendered me perfectly helpless" (460–1). Then, after narrating the "Dummer" chapter, she begins her next chapter with the words "during my illness" (491) and goes on to describe the heartbreak of having to be separated from one of her children because of the illness. With the letters acting as intertext, along with the dramatic placement of this chapter out of historical chronology and with its frame of reference to her illness, I can begin to read the chapter as a symbolization of Moodie's subjectivity during her suffering from mastitis and from the stress of her children's illnesses and the separation from her daughter. For example, her title draws attention not to the woman she and Emilia go to rescue, but to the "walk," the long cold journey through the "tangled maze of closely-interwoven cedars," through the "interminable forest" on a frigid winter day when they fear, as Emilia confesses, they may die of hunger while trying to bring food to a starving woman (479). This journey, cast in the language of a mythic task, would seem in tone, like most of the chapter, to be an overextended, melodramatic account of a common pioneer act of charity. If it is read in the context I suggest, its tone reflects the trauma of a psyche that cannot speak its conflicted nature, a body that must not speak its suffering, except allegorically. Thus the walk becomes the heroic journey, which like all myths must symbolize more than itself.

The first ten pages are devoted to making Moodie's servant Jenny into a kind of mythic hero, a woman who has devoted herself above the call of duty to the people she has served. It is through her that Moodie learns of Louisa Lloyd's desperate situation, abandoned by her husband, with a family of children to feed. The mythologization of Jenny and her origins is not necessary if all Moodie wants to do is explain how she heard of this woman's plight. But given that this is the symbolic account of her own suffering, then Jenny was the true hero that rescued her from starvation through her work in the fields with Moodie and her nursing of both the children and Moodie during the winter.

Moodie ends the section extolling Jenny and outlining Mrs Lloyd's situation with this information: "The year of the Canadian rebellion came, and brought with it sorrow into many a bush dwelling. Old Jenny and I were left alone with the little children, in the depths of the dark forest, to help ourselves in the best way we could" (472). Two paragraphs later, praising Emilia for her contribution, Moodie adds that she is especially grateful for her help "in the dark hour of adversity, and, amidst the almost total neglect of those from whom nature claimed a tenderer and holier sympathy" (473). These editorial interruptions set up the possibility of a shift in our reading and make many seemingly melodramatic expressions fill with new meaning. For instance, Moodie, in explaining her inability to contribute to the support of Mrs Lloyd, says, "Tears sprang to my eyes, and I thought, in the bitterness of my heart, upon my own galling poverty ... and the thought of my incapacity gave me severe pain" (474). If we decode the encoded world of enforced female silence through knowing the physical pain that Moodie suffered because of mastitis, brought on by overwork, worry, and poverty, such phrases begin to create an alternate discourse, one informed by and informing all the detail of feeling that follows.

Moodie's choice of the mythic journey as the narrative form for her chapter is suitable. In this long and complex text she has tried to adopt the voice of the intrepid but humorously ironic traveller in a strange land, a voice her English readers would be used to, would trust. Somewhere in the Brian chapter, that voice begins to undergo a radical change, as Moodie the observing, ironic traveller, through the simple act of learning to milk a cow, through the experience of spending one night alone with her child, worried and frightened for her husband's safety, moderates her stance of observing traveller with that of the mythic journeyer, an actor in her own story, and begins to write the narrative of that journey inside the shell of the other story. It culminates in "The Walk to Dummer." But we should note that Moodie's own story, although exposed by this intertextual and contextual reading, remains inscribed inside a gap in an otherwise androcentric tale. She ends her chapter by telling the reader that she "wrote to Moodie an account of the scene I had witnessed, and he raised a subscription among the officers of the regiment for the poor lady and her children" (488). Thus, the patriarchal frame is restored, the husband who a moment before was almost directly chastised, is restored to his place; the doubled discourse continues.

In speaking of the ways in which the twentieth-century autobiographer Maxine Hong Kingston combines aspects of "techniques usually associated with myths and tales together with techniques more usually associated with non-fiction" to extend the possible realms of fictivity, Victoria Myers says that the purpose of this narrative strategy is for the autobiographer to identify "the perceiving self" and also to "locate it in her effort to extricate her voice from the many already existing voices of tradition, myth and story in her speech community."[12] With regard to nineteenth-century writers such as Moodie, I would revise Myers's statement to say that such a woman wished not to "extricate" her own voice, but to inscribe it within, to hold it in dynamic balance with the other voices of her community, voices that her sense of the othered nature of her identity makes her own. This cannot be done merely by a discourse that interrupts narrative in order to break its hold on us. Such a voice must make its own narrative strand to be interwoven with other narratives, an enabling mythology intertwined with many other mythologies, perhaps imprisoning ones by our standards, but ones in which Moodie nevertheless wishes to keep her place.

Thus, as de Lauretis observes, narrative is both "attractive," in that it is the mode by which inscription of the self-facilitating story can be made, and a place of "suspicion" where all the old master narratives await the woman writer. Moodie learned that the only way to "position oneself outside of that [patriarchal] discourse is to displace oneself within it," as de Lauretis suggests to contemporary women dealing with a patriarchal discourse in cinema.[13] But the modern film critic has also suggested that as well as displacing oneself inside the imprisoning discourse, the resisting woman can "refuse the question as formulated, or ... answer deviously (though in its words), even to quote (but against the grain)" in a complex effort to negotiate "the politics of self-representation" (7).

No nineteenth-century woman was more sophisticated in her knowledge of the devious purposes to which narrative could be put and of the politics a woman encounters in self-representation than feminist writer Anna Jameson, who visited Canada in 1836–37, just before Moodie's terrible winter of the rebellion, and who wrote of her experiences in *Winter Studies and Summer Rambles in Canada*.[14] Anna Jameson was certainly ready for the subversive tasks her text was to undertake, ready professionally and personally. Like Moodie she was recognized as a professional writer before coming to Canada, but whereas Moodie was only twenty-nine when she immigrated, known as "a writer of promise in literary circles,"[15] Jameson, at forty-two, had published six important works, including three biographies, the diary-style novel *Diary of an Ennuyée*, and a book of literary criticism, *Characteristics of Women*, which analyses Shakespeare's heroines. As well, she had already written one travel book, *Visits and Sketches at Home and Abroad*, and was a prolific letter writer. She was certainly as aware as Moodie of the useful disguise the travel persona could offer a woman wishing to represent the self, but whereas Moodie's primary skill lay in her ability to manipulate the narrative forms of sentimental romance and the short character sketch, Jameson's writing background gave her skill in several discourses: the novel, the diary, literary criticism, the travel journal, historical, biographical, and essay discourses as well as the private (but very demanding by nineteenth-century standards) genre of the personal letter. She was also a self-taught scholar who knew not only how to research, but how best to use her results through vivid narrative choices.[16] Jameson uses every one of her skills to manage her subversive act of female self-representation, forbidden in androcentric discourse. Hers is the most spectacular example I have found among early women writers of the ability to shift the terms of representation to her own autobiographical needs, to undercut old identities and build new ones, to inscribe her own desire by using the discourses of the patriarchy, brilliantly and subversively, against the grain of their own habitual functions.

One of the reasons Jameson was able to do this so well is that she had reached a moment in her personal as well as her professional life when she needed to make a great change. Her Canadian experience facilitated that change. She had married her husband, Robert Jameson, in 1825 – despite her reservations about their compatibility and her independent financial status, which her writing gave her – because he seemed so supportive of her career. But this changed and a great distance grew between them, a distance that became physical when he became first chief justice of Dominica and later attorney general of Upper Canada. Although he may well have wanted her to join him there in 1836 to help his chances of promotion to chanceller, her movitation in going was more to arrange a legal separation and to gain the opportunity to write about the experience of a visit to a new land. As Clara Thomas observes, "She walked a fine line ... between writing a frank, truthful and saleable account and one which might hurt her husband's reputation – or her own."[17] However, Jameson was not only expert at walking that fine line that colonial, marital, and publishing politics demanded, she was also very good at negotiating the fine line between her various "legitimate" discourses and her subversive discourse of female self-inscription.

She begins by giving us an introduction that offers various decoding devices by which we may read her text for its autobiographical agenda: "I would fain have extracted, altogether, the impertinent leaven of egotism which necessarily mixed itself up with the journal form of writing: but in making the attempt, the whole work lost its original character – lost its air of reality, lost even its essential truth ... It was found that to extract the tone of personal feeling, on which the whole series of action and observation depended, was like drawing the thread out of a string of beads – the chain of linked ideas and experiences fell to pieces, and became a mere unconnected, incongruous heap" (10). This is not the only way in which Jameson subtly announces her autobiographical intentions while seeming to apologize for what the form necessitated. She also "throws" herself upon "the merciful construction of good women" (10), thus announcing her chosen audience, and claims she will abstain "generally from politics and personalities," viewpoints that might show the distance between her and her husband (12). In fact, she does no such thing, the political Anna being a very large part of this text. As well, she begins her chapters with German-language epigrams, which often speak to her personal emotions and her female condition. Any reader giving notice to them (as the first reader of much of this account, the German Ottilie Von Goethe, must have) has a keen appreciation of just what emotional overtones the facts of the chapter should receive from the reader.

Since I have explored Jameson's detailed mapping of her winter in Toronto and her summer travelling on the Great Lakes in more than one venue, and named her complex genre bridging an "epistolary dijournal," I do not wish to retrace those mappings here.[18] The additional contour I would like to map is Jameson's necessary involvement, as the result of performing the act of self-representation, in what Bella Brodzki would call the "maternal pre-text," that powerful imaginary and/or real precedent that "the daughter's text, variously, seeks to reject, reconstruct and reclaim – to locate and recontextualize." I have found that early nineteenth-century women are not as obsessed with their personal mothers as are the women born later in history, especially the twentieth-century autobiographers studied by Brodzki, perhaps because most of them were very close, in terms of psychology, role, and belief, to their mothers. They may have lived in a female ghetto, but inside that ghetto there was the solidarity ghetto life often brings to the individuals who must live there. A woman growing up in our century often suffers from a much more profound dislocation of her identity from that of her mother, and these dislocations necessarily inform women's maps of self-representation. In this regard, Anna Jameson was in many ways a very twentieth-century woman, having performed from the age of sixteen the roles of breadwinner and career woman, and on coming to Canada she was already in the process of evolving her mature feminist positions. With her Canadian adventure she began to map the forbidden territory of the woman separated from her husband, a position that could easily make a female an outcast from society in her time (the force of this social custom is shown by the fact that to the end of her life Jameson was careful to represent herself as married to Robert Jameson). I believe that, with these agendas of her own and our age pressing upon her, Anna Jameson at forty-two had a great need to construct an enabling maternal mythology that would help her live outside of the male-defined roles of nineteenth-century women. She sought her maternal pre-texts first in literature and then in what she called the "wild expedition" of her two-month journey into the interior of Canada.

The early part of the text, in which she describes her winter in Toronto, which she spent observing the local scene, writing meandering accounts of her reading to her friend Ottilie, and doing some translating, is strewn with references to women. She discusses the interpretation of women by male writers, the conditions of work for actresses, the phenomenon of the Madonna image in art, her yearning for female friends. She even compares woman's heartache to the "ringing" of trees in the Canadian forest (65). She takes time, while reading Boswell, to scold Dr Johnson for saying that men are "'held down in conversation by the presence of women' – held up rather, where moral feeling is concerned" (87). She muses on the idea that "female character rises with the pressure of ill fortune" (101), and decides that since the "tyranny of circumstances" in the real world is always pressing on women, it is inevitable that their characters will respond to this situation. Whenever possible she praises women writers, including Mme de Stael, and male writers who construct strong and interesting female characters. But in contrast to the "rambles" section of the text, the "studies" section seems preparatory, the place where we get to know our narrator, her intelligence, her humour, her encyclopaedic knowledge, and her difficult situation in the new country. Once she decides on her "project," a much more confident and directed Anna emerges, one who, after deciding firmly that she will undertake the Great Lakes expedition despite the disapproval of Torontonians, concludes: "The French have a proverb which does honour to their gallantry, and to which, from experience, I am inclined to give full credence – 'Ce que femme veut, Dieu veut' [What a woman wants, God wants]. We shall see" (181).

Within days of starting her expedition she meets one of the women who will be her mentor, surrogate sister, or mother on her voyage of self-discovery. Mrs MacMurray, the half-Indian wife of a missionary, whose Indian name, O-ge-ne-bu-go-quay, means "the wild rose," immediately impresses Jameson with her manner and her voice. "She speaks English well, with a slightly foreign intonation, not the less pleasing to my ear that it reminded me of the voice and accent of some of my German friends. In two minutes I was seated by her – my hand kindly folded in hers – and we were talking over the possibility of my plans" (194). This woman, her sister, Mrs Schoolcraft, and their mother, Mrs Johnson (Oh-shah-gush-ko-da-wa-qua), are to become not only the surrogates for her beloved German friend Ottilie, but her loving guides into a stronger sense of herself and of her feminist philosophy: "The sight of Mrs MacMurray seemed to give something definite to the vague hope which had been floating in my mind ... This rencontre, which some would call accidental, and some providential, pleased and encouraged me" (195). The last two-thirds of the text, 350 pages, circle round these women; for whole sections they will seem marginal, then return again to the centre of Jameson's consideration, fading for another moment as a new subject of interest arises, but quickly reconnecting as Jameson's rambles become more and more a mothering into being of her new consciousness.

Brodzki proposes that women narrators of the self have a "linguistic disability or instability and cultural disorientation" that "pivots" on the mother. I propose that these three native women figures, Mrs Johnson and her daughters, become the pivot that ends Anna Jameson's disability. It seems almost laughable to figure a woman of Jameson's accomplishments and erudition, an expert articulator of ideas, as having a "linguistic disability," a "cultural disorientation," yet that is exactly the problem of well-educated, scholarly women within patriarchy. Even as feminists, we live within the culture and discourses of patriarchy. We may even, at times, be at a special disadvantage when it comes to fully realizing the female self, in that we may be imbricated by and implicated with (if we hold any discursive power) the patriarchy's agendas in sophisticated ways that are hard to undo. What these native women give Jameson (and they seem to be very aware at times that they are educating her) is a place outside her own culture, in a culture that has had to deal in an entirely different manner with gender differences, from which she can measure what she has come from and decide where she is going. Her learning is facilitated and intensified by the loving, maternal context in which she receives her lessons: they become the "primary source" of both "speech and love" that, as Brodzki puts it, "engenders subjectivity through language" (246).

In *Technologies of Gender* de Lauretis speaks of the need that feminists have for an "elsewhere," which is "not some mythic distant past or some utopian future history; it is the elsewhere of discourse here and now, the blind spots, or the space-off, of its representation. I think of it as spaces in the margins of hegemonic discourses, social spaces carved in the interstices of institutions and in the chinks and cracks of the power-knowledge apparati" (25). I agree with de Lauretis that in this time we can find no literal "mythic distant past or some utopian future history" that will properly construct for us non-patriarchal identities, but I believe that Anna Jameson had an advantage over us; there was still an elsewhere when she journeyed into the wilderness. Not for everyone, not for people so committed to the discourses of patriarchy that they saw the native people as savages, not for those who came to profit from aboriginal people, not even for the proto-anthropologists, admiring, but committed to containing the native peoples inside a discursive appropriation, such as Alexander Henry and Henry Schoolcraft, whose works Jameson studies and questions. That elsewhere was not unspoiled and it would not be there for very long; Jameson and the women she learns from recognize this tragic fact. But for those who could, like Jameson, imaginatively embrace the other culture, give oneself to it in loving ways, be mothered into it, there was a way to learn from native culture, rather than to appropriate from it.

I identify the principal features of the process Jameson goes through as centring around orality, intimacy, and ritual. Contrasting the "studies" portion of the text with the "rambles," one is struck by Jameson's preoccupation in the first with narratives in books and in the latter with the narratives of the oral tradition of the Chippewa. She writes into her text stories that her mentors and their relatives have told her, such as the tale of Mishosha, through which she became aware of the mythic structure of Indian tales and their similarity to Ovid's recountings. She obviously feels that her recording of these stories fulfils an Ovidian purpose, as she includes many, and all of them are artfully retold in great detail. Most are told by the voices of the three women whom she has come to care for so deeply, and her absorption of Indian culture has much to do with the intimacy of her relationships with them and the rituals they help her enact. That intimacy is grounded in orality as well, as Jameson continually speaks of the sound of the native-inflected voices, "the soft-plaintive voice" (377) of the suffering Mrs Schoolcraft, whose health seems to improve as she travels closer to her Chippewa mother, singing aloud to Jameson as they cross the waters. Jameson feels like "the unweaned child in its cradle" who has an "unconscious trust and love" (443) in that voice. She finds that "the accent of the women is particularly soft, with a sort of plaintive modulation, reminding me of recitative. Their low laugh is quite musical, and has something infantine in it" (389).

The intimate touch and the sound of these women come together for Jameson when she meets the mother: "Mrs. Johnson speaks no English ... but in her own language she is eloquent, and her voice, like that of her people, low and musical; many kind words were exchanged, and when I said anything that pleased her, she laughed softly like a child. I was not well and much fevered, and I remember she took me in her arms, laid me down on a couch, and began to rub my feet, soothing and caressing me. She called me Nindannis, daughter, and I called her Neengai, mother (though how different from my own fair mother, I thought, as I looked up gratefully in her dark Indian face!)" (455). This experience of being mothered is a turning-point for Jameson in terms of her personal well-being and her keenness to understand her own position as woman in white culture in comparison to the Indian woman's position. Her task is facilitated by her ritualistic entrance into Chippewa society when she shoots the rapids at Sault Ste Marie, after which "my Neengai ... laughed, clapped her hands, and embraced me several times. I was declared duly initiated, and adopted into the family by the name of Wah, sàh, ge, wah, nó, quà [woman of the bright foam]" (462).

Her inquiries into native culture emphasize two aspects that differ from white culture, the nature of language and the treatment of women. In the first regard she becomes fascinated by the special rhythms of the language, recognizing how dependent it is on repetition in its oral tradition of song and story: "In their speeches and songs they are emphatic and impressive by the continual repetition of the same phrase or idea; and it seems to affect them like the perpetual recurrence of a few simple notes in music, by which I have been myself wound up to painful excitement, or melted to tears" (472–3). The view of language Jameson is discovering is one that combines its symbolic and pre-symbolic or emotive functions, language as love as used by the mother with the young child, and language as meaning, the kind of mapping of self and other that the child learns as she begins to map herself and the world.

Her continuing investigation of the position of native women and the comparison of that position to her own culture yield her anthropologically prescient conclusions, which she casts as rhetorical questions: "Do you not think ... that the true importance and real dignity of woman is everywhere, in savage and civilised communities, regulated by her capacity of being useful; or, in other words, that her condition is decided by the share she takes in providing for her own subsistence and the well-being of society as a productive labourer? Where she is idle and useless by privilege of sex, a divinity and an idol, a victim or a toy, is not her position quite as lamentable, as false, as injurious to herself and all social progress, as where she is the drudge, slave, and possession of the man?" (519). In fact, the passages at the end of the text, in which Jameson discourses on the condition of women, seem especially oral and rhetorical in their construction, showing she had absorbed the important features of oral style present in the Indian orality of her women mentors.

The processes of personal and intellectual change that Jameson goes though in her "rambles" are facilitated, as well, by qualities she has brought with her that are shaped and intensified by her two months in the wilderness. Because she is already an accomplished scholar, she is able to use patriarchal discourses well; however, as a good feminist she has refused "the question as formulated," as de Lauretis puts it, not asking how she can study the native peoples from the point of view of an objective, superior observer, but discovering instead ways she can involve herself completely, how she can use that "tone of personal feeling," which she refused to extract from her journal account, to come to her new self-representation as woman and as feminist. She knows how to answer questions "deviously," that is, by asking them seemingly uncontroversially, winning the reader's allegiance while still using the discourses of patriarchy, but at the same time drawing the reader towards radical conclusions. This is especially true when she makes her detailed comparison of women in white and native culture, a comparison that neither denigrates nor romanticizes the aboriginal people and never makes the mistake of confusing her own subject position with that of women who have had to live with the rigors of subsistance life. As she asserts, her own "taste" is for the civilized existence, but she prefers "the Indians on the score of consistency: they are what they profess to be, and we are *not* what we profess to be" (460).

Much of her skilful rhetoric is due to her ability to use sources such as Schoolcraft – whose work on Indian customs is admirable, but coloured by his place as missionary – and sources such as Alexander Henry – whose anecdotes on native life are fascinating, but often made to serve Henry's economic interest as a trader – using them subversively by "quot[ing] them against the grain."

In fact, all the strategies proposed by the feminist theorists I have quoted in this study are part of the cultural and literary repertoire of this nineteenth-century feminist, and in her relationship with the three Indian women who mentor her, she is my paradigm as a reader of women's self-representation in language. She becomes, through her relationship with three native women, the daughter and sister and, through her text, the mother of the subjective cultural place she wishes to map. Through mapping that culture, she finds the language she needs to "reconstruct and reclaim – to locate and recontextualize – the mother's message" and thereby write herself into language, to inscribe a female subjectivity that, like the wild landscape she met in the Great Lakes country, she at first had no words for: "I wish I could place before you in words, – but I despair, unless words were of light, and lustrous hues, and breathing music" (371).

The Anna of Jameson's text finds her "music" in the orality and intimacy of her mentors' world and brings something of what she found in them and in herself back with her. Her ability to do this is largely a function of her ability to bridge many discoursive communities, both literary and in the larger cultural area of the then embryonic discourses of the social sciences. Her style in this regard exhibits many of the best features of the personal essay informed by the factual and research base of the more formal scholarly essay. Graham Good marks the heart of this form in *The Observing Self:* "The heart of the essay as a form is [a] moment of characterization, of recognition, of figuration, where the self finds a pattern in the world and the world finds a pattern in the self."[19] This moment occurs because the essayist, though "prepared by careful attention and observation," is able to bring a "spontaneous" attitude, one that does not apply a "preconceived method" (22), to the experience. In this way the "essay is an act of personal witness" (23). I find that this particular generic orientation, one especially suited to the traveller stance, is one of the reasons both Moodie (her sketches are very essayistic) and Jameson succeed in so much of their inscription of female subjectivity. The essay form not only allows a speculative, open-ended enquiry, a joined sense of self and other, a spontaneity suited to its purpose, but allows for a catalytic form facilitating movement between contrasting generic positions. It is in its ability to negotiate a path between various features of narrative, drama, and poetry that the essay creates the space for female inscription of self.

Thus, the map I trace contains both aspects of personal psychology, the palimpsest of self and others that these women inscribe and a set of generic overlays. As one might find the features of mountain chains and river systems overlaying one another in a map, so reading for the features of various strategies of inscription reveals the contours of women's autobiographical writing. But as well, positioning these pychological and generic features are two "meridians" of the self living and constructing itself in the world: the Canadian nature of the experience, entailing a discovery of the new land and one's place in it (which help to identify common features in these accounts), and the place of the maternal pre-text in the individual stories. While I emphasized the first in the early women's accounts, as all of them, in one way or another, underwent a pioneering experience in Canada, I will emphasize the second in the women's accounts I am about to consider, as I move to the consideration of the lives of women who have become caught in the conflict of the competing cultural agendas of twentieth-century life. Interestingly, the sense of the place that is Canada does not disappear from these later accounts, but interweaves itself with the desire for a maternal pre-text as it did in Anna Jameson's text, the early nineteenth-century exploration of self and other that often feels so twentieth century to contemporary readers.

PART TWO

On Becoming
a Twentieth-Century Woman

When Anna Jameson was leaving the Great Lakes, Queen Victoria had just come to the throne. Jameson mused on what effect a woman in that position might have. Her observations regarding the young queen show a view of womanly possibility as well as an awareness of the patriarchal setting it must survive: "If she be but simple-minded, and true-hearted, and straightforward, with the common portion of intellect – if royal education have not blunted in her the quick perceptions and pure kind instincts of the woman – if she has only had fair play, and carries into business plain distinct notions of right and wrong – and the fine moral sense that is not to be confounded by diplomatic verbiage and expediency – she will do better for us than a whole cabinet full of cut and dried officials, with Tallyrand at the head of them."[1]

Her statement contains, for a reader like myself, reading with a 150 years of hindsight, both an irony and a warning – an irony because the years of Victoria's reign mark a reactionary societal phenomenon in regard to women's place. The phenomenon has been described in accounts as diverse as Charlotte Perkins Gilman's 1904 book *Women and Economics*[2] and, more recently, Ann Douglas's *The Feminization of American Culture*.[3] Gilman analysed the public/private split of an economics that confines women to the home, where without power, but with much responsibility, a woman must become the "moral mother," the figure who through her own example advocates a high ethical standard for those in her household. She has no power to enforce this standard, and as Barbara Welter has pointed out in "The cult of True Womanhood," this was the way the industrial/capitalist male public world needed it. Such a state of affairs allowed the existence of an expansionist, imperialist, money-based economy where few ethical standards could be enforced, cushioned by a home environment where an impossibly high moral standard was advocated, where the male conscience could rest secure in the false belief that it lived in a moral world. Ann Douglas describes more fully the late nineteenth-century society that this led to, one in which women were encouraged to think of themselves as powerful arbiters of moral goodness, were allowed a limited sphere of effectiveness in the arts, in the church, and in the various fashionable social and entertainment structures of their world, and of course on the domestic scene, but were never allowed to exercise that power where it might really matter, in the world of economics, that is, the world of government and business.

In Britain, Queen Victoria operated as a central figure in this feminization, representing all that was morally correct as Victorian wife and mother and serving as living symbol of the power and rank such correctness gave to a woman. Of course, the power was largely illusionary, for the world was actually run by the same kind of "cabinet full of cut and dried officials, with Tallyrand at the head" that Jameson imagined might yield to the "pure kind instincts of a woman" like the young Victoria. Such is the irony of history, that the very belief in the moral, true-hearted nature of women that allowed Anna Jameson to construct a self that led to much personal success and independence was the same belief appropriated by patriarchy to limit and curtail female power.

Thus, as a feminist who admires Jameson, I am struck by the irony in Jameson's words. Viewing her statement as warning, I see its applicability to our current situation when I read Ann Douglas's autobiographical introduction, in which she worries that twentieth-century academic women may be in exactly the same position as our nineteenth-century sisters, that is, ripe to have our campaign to revise culture through women-centred theories appropriated once more by the patriarchy. I therefore find myself in a seeming paradox. Jameson's view of women as possessing a "fine moral sense," a true-hearted goodness, which by implication is not possessed by men, can become a trap for feminists, the essentialist trap whereby we propose a difference between men and women only to be implicated in confining women inside patriarchal definitions of that difference. At the same time as I heed this warning, I am also aware that to construct gender based on biological differences of sex is a powerful way (in which we are all encouraged, both by forces outside ourselves and by the very physical differences between us) to map ourselves and our places in the world. Somehow, as reader, I must embrace this difference and its positive possibilities without falling prey to essentialism. To do so I must re-examine my own subject position as reader.

The mapping of the autobiographical accounts of early Canadian women leads me to take another look at my introduction to Part 1, in which I write of my own foremothers. In reading what I wrote about my admiration for their fine qualities, their strength, devotion, and moral leadership, I now see that if I only measure them by the male-absent domestic scene, I too am in danger of the essentialist trap, of praising and therefore advocating an inscription of female selfhood that celebrates their domestic and community effectiveness while advocating the continuation of their limitation of power. I have to remind myself that both my grandmothers ended their lives in positions of great powerlessness. The qualities of leadership and moral authority that I saw in my paternal grandmother as a middle-aged mother running her farm do not change the fact that she ended her life dependent on the care of her daughter-in-law, with nothing but the latchkey to her long-gone home to remind her of her place in the world. The active community service of my maternal grandmother as midwife, as emotional and financial resource for generations of women, did not keep her from an old age in which she owned nothing and was powerless even to decide her place of residence.

My grandmothers lived the lives of working-class rural women. My mother, however, like many of her generation in Newfoundland, moved into the middle class. Because she and my father had educational advantages unavailable before their generation, they were able, with hard work, to construct a lifestyle in which the mother remained in the home while the father worked at a secure and continuing position. However, since they still lived in close community with their large, extended, working-class (but upwardly mobile) families, my childhood was not typical of a child growing up in a middle-class, nuclear family. As well, since my parents, as Newfoundlanders, certainly did not have the financial resources we associate with the middle class today, since they still had important financial obligations within the extended family, and since they always insisted that educational expenditures come first, I rarely had the feeling that I was, on a day-to-day basis, much better off than many financially strapped Newfoundlanders. When I was a very young girl and lived in my parents' house, the best times I remember were when one or more of the women in my mother's large extended family, or from among her many community contacts, came to our home. This happened often, as my father travelled in his work and my mother was frequently left alone with five young children. Since my mother had six sisters in her own family, as well as sister-in-laws, cousins, and nieces, and since she belonged to female church and community organizations and lived in a neighbourhood full of women not working outside the home, her house was a place where women's voices, women's stories, shaped my development as a person, my mapping of my sense of my self and the world.

Children were not always welcome additions to these conversations, since matters not considered suitable for their young ears were often discussed. I remember an occasion when my mother and her mother were reminiscing about the days of midwifery. My mother observed that the hardest times for her were the weeks when her mother was away on a case, especially one that required my grandmother to sleep away from home. Not understanding, I asked my grandmother why she had to stay at the newborn's house after the baby had arrived. She explained about caring for the needs of the new mother and child and then, in quite another, rather bitter voice, said, "And sometimes you had to sleep in the woman's bed to keep the husband out!" My mother quickly stayed any elaboration or any more questions by warning, "Don't tell the girl that!" and my mind teemed for a while with the possible dangers of adult males, the very figures all my female relatives taught me to respect and revere.

My grandmother's slippage into a forbidden discourse and my mother's silencing of that discourse were important in my conditioning as a female person. I learned very quickly that silence was not only proper, but an important way of learning. If I remained unobtrusive, helpfully brought the tea cups, placed myself in just the right peripheral place in the kitchen, sipped my own milk-diluted tea without slurping, I could often overhear amazing stories. As I grew to be a more skilled listener, I found that crucial moments arrived in conversations, silences in which I knew there were words that could not be said. Sometimes if the silence felt just right, I could phrase a question that would lead the speaker further into the unknown. This was a risk, though, for it brought me to the attention of my mother, who would then, to her horror, discover it was way past my bedtime. On those nights my mother sometimes found me sleeping on the stairs, where I had placed myself in the hope of hearing what could not be said in front of me. Often, however, the effort to overhear led to nothing, as the subject so close to the surface in that pregnant silence was not given voice after the child's question.

I cannot pinpoint at what age I became aware that there was another world that was forbidden to me in a much more effective way than the one represented by the silence at the tea table. I must have been very young because I can remember watching my father read the paper and thinking that the key to being allowed to sit in the comfortable living room while the dirty work of dishes was being done after supper was to be able to read. I wanted to read desperately. I would watch my father's posture, his eyes moving across the page, the concentrated expression of his face, trying to find the key to this wonderful power. I remember as well that, late in the Second World War, a jeep and uniformed driver came each morning to our home to pick up my father to take him to his work, an activity that was hazy in my mind except that I knew it involved the protection of our Newfoundland coastlines, the very survival of the safe world I lived in with my mother. But what interested me was not survival, but the wonderful machine, the jeep, and the way the driver manipulated the wheel and the various buttons and pedals and sticks that made it roar off with my dad. Now there was a world I wanted!

I must have been eight or nine when I heard my parents talking regretfully about the fact that my father must live without his very efficient secretary, who would be leaving his office. Amazed that anyone would want to give up that huge desk I had seen her sitting behind and that wonderful typing machine, the telephones, and the office full of busy people, I asked why she was leaving. "Oh, she's getting married, " mother said. "So?" asked I. "Well, they don't keep married women," my mother explained, as if she was surprised I did not know this important fact of life. My father went on to explain that it wasn't fair for a married woman to keep a job that might go to someone else, especially since she had a husband to support her. I still remember the feeling of shock, of disappointment, and a kind of embarrassment and shame at having envied my father's world and having thought that it might someday be mine. I was silent on the subject of that world for a long time. Now when I read Freudian theories of female development involving penis envy, I immediately assume that the term is used figuratively, could not possibly refer to those seemingly pointless appendages that my girlfriends and I occasionally glimpsed and laughed at as children, pleased that our own bodies were so much more smoothly and sensibly made. When I read "penis-envy," I always infer the power of jeeps and jobs and newspapers.

A few years ago, when I was talking with my father about my own modest success as an academic and writer, he observed that a position senior to the one he had occupied on retirement was now for the first time being filled by a woman. We talked for a while about the great technological, historical, and cultural changes we had both lived through, and he concluded that soon all the workplaces of business and government would be staffed by women. "They just work harder and they are better at managing people," he said, shrugging with the philosophical gesture of a gentleman long retired from the fray. "I don't know what we are going to do with the men!" He seemed suddenly aware of the implications of his observation. I laughed and told him not to worry, I was not as optimistic about the possibility of a female takeover as he was.

When I look back on my own construction as a female person, from the position of an academic vitally concerned with the ways in which females map identity, I realize that many of my ways of knowing both myself as a female person and the world in which I was to act out my personhood were contextualized always by my relationship with my mother and the women who talked and were silent in her kitchen, and by the more distant, but very desirable, world in which my seemingly heroic father moved. I am aware that, like the women who pioneered in Canada and underwent great changes in self that caused them to write of the experience, I too have lived on the cusp of a great change in society. I grew up assuming that I must accept the traditional domestic place of women in my culture but later found that I not only had access to paths that had formerly seemed forbidden, but indeed, was expected to fill many roles, sliding back and forth between public and private roles in an often dizzying improvisation for which my training had not prepared me. When seeking the facilitating theory that will help me read the accounts of women who also experienced something of this great change, I want to keep this historicity of my own cultural situation in mind as a means both of avoiding essentialism and of helping me read their accounts always in their historical, cultural, and personal contexts.

While the literary perspectives of the theorists I gave emphasis to in the first chapters were suitable for consideration of those accounts, I find now that I need to refer to the theories of feminists working in the social sciences. Nineteenth-century women confronted a different face of patriarchy then do women of my own century. Theirs was a world defined by patriarchal religious and imperial values and informed by a literature largely supportive of that world. Twentieth-century women confront a situation in which social sciences such as psychology, sociology, and anthropology, as well as the practices of more science-based activities such as medicine, have worked to create new cultural (but still patriarchal) definitions of women. Thus, it is inside these disciplines we will find the subversive work of feminists that will aid the kind of literary mapping I undertake. Theoretical accounts of women's development can be helpful to me in contextualizing twentieth-century accounts, especially in reading the silences they speak. As well, the different actualities of the individual lives recorded in the autobiographies of these women will inform these theories. I would like to summarize briefly some of Nancy Chodorow's findings on female development, some of the epistemological research of the authors of *Women's Ways of Knowing*, and some of Carol Gilligan's findings on female ethical development in order to move away for a time from the more literary and genre-based mapping I have been making. The reason for this is that the books I will highlight in this chapter are neither by women who thought they were writing for a private audience, nor by women (except for McClung) who had literary reputations at the time of writing. What I am interested in is the way their perceived development as females affects the generic and stylistic choices they make. This will allow me to speculate on the way gender affects genre, and to make comparisons with the literary women who are the subject of the following chapter.

Chodorow, working out of a Freudian-based model in *The Reproduction of Mothering*, proposes several differences in the early development of males and females in Western culture. Chodorow finds that the "feminine Oedipus complex is not simply a transfer of affection from mother to father and a giving up of mother" as Freudians propose for male children.[4] Because most of their nurture and early care are given by same-sex individuals, "girls come to experience themselves as less separate than boys, as having more permeable ego boundaries. Girls come to define themselves more in relation to others" (93). As well, Chodorow points out, the feeling the mother has that the girl child, is more her "self" than the male child leads to the girl being held in a symbiotic relationship longer. But further, the "nature of the attachment is different." Since the girl experiences a "continuation of the two-person relationship of infancy" (96) for longer, she remains preoccupied with the connected nature of "issues of dependence and individuation" (97) more than the boy child. Even when girls eventually transfer their attention to the father as other, a means by which both sexes develop as individuals and out of the symbiosis with the mother, the attachment is likely to be quite intense, a replication of the "equally strong and passionate attachment to their mother" (96). In fact, Chodorow finds that the nature of the early "preoedipal attachment of the girl child to her mother largely determines both her subsequent oedipal attachment to her father and her later relationship to men in general" (96). Most intriguingly for one like myself, concerned with how factors in development affect our construction in language, Chodorow concludes that the more nuanced and complex development of females leads to behaviour patterns of some ambivalence. She finds that "a girl alternates between total rejection of a mother who represents infantile dependence and attachment to her, between identification with anyone other than her mother and feeling herself her mother's double and extension. Her mother often mirrors her preoccupations" (138). The pattern of ambivalence outlined by Chodorow should offer insight into the subtle ways in which women engage the maternal pre-texts of their writings.

The authors of *Women's Ways of Knowing* find that different development leads to different ways of mapping the world and the self, that is, a different language of learning. Women, for instance, often value listening as a way of learning more than more active pursuits of knowledge. Many express the conviction that they have an inner voice that leads them in their search for knowledge, one that informs them about the correct paths they might choose. The authors of *Knowing* contend that the most successful pattern for women is to become *connected* rather than *separate* knowers: "Connected knowers develop procedures for gaining access to other people's knowledge. At the heart of these procedures is the capacity for empathy."[5] They propose an epistemological development for women that briefly stated involves four stages. The first involves a "silence" in which women are "selfless and voiceless" and accept the word of external authority. A second way of knowing is the stage of "received knowledge and procedural knowledge" in which women obey the sex role stereotypes of our society, whereby they seek "gratification in pleasing others," obeying the rules, and fitting into pre-set patterns. In a third stage, the position of "subjective knowledge," women tend to construct "a space for the growth of self" and often develop a sense of the inner voice, which is a kind of private authority replacing external authority. But in order to develop what is called a "constructed knowledge," the mature female thinker must "learn to speak in a unique and authentic voice" (134) that combines the inner voice with knowledge from the external world. In fact, the authors of *Knowing* find that women who do not develop an integrated way of knowing, who do not achieve a connected knowledge, find themselves in a painful state where "thinking and feeling are split asunder; they feel fraudulent and deadened to their inner experiences and inner selves" (135). This search for an authentic voice must have profound effects on the way women use our culture's literary genres.

As one concerned with the ways in which language shapes thought and indeed *is* thought, I find it interesting that the authors of *Knowing* note how often women tend to "ground their epistemological premises in metaphors suggesting speaking and listening" rather than the "visual metaphors (such as equating knowledge with illumination, knowing with seeing and truth with light) that scientists and philosophers most often use to express their sense of mind" (18). I think immediately of Anna Jameson and her fascination with the voices of her mentors and with the orality of Indian language, which expressed a sense of the communal nature of language. I think of my own oral culture of the tea table and wonder if this metaphor is an important one in the autobiographies of twentieth-century women. Carol Gilligan calls her study of the ethical development of female persons *In a Different Voice*, embedding the metaphor of "voice" in her title. In wishing "to restore ... the missing text of women's development," she indicates that "text" and "voice" are connected.[6] Her research in modifying male-oriented ethical development rating systems teaches her that "from the different dynamics of separation and attachment in their gender identity formation through the divergence of identity and intimacy that marks their experience in the adolescent years, male and female voices typically speak of the importance of different truths, the former of the role of separation as it defines and empowers the self, the latter of the ongoing process of attachment that creates and sustains the human community" (156).

While these theories are helpful to my mapping, it seems to me that all of these social scientists assume a particular and fairly stable idea of the family situations in which children grow up: this is the nuclear family with two parents, both of whom obey the stereotypical roles assigned in Western culture, the mother nurturing, the father distant but powerful, the economic resource of the household. Such a pattern assumes the so-called normal factors of middle-class values and heterosexuality and does not allow for factors such as alternate sexual orientations, ethnic variation, racial oppression, poverty, the interruption of family life by war, immigration, or death. But this is the nature of psychological and sociological studies; they must establish norms to do their work. And their findings can be helpful if used to inform rather than dictate the compilation of autobiographical writings by women. In fact, what the study of actual accounts offers, as Gilligan discovered in having her subjects write autobiographical reports and as the authors of *Knowing* show through reprinting many of the oral statements of their subjects, is the nuance and difference that exist within certain general features, and the way in which the presence or absence of certain factors can make the difference that gives each of us the conviction of our uniqueness. It is this balance between pattern and difference that I would like to highlight as I explore the autobiographies of women who undertook to achieve some special mission in the public world, a mission that involved them in issues of identity as well as achievement.

Being aware that I am especially attracted to those accounts and theories that verify my own experience of the world, I have offered a personal account to my readers in order that they may include it in their own assessment of the validity of what I say. As well, it will serve as a reminder to me that although I may legitimately seek what is similar in my own experience and others', I must also make room for what is different.

4 Achieving Women / Achieving Womanhood

> Resisting the shape of male autobiography is only the beginning. The female autobiographer must also resist cultural pressure to remain silent. The pressure is all the more intense if she wishes to speak as a mother, for as recent feminist and psychoanalytic theorists have shown, the central project of our (patriarchal) culture necessitates the mother's absence.
>
> Gail Twersky Reimer, "Revisions of Labor in Margaret Oliphant's Autobiography"

> A factor that recurs with remarkable frequency in the backgrounds of these women is the identification with and dependence upon, the father; and either loss of, or alienation from, the mother.
>
> Elaine Showalter, *A Literature of Their Own*

> When I speak of gynocentric myth and feminist myth-making I do not refer to tales of reified gods and/or goddesses but to stories arising from the experience of the Crones – stories which convey primary and archetypal messages about our own Prehistory and about Female-identified power.
>
> Mary Daly, *Gyn/Ecology*

The "father" of academic theories of autobiography, Georg Misch, observed that such personal writing flourishes in times when people find themselves seeking "to regain the harmony and inner tranquility" of a right relationship with all of existence, and in such times "actual personal experience" becomes the "driving force" which leads to "an insight into those deep layers of human existence in which passion and suffering and the feeling for the infinite" obtain "the character of positive values."[1] The present can be considered such a time, since we live in a society where so many past patterns have been overturned without our sometimes realizing or admitting the change. Often, values we profess fly in the face of facts we live with. In such a time the autobiographical mode, as one critic puts it, "can be an authentic way of establishing the truth of our experience. The individual is real even when the culture is not."[2] In the last few generations great change has especially had an impact on women, but many women, rather than having the conviction that they were "real," have felt quite the opposite, that they were not real. They have felt lost, dislocated, unfit for the contending and conflicting roles to which a very real and ever-present and intrusive culture subjects them. Our culture uses images of the bodies and personalities of women to sell everything from cosmetics to cars, and tells us we must dress like whores but love like super-mothers, learn like scholars but act like fools, work like navvies but look like leisured courtesans. Faced with such conflicting images, women today often feel unreal and have a sense of lost values and unmarked paths, of being thrust into what Sandra Frieden calls, in her exploration of German women's autobiographies, "a life without role models."[3] This sense of dislocation is, in our century, one shared by women in many parts of the world. As women enter the public roles once labelled masculine and try to integrate that change with the identity patterns developed in the private world labelled feminine, social scientists become interested in their development as psychological and sociological entities. Whereas formerly the typical human models of these disciplines were gendered male, in the last decade publications like the three I have referred to in the introduction to Part 2 indicate a new interest in women's identities.

The achievement focus of this chapter is not one I choose arbitrarily. I find that it is the autobiographies of such women that offer the material that can allow us to realize in the fullest possible way the identity markers the theorists speak of, and to inform our theories with the variety of lived experience and writing choices these writers make in constructing their experience in language. But as well, in reading many women's autobiographical accounts from the late 1700s to the present, I notice a distinct change as the pioneer period ends. The end of the settlement period in Canada coincides with the rise in consciousness concerning women's roles that occurred in the late nineteenth century with the growth of the suffragette movement. In our own time economic and technological changes have allowed women to have a measure of control over their reproductive lives and to increasingly take on work outside the domestic economy. Some of the most lively accounts are ones in which settlement and women's issues overlap, as they often did at the turn of the twentieth century. The feminist Georgina Binnie-Clark wrote two autobiographical accounts of her life, first as a visitor from England and later as a farmer on the Saskatchewan prairie.

A Summer on the Canadian Prairie is on the surface a light-hearted travel account telling of the foibles of well-to-do sophisticated English gentry who are ill-suited for the hard work of the frontier, a kind of updating of Moodie's travel writing and her warning to "gentlemen" settlers. However, beneath the surface light heartedness, but not very far beneath that surface, is a none-too-disguised effort to discredit a brother, Lal, who in the opinion of the narrator is dependent and shiftless. The young man holds first place in the father's affections, a place the narrator envies. The father has sent the daughter out to see how Lal is making out on the prairie, and in habitually defining her own strength through the disparaging of her brother, who acts as a kind of negative other, the narrator sets up a situation in which she must inevitably deal with male and female differences. Making the most of strategies of indirection, Binnie-Clark often puts her criticisms into the mouths of seemingly impartial settlers. One immigrant observes: "In England I used to think that men worked whilst women gossiped. On a prairie settlement the women work, and it isn't the women who gossip. I owe one debt to my life on the prairie, and that is a fair appreciation of my own sex."[4] This kind of statement, attributed either to her travelling companion, Hilaria, or other women, nevertheless has the same diction and tone as the voice of the narrator, a narrative voice the author is not at great pains to define as different than her own. The fact that the book is dedicated to her father indicates that the effort is directed towards winning him to a more positive assessment of the role of women, especially that of his daughter, and that she seeks to rival her brother's place in the father's world.

Towards the end of *Summer*, Binnie-Clark begins to drop her disguises and her bantering tone and observes bluntly: "You can't get over the fact that in the entire settlement we are the only real failures. Our two men [Lal and his gentleman friend], who have had more advantages than the rest of the neighbors put together, are the only ones who have failed. And it isn't because they are helpless: it is because they won't lend themselves to small beginnings" (272). Susanna Moodie could have told Binnie-Clark this truth about gentleman immigrants, but one of the features I find interesting in this account is its emphasis on the sibling rivalry, as if in emerging from former definitions of womanhood that are too narrow for the modern world, this writer finds the new grounds of her self-definition already occupied by her brother. The conclusion I draw is that, for Binnie-Clark, her father's approval of her pose as "son" is an important factor in self-identity, and therefore identity becomes a male-defined rivalry for the father's approval. I find this identity problem is a common one for women writing autobiographically in the twentieth century.

However, on examining the second book Binnie-Clark wrote about her Canadian experience, *Wheat and Women*, I find the tone of her first book – the travel persona telling amusing anecdotes in a winning, almost cute, manner, a discourse that seems almost a direct address to the father – is abandoned in favour of a much more discursive, descriptive, and sometimes polemical style, producing a more public tone than the first book. This book tells the story of her setbacks and successes as a farmer of her own land. Earlier cloaked sarcasms concerning brothers have turned to open disapproval of the ways in which women are treated by male governments as well as male individuals. Binnie-Clark actively campaigns for the rights of women farmers and is most offended by the injustice built into the system by which a woman "may be the best farmer in Canada, she may buy land, work it, take prizes for seed and stock, but she is denied the right to claim from the Government the hundred and sixty acres of land held out as a bait to every man."[5]

However, in addition to her abandoning the tone of the dispossessed daughter who seeks the approval of her patriarchal father, and adopting an independent position as feminist criticizing a patriarchal government, another change occurs from the beginning of the first book to the end of the second, one less to do with polemic and more to do with a changing image of her own identity as woman. Whereas in chapter 2 of the first work her example of appropriate feminine behaviour is herself as fine and sensitive literary companion to a shipboard male "philosopher and ... comrade" (15), much later in the same text there is a shift as she starts to notice women more than men and begins to build an image of maternal behaviour: "I sat down ... and glanced round the garden, which was racing towards a fulfillment of the promise, and the end of the story of what a brave, patient, loving English mother can accomplish under the stress of circumstance" (276). In the second book Binnie-Clark seeks her own end of story. She figures Canada as "the virgin side of the Great Mother" who asks from her children "courage and kindness, swiftness and patience, strength and sympathy, unflinching purpose, unfailing energy, untiring philosophy." This devotion will produce a people that are of the "old giant kind" (312–13). This change from the father-preoccupied discourse in the first book to the ringing tones of the "great mother" image in the second indicates a movement away from male-centred self-definitions to more female-centred ones for this feminist writer. There is no doubt that her pioneering experience had the same radical effect on her as on earlier women, whereas her cultural and historical situation has allowed her to draw more consciously feminist conclusions.

However, it is important to note that Binnie-Clark uses a mythic image of motherhood. The father in the first text seems a very real, personal father. Although largely extra-textual, he does not seem mythically godlike, merely economically powerful. The brother figure is a very mundane sort, and the rivalry between him and his sister an everyday kind, often comical. That she must cast the mother figure in mythic terms indicates the need to inscribe a different story, one that cannot be found easily in the world. Stephanie Demetrakopoulos describes this fairly common phenomenon in women's autobiography as one in which present-day women wish to reconnect with a mythic concept of the world view expressed in the matriarchal Eleusinian rites of a world in which women were, as Binnie-Clark says, of "the old giant kind" and the relationship of mother and daughter was full and rich in scope. The appearance of this myth-based trope at the end of a text noted for its rather down-to-earth practical narrative discourse alerts a reader trained in literary tropes to the possibility of the maternal pre-text.

Why and how the maternal pre-text actually makes its appearance in written accounts is easier to decode if I view it alongside the social scientists' formulation of a typical girl's psyche in the maternal relationship. If Binnie-Clark is any example, real mothers are noted by their absence, and father identification is more obvious. Even if the a girl like Binnie-Clark had a preoedipal relationship with the personal mother, there is little evidence of its influence in the girl's conscious world, which would seem to be largely dominated by the father. Not only would she seem to have completely transferred her intense feelings concerning identity to her father, but the mother does not remain a figure of identification, either negative or positive. The most notable feature of the mother is her absence. As well, as a literary reader, I suspect that when a writer starts to appeal to the rhetoric of myth, she is more than likely seeking a configuration of her own life that her culture excludes, seeking to inscribe a new, or long lost, subjectivity.

An autobiography that illustrates more clearly the ways in which paternal and maternal influences shape the achieving woman is Martha Black's *My Seventy Years*. It does so because Black chooses to deal in some detail with her childhood. She narrates in a very readable combination of narrative and essay her beginnings in a prosperous and close-knit Chicago family, where women's roles were narrowly defined by the example of Black's devoted, modest, uncomplaining, and completely subservient mother. Black describes her parents' reaction to her birth. The father complains to his wife: "Susan, I am disappointed. I expected a boy." The mother replies meekly, "Yes, I know, I am so sorry."[6] The recounting of this moment – one she would have had to have heard from family members, thereby implying her insufficiency – as well as the re-creation of an incident in her childhood in which she physically attacks a little girl for behaving with prescribed feminine submissiveness, outlines the conflicted nature of Black's identity. Further, her obvious admiration for her father, whom she describes as single-handedly saving the family and their fortunes during the Chicago fire, indicates Black's desire to be more like the boy her father wanted than the daughter her parents expected her to be. To add to the conflict, Black claims to admire her mother and denigrates her own independent and assertive childhood self. She observes: "To-day I am grateful to that dear mother of mine who so wisely showed me the unhappiness that inevitably follows ungovernable passion, vanity and covetousness. Of course, being naturally hot-headed and vain, I was not cured for ever of those faults" (37).

Black's language indicates first a condemnation of her "passion, vanity and covetousness" and a gratitude to her mother, an acceptance of her feminine standards. But the phrase "being naturally" mediates the self-condemnation and is an indicator of the kind of formula Black is to follow in her writing. Gail Reimer describes something like this strategy in analysing Margaret Oliphant's autobiography: "Each articulation of her own perception of self and world is followed by a gesture of suppression." Reimer attributes this suppression to Oliphant's "effort to translate her experience into the culture's terms."[7] While the correct female novelist at the heart of Victorian patriarchy is so enclosed by patriarchy that all experience is seen through that glass, such is not exactly the case with this American woman who became a distinguished Canadian. Black first proposes the correct societal mode, then partially undermines it with expressions such as "naturally" and tempts us further into her non-feminine life story with phrases such as "I was not cured for ever of those faults." In fact, just before this observation, she has offered the reader a version of her feisty childhood self that has solicited the reader's admiration for her pluck and independence. At other times she will suppress one obvious unfeminine thought or activity by censuring herself and let several others go uncensured, even dramatically and winningly re-creating them for our vicarious pleasure. This nuanced version of articulation and suppression of self is the strategy Black uses to maintain her ambivalent identification with her entrepreneurial father and her saintly, but passive, mother. Interestingly, the articulation often occurs in the narrative sections of the text, whereas the essayistic commentary is used to present a correctly feminine ideology. Thus, the reader who pays more attention to narrative may glean quite a different impression of Black than the reader who takes her at her stated opinion. Further, it is worth noting that narrative, in literature and in life, has its roots in the earliest oral culture, whereas the argument of essay is one that needs the printed text, or at least the Socratic forum, as its base. For Black, narrative is a means of inscribing an alternative, forbidden, non-patriarchal self, her own embedded arachnology, contextualized and hidden inside a safe, moralistic feminine surface.

I want to consider, too, the possibility that the reason this other inscription is possible is that through her actual life experiences Black was offered an unusual opportunity to realize quite fully the intense interpersonal and often conflicting attachments that Chodorow notes in female subjects. It is in paying close attention to the historicity of a woman's life that we can once more see the interconnection of theories of female subjectivity and experience in the world.

Black leads a conventional life until her thirties, marrying and having two sons. Although she complains of the confining life of young motherhood and the wandering eye of her husband, she accepts her place, since it means being connected to others in a close family life and having the parental approval she needs. She might never have rebelled if history and her husband had not taken a hand. She and her husband decide to go on the great adventure of their lives, to pan for gold during the Yukon gold rush. Black presents this as a mutual decision, but what happens afterwards is obviously a combination of accident, personality, place, and the fact of being caught up in one of the last great rushes to affect that portion of the pioneering North American population that seems to have become mobile by definition. Waiting in San Francisco for the boat north, Black's husband decides he prefers the Hawaiian Islands. It is at this point, when she is about to take a path not in keeping with wifely submissiveness, that Black begins to use the elevated language of the mythologizer: "It was the pivotal point of my life – my destiny. The North Star, my lodestar, beckoned me. It lured me onward. My whole being cried out to follow it" (92–3). The myth-making, elevated language, here somewhat like the inner voice of the second-stage knower, indicates a woman seeking to extend or break cultural role models, yet with no clear idea of how that other self is to be contained in language.

However, I also wish to point out that whereas psychological models often see identity as complete in childhood and contextualized entirely by the familial situation, researchers such as the writers of *Knowing* indicate that some female development does not occur until adulthood. My reading of autobiography would indicate that many women are middle-aged before the full contours of their personalities are mapped. This may be partially a result of needing to fulfil marital and child-bearing agendas, of needing to accommodate the realities of living in a female body in a society that does not make it easy to combine diverse roles, but it can also be the result of the unstable, contradictatory, and fast-changing nature of twentieth-century life in the Western world. This is especially so for women, where such change factors as pioneering, gold rushes, and wars, as well as changes in reproductive and domestic technologies, can take them out of known contexts much more fully than men.

Left largely to her own devices in San Francisco, with only a compliant brother to convince, Black takes her escape route north to adventure and the fuller realization of her contentious selfhood. The Yukon proves the place where her independent headstrong self, the part of her that emulates her father, can blossom, but as well she redefines the idea of maternality that her mother exemplified. She not only crosses the Chinook Pass in winter, sets up placer claims of her own, and begins a business employing (and successfully managing) several men hostile to female entrepreneurship, but also delivers her own baby in a small shack. The arrival of the child is given the kind of elevated treatment that she gives her decision to go north. In images reminiscent of the Holy Mother, Black describes the "men-folk" gathering around her, as she, like the virgin with her divine son, receives their gifts. Those of us not keen on images of virgin birth are left to speculate on whether or not the Hawaii-bound husband is the father. Black does not comment on such commonplaces. Her remarks on father, pregnancy, and child are limited to an observation on her incredibly easy labour, which she finds is, "Mother nature's gift to women who live a natural out-of-doors life such as I had done" (130).

Despite her success, she finds the hand of patriarchal culture far-reaching. It arrives in the form of her father, who convinces her to bring her child home and live with him and her mother. Meekly she goes, but the experience of returning to the old place and thus to the old identity makes her so physically ill that her parents have to agree to let her go north again. Later in her life, her marriage to George Black, whereby she becomes the gracious wife of the Yukon's commissioner and his exemplary spouse when he is speaker of the Canadian Parliament, allows her to exhibit her mother-defined role as pleasing and passive spouse, but gives the more flamboyant Black some scope as well. However, it is her role as member of Parliament for the Yukon, undertaken when her husband becomes too ill to carry on his duties, that allows Black her most satisfying combination of the two strong pulls in her personality. This is indicated by the event with which she chooses to close her account, and which she points to as the culmination of her career: her moment of rebellion in the House of Commons.

The Commons is about to send a message of sympathy to Queen Mary on the death of George V. Her house leader has declined Black's private suggestion that the sympathies of the women of Canada be added to the telegram. Torn between obeying her male leader and her need to speak on behalf of women, she finally rises to speak, publically offering sympathy to "Her majesty the Queen [who] has set the women of Canada an example of devotion to family, devotion to business that comes up every day – an example by which we must all profit" (314). The mention of devotion, her mother's chief characteristic, and of business and profit, her father's preoccupations, in the same sentence joins together the significant others that have shaped Black's personality in an utterance that may seem rather pointless in our own time and place, but that symbolically allowed Black to speak her agency as a subject in a way that obviously gave her much satisfaction. The actual experience of speaking in a voice that one feels is uniquely and authentically one's own cannot be defined by any politically correct feminist code. It is appropriate that Black manages this joining of her two selves through an act of praising a conventional mother figure, in a context in which she had always felt safest (the Canadian Parliament in the 1930s being at least as respectably patriarchal as the family she grew up in) and in a moment of rebellion against her house leader, an authority figure who has just told her in symbolic terms to be the kind of female she has always rebelled against being – the silent, obedient girl. She has been given this occasion to speak in her own voice by many fortuitous happenings, happenings she seemed always fully ready to take advantage of, allowing the pull of her psychology intertwining with the fortuitous history of her time to produce the agency of her self-actualizing acts.

Many Canadian women caught in similar psychological positions and historical opportunities have written of their lives. They range from the self-effacing Luta Munday, who displaces her identity into her husband's even in her title, A Mounty's Wife,[8] to Mina Hubbard, who while modestly signing herself as Mrs Leonidas Hubbard in the first edition (1908) of A Woman's Way through Unknown Labrador and allowing the search for her husband's fate in the wilds of Labrador to be the occasion of her autobiographical travel account, nevertheless has the spunk to undertake an incredible journey never tried by a white woman, and manages to give her own story equal time with the husband's sad tale.[9] These women's achievements range from those of Alice A. Chown, who, deliberately imitating the diary style to emphasize the empathetic and interpersonal nature of her commitment to various ideological causes, gives an account in *The Stairway* of a lifetime of breaking barriers as a socialist feminist,[10] to those of Flora Eaton, author of *Memory's Wall*, who as wife and widow of one of the scions of the famous merchant family, living at the centre of a booming Canadian expansionist economy, herself the family firm's legal head after her husband's death, nevertheless manages to relate an account centred on what would seem rather fleeting and peripheral social successes and trivial personal accomplishments. Yet for her these expressed her voice.[11]

One Canadian autobiographer, shaped by the fortuitous intersection of the pioneer adventure and the feminist consciousness, affords a sophisticated and conscious voicing of the opportunities, the ambivalences, the successes and failures that map the subjectivity of such women. Nellie McClung, the writer and feminist, wrote her first autobiography, *Clearing in the West*, in the style of an inspirational novel for young women, a form in which as a novelist she was quite proficient.[12] It tells the story of her birth on a marginal farm in Ontario (she too was expected to be a boy by her men-folk), the family's move when she was a young girl to a pioneer Manitoba farm, and her growing feminism as a young working woman, and ends with her marriage. The tone of the book reveals an effort to show herself as a confident positivist about family and society, projecting an image of a woman who conforms to conventional femininity while pursuing achievement and success not always sanctioned in her world. Much is left ambiguous and unstated by the happy-ever-after tone of this novelistic autobiography. In the second autobiography, *The Stream Runs Fast*, McClung varies her stylistic approaches in an attempt to accommodate a mature view of her life as one of many dimensions, not all of which can be formulated in a female version of the progress-of-the-hero novel.

In the preface to the second book, McClung remarks on how she has used her life: "Like the impatient prairie farmer, I have cropped it too steadily, forcing it to yield. Now I can construct a new life on a new pattern. For the first time in my life I can disregard the clock and the calendar and write as I please."[13] Besides the literal meaning of these words – telling us she has lived a busy, hurried life, with not enough leisure to write in the way she would like – the simile implies another possibility: that McClung has forced her life, making a pattern against the expected one, one that gave problems to herself and others. As well, to have "cropped" one's life means to cut it off, not allow its full possibility. The phrases "construct a new life on a new pattern" and "write as I please" also encode more than their literal content, for the second autobiography does "construct," with its content and its style, a darker, more nuanced account of the life of an early twentieth-century feminist than does the first book, offering more insight into the conflicted psyche of an achieving woman.

McClung's feelings of being drawn by very different role models begin early in life, as she describes in *Clearing*. When one of her most admired influences, her schoolteacher Mr Schultz, presents her with a version of the Riel rebellion that makes the Métis people less the guilty party than McClung's mother, Mrs Moonie, would have them, her mother threatens to call in the school board to have Mr Schultz straightened out. McClung feels so disconnected, so torn between admired others, she becomes physically ill and cannot attend school. Since success at school is the way McClung thinks she can overcome the limitations of being female in a prejudiced society, the situation is a desperate conflict for the young girl. It is interesting to note that, like Martha Black, when this female subject feels herself profoundly split between two people who represent important features of her identity, she manifests it not in a conscious way, in terms of inappropriate or rebellious behaviour, actions suitable to an identity defining itself through separation, the kind of reaction we might see in a hero's story, but in an unconscious way, in terms of physical illness, a rebellion that hurts the self more than it hurts any significant other, but that has the benefit of drawing the child to the closer attention of the care giver, the mother.

Fortunately, Mr Schultz is sensitive enough to see that he must smooth the rough waters, and resolves the young girl's conflicts of loyalty by telling her to "learn all you can from your mother ... You'll be proud of her skill when you grow up" (177). When, later, McClung sees her mother ministering to the physical illnesses of a group of Indian people who visit the Moonie farm, her desire to be like her admirable mother grows. This incident bristles with ambivalences with regard to the identity formation of the young girl. Mr Shultz, the male figure, who should be a representative of the male privilege that McClung is to fight as a feminist, not only is the racially tolerant figure, but is maternally sensitive to the girl's distress. The mother, who, if Chodorow and others are correct, is the figure at the heart of the girl's first self-identification, offers McClung on more than one occasion an ethical standard rife with racism, and yet through her behaviour towards individual human beings, she is a constant source of inspiration to McClung. As well, the mother plays the role of moral mother in family life, but her judgments are often, if not immoral, then at least ungenerous. At the same time, she is a woman of great vigour and decided opinion, and one has no problem seeing why the example of her energy and determination helped to construct the personality of Canada's most distinguished feminist. As a woman, McClung will often find herself in dichotomous situations, advocating equality for women but exhibiting racial prejudice against non-British Canadians of either sex. Further, McClung, though an active writer and feminist, continually emphasizes her place as mother, carrying out many of the same acts of individual caring that her own mother did. The degree to which her reputation as good mother worries her is indicated by an incident she relates in *Stream*: her oldest son, finding her younger son covered with dirt from playing on the riverbank, insists on taking the boy home down the back lane instead of the street, since he knows his mother would not want the neighbours to see that a feminist has dirty children![14]

As a woman, McClung also reveals signs that even though her intense need for approval may have begun in her difficult relationship with her mother, male figures like Mr Shultz have profoundly shaped that need. She becomes very dependent on the good opinion of men, seeking both the approval of an older brother and public approval of men outside her family. But in becoming Canada's leading feminist, she is bound to disappoint these men, since they, especially the brother, hold very patriarchal opinions of the place of women.[15] In an amusing but rather sad twist of her need to seek approval as a womanly woman, she attempts to defend Cora Hind, who was often under attack for her courageous stands as a journalist, by pointing out the detail of Hind's dress and appearance, as if her feminine attire could modify patriarchal opinions of her feminism.

In some ways McClung makes up for the insufficiencies of her mother as role model by developing an intense admiration for her mother-in-law. In fact, this admiration would seem to be the reason she married her husband: "I felt sure Mrs. McClung's son must be the sort of man I would like. She had all the sweetness, charm and beauty of the old-fashioned woman, and in addition to this had a fearless, and even radical mind"(*Clearing*, 313). As well, Mrs McClung gender-balances the household chores, a change in the division of labour that impresses McClung immensely. McClung's admiration is for a woman who keeps a foot in both worlds, as McClung tried to do all her life. Her mother-in-law is to be the woman who leads her into work for temperance organizations, McClung's training ground as a feminist. When McClung's own mother meets her future husband, Wesley McClung, she observes that her daughter has "more sense than I ever gave you credit for ... I like your young man – I couldn't have picked out a finer one myself. Now, if you cannot get on, I'll be inclined to think it will be your fault" (375–6). The mother's judgment epitomizes the daughter's ambivalent position: inside the compliment to her good judgment is the implication that the daughter is good not because of the value of any quality of her own, but because she is loved by a good man. As well, the moral mother puts the full responsibility for the success of the union on the daughter, thus making another generation of women into moral mothers. The idealization of the son-in-law is a particularly pernicious but effective way that mothers can keep daughters in traditional positions of powerless responsibility.

It would be simple enough for me, as reader, to make the traditional patriarchal judgment of such an identity situation, that is, to blame the personal mother for her hypocritical stands. But to do so is to ignore the fact that McClung's mother has been shaped in her own identity in exactly the way patriarchy shapes women for its own needs. Mrs Moonie, trained to value men more than women, gives unqualified approval of her son-in-law. Trained to uncritical acceptance of patriarchal racial stereotypes as well as its view of woman's place as nurturer, healer, she expresses both racial prejudice against natives and the desire to assist individual native people. Accepting the typical place of woman as morally responsible but otherwise powerless, she places incredible psychic burdens on her daughter, releasing men from a similar responsibility. In this way, the special nature of female psychological formation combines with a cultural history of patriarchal definitions to produce a continuing sense of tension and stress for women like McClung. That such a female person plays an important part in the history of feminism creates a crucible for psychological development for the adult woman that is both remarkable and illustrative of an important feature of female identity in our century.

The form of the first book, which deals with these early formative stages of McClung's life, is, as illustrated, in contention with much of what McClung needs to say about her life, and she seems to realize this herself, since in her first chapter of her second autobiography, she jokingly summarizes her own ending: "*Clearing in the West* ended in the approved manner. The two young people stood on the rear platform of a 'mixed' train and saw the sun break through the dark shoulder of a rain-cloud and knew that 'tomorrow would be fine'" (2). In the second work, McClung seems intent on breaking out of the approved manner and showing that the typical happy ending of marriage that women are given in the form of the domestic novel is a sham.[16] She wishes to allow for more of the ambiguity and tension that result from living a life of public accomplishment within a framework of conventional wifehood and motherhood.

For example, she describes the depression and panic with which she greeted her first pregnancy: "It was a low moment in my life; surely a climacteric, when the eyes that look out of the windows are darkened. Many bewildered women have gone down this same dark road" (17). On the conscious level of her discourse, it is courageous of McClung to confess that motherhood was not the unqualified boon that her contemporary societal image of correct maternal attitude would have it. But as well, the language of the passage reveals a deeper problem. The phrase "the eyes that look out of the windows" characterizes the female psyche as in a "housed" condition, as it is in such formulations of femaleness as "the angel in the home." But McClung's image would indicate that she is no angel inside her windows, but rather a prisoner inside her own body, the prisoner on a reproductive road she does not choose and a prisoner also of the definitions of maternality current in her time. The fact that she thinks this realization must be a "climacteric" moment in her life indicates how profoundly her optimistic views on marriage and childbearing must have changed when she faced motherhood herself. This fear of becoming a mother would indicate that her identity formation through contact with her own mother was much more problematic than the smooth and humorous surface of the first autobiography would indicate.

I note, as well, another important factor in McClung's identity pattern: her desire to make common cause with other women, as indicated by her observation that "many bewildered women have gone down this same dark road." The tendency to universalize her own condition would become a typical strategy for McClung and one that would allow her the energy and commitment of her feminist stances. Almost all of her most important political activity would be on behalf of women who were legally or economically oppressed, like the garment workers she defended in her ground-breaking feminist activity in Manitoba. But her courageous and imaginative work also speaks to a darker ground of formation. It is in the ambivalent, unsatisfying, and very intense relationship with her mother, herself crippled by her patriarchal construction, that the driving power of McClung's feminism can be found. Her relationships with mother surrogates and men and the cultural situation of her time may have shaped and directed McClung's feminism, but its origins are in her relationship with her mother. To map the influence of this first relationship as it interweaves with the life history to create a female subjectivity is to trace, in McClung's case, both an amazing accomplishment and something in the nature of a female tragedy.

In *The Fighting Days*, a play about the early western Canadian feminists, Wendy Lill makes it obvious that McClung was the feminist who compromised her ideals, was less heroic, less pure than others. Lill's perception of McClung's failure centres around her attitudes to the First World War, an event that divided feminists and diluted the zeal of the movement. In England the marches and hunger strikes were abandoned; women who had very recently suffered the indignities of forced feeding and imprisonment at the hands of a patriarchal government put their energies fully behind that same government. In Canada the change was less dramatic, but just as real. As a radical feminist, McClung believed that war was murder. She was particularly upset that women so easily gave sons to the cause, characterizing them as being like Abraham, who so easily accepted his son's sacrifice.[17]

However, in the second autobiography she speaks very little of her opposition to the war, dwelling instead on the difficult time it was for her family because her oldest son, Jack, had decided to serve. In this she does not fulfil the early promise of openness about female life indicated by her confession regarding her first pregnancy. She had planned to follow the advice writer Laura Salverson gave her and "break down and tell all!" (145), but in speaking of her son's life, she cannot. Here lies the great problem for a feminist who is also a mother within a traditional patriarchal societal and familial structure: Jack's mother cannot very well condemn war as murder without condemning her own son's activity, an activity encouraged by every societal agency, including the family, that the patriarchy could muster. This, after all, was the war to end wars, according to the propaganda of the time.[18] To be a feminist mother is to realize the full unfairness of patriarchal structures and to be simultaneously silenced by the fear of harming the child who must live in those structures.

It is here that we can map Gilligan's identification of women's relational moral standards in the nuance of a lived life. We can trace just how compromised a woman who follows such a standard inside patriarchy can become. McClung's decision to put attachment ahead of the separation idealism of the ego-self also involves her in a necessary hypocrisy. It is interesting to note how she handles that hypocrisy in *Stream*, how the results of her compromise – made for her son and for the sake of the personal attachments of family – work against her, and how she comes to terms with the tragedy this brings to her. In recounting the war years, she dwells on the sadness of moving to Edmonton and leaving Winnipeg friends and family, on her maternal anguish on parting from her oldest child, and on the more positive uses that feminists made of the wartime mentality and its concomitant desire for reform. But the "climacteric" nature of the experience of sending a son to war, like the experience of bearing him, cannot be entirely removed from the written account; it enters under other disguises, through a rhetoric typical of women who find they cannot speak in their own voice: through the seemingly comic words of a woman of a lower class than the autobiographer, a woman who can speak because she does not know the import of her words. At the train station where McClung bids farewell to her son, she meets a woman with eight children who is saying goodbye to her husband, who is also going to war. The woman observes bitterly: "There should be a lawr to stop a man from going who has eight children. But what can a woman do but just take what comes. 'E'll be a 'ero and I'll be a drudge with bunions on my feet" (140).

Placing one's rebellion in the mouth of another woman may be a compensatory strategy for the writer, but when McClung is dealing with the actual facts of her own life and her son's, such a rhetoric cannot express what she needs to say. She tries to make an additional compensation by making her son the hero of a good part of the text, detailing how he seemed to make a successful adjustment to his peacetime position as eldest son after the nightmare of his war experiences, becoming a scholarship student and a successful attorney. But as McClung observes, "A wound in a young heart is like a wound in a young tree. It does not grow out. It grows in" (195). McClung sets this simile off by giving it a separate paragraph, but she cannot find words to tell the full tragedy of her son's life, and by implication the tragedy of her own life as mother and feminist. Once again, the intertextual reading of biography with autobiography reveals the full texture of McClung's stifled voice. Jack McClung committed suicide while his mother was writing *The Stream Runs Fast*, and we must turn to Candace Savage's biography to learn the weight of this fact in McClung's life. A close associate of McClung's is quoted as saying that "Jack's death was the greatest calamity in Nellie's life, and she did not rebound easily" (198). One of the ways McClung attempted to "rebound" was by devoting a good part of her later life to peace initiatives, highlighting in *Stream* her work as one of Canada's representatives in the League of Nations in 1938. Despite the fact that she completed her second autobiography during the Second World War and patriotism and militarism were the national mood, there is a noticeable emphasis in this second text on the importance of the search for world peace.

Both of McClung's autobiographies are subtitled "my own story," but the first book presents quite a masculine-defined young woman who is more the central character of her own story. The second book, more episodic, more openly feminist, yet still using humour and indirection as strategies of disguise for unpalatable positions, indicates the author's need to develop a non-novelistic style, yet one that can combine the qualities of narrative with those of a more personal and philosophical essay style in order to express the complexity of a feminist life lived inside the traditional female roles of patriarchal society. McClung was a woman in her fifties when she wrote her first book, a woman who had achieved success as an active feminist, mother, and writer. The second, written ten years later, is the book of a woman who has suffered the suicide of her beloved son and seen her accomplishments eclipsed by depression and war. These events of the personal and public life have an effect on the subjectivity of the autobiographer. The authors of *Knowing* demonstrate the possibilities of female development in adulthood, but perhaps do not mean quite so late as a woman's sixth and seventh decades of life. But even the limited confessions McClung is willing to make in the second autobiography indicate that the writing of the life can be the agency of a changed subjective position even in old age.

McClung sums up her philosophy late in *Stream* with this advice: "Do not look for safety in this world. There is no safety here. There is only balance" (316). The word "balance" takes on an ironic meaning given the female life events McClung has mapped in this autobiography. However, when I say "mapped," I mean always to imply that the mapping is as much mine as McClung's. To read the full tragedy of her son's death, to find his suicide, one must read McClung intertextually with her biographer's book. To read the full tragedy of the compromise of her feminism, one must read her words from a position of feminist subjectivity. This latter can be illustrated by McClung's account of her move from Manitoba to Edmonton, at a moment when everybody predicted that she would become the first woman cabinet member in history. Supposedly the move was undertaken for the husband's work, but it is one McClung admits had other benefits:

I knew I could persuade people, and I knew I had a real hold on the people of Manitoba, especially the women, but I also knew that the whole situation was fraught with danger for if I, as the first woman to hold a Cabinet position failed, it would be a blow to women everywhere. I could easily undo all I had done for I knew the world would be critical of women for a long time. If a woman succeeded, her success would belong to her as an individual. People would say she was an exceptional woman. She had a "masculine" mind. Her success belonged to her alone, but if she failed, she failed for all women everywhere. With this in mind, I hadn't the nerve to go on to the sixty-four-dollar question. I said nothing to anyone but it reconciled me to the move. I felt I was being let down over the wall in a basket. (143)

McClung puts her finger on a great problem for all feminists in her day and our own, the ability of the patriarchy to reappropriate credit for women's work, women's accomplishments. The widespread cultural myth that a woman who achieves is unwomanly, is manlike, in combination with the contradictory tendency of patriarchy to generalize a female's failure to all females, removes the possibility of a female tradition. This kind of reappropriation can be seen in literary and cultural documents to the present day. In literary texts of the present time, for example, the figure of McClung has become the symbol of a judgmental snob[19] or, as in Lill's play, the figure of the sell-out, used as a straw woman to highlight the courage of feminists who were not mothers and who seemingly did not allow themselves to be appropriated by the patriarchy.

However, there is enough of a grain of truth in these accounts to encourage me to look at McClung's philosophy of balance to see how it can lead to a feminist's complicity in her own appropriation. In this confession of her relief on leaving the public success behind to start over in Alberta, we can read the ways in which a female life can lead to a fear of success, the fear of how success would make one lose connection, relatedness, with other women by failing in a high-profile position. The statement also reveals McClung's constant awareness and trepidation about the judgment of the patriarchal world. While it is not unrealistic of her to observe that that world would be "critical of women for some time," perhaps too sharp an awareness of the opinions of patriarchy can lead to a position of compromise that defeats feminists far more effectively than direct opposition by patriarchal forces.

At the same time, I do not mean to downplay McClung's own sophisticated awareness of her problems as a feminist, nor do I want to be guilty of failing to see the import of her concluding biblical reference. In the Christian Bible the figure who is let down over the city walls of Damascus is Paul, of whom God was supposed to have observed: "It is hard for thee to kick against the pricks" (Acts 9:5). It was certainly difficult for McClung to do so, and I think she means a very deliberate comparison of her own vulnerability to Paul's in this reference. She knew she was often daunted by opposition, as was Paul. But by a feminist decoding of other implications encoded in the biblical reference, I can also point out that it was at Damascus that Paul was baptized and first publically declared himself a Christian as it was in Manitoba that McClung became a feminist and first voiced her position. After escaping the assassins waiting for him at the gates of Damascus, Paul went on to establish the church that changed Western patriarchy into much of what makes our own patri-archal culture possible. In making this reference, McClung seems to invite us to see her own position as subject in a similar light: that of her being (at least one of) the female type of Paul whose writing stands as the origins of a new cultural order. If this is so, it is interesting that she chooses Paul as her patriarchal precursor, the man who not only institutionalized Christianity, but also went a long way towards instituting its misogyny. It is a wry comment on the ambivalence of McClung's own male definitions and her rebellion against them that she chooses such an ambivalent (for a feminist) father figure to begin her own mythologization.

Indicative of McClung's problem as a feminist implicated in pre-serving patriarchal structures is the generic effect of her position. Her choice of writing forms, while moving out of the more novelistic style into a memoir/essay style, still imposes a silence on aspects of her life. For example, the revelation of the "dark" aspects of preg-nancy cannot be followed by an exploration of the embodied nature of the experience. A revelation of the wound received by the son at war cannot be followed by a mapping of maternal feeling vis-à-vis the child and the world into which she birthed and raised him to become, ultimately, a suicide. Therefore, although the memoir and the essay styles can provide women with a way of avoiding the pitfalls of egocentric autobiography, a way of writing themselves into the gap in patriarchal discourse, these forms cannot provide the fully intimate knowledge of a lived female life. In the end, they are genres through which one observes, objectifies, the self. Certainly as they were prac-tised in McClung's time, the memoir and the essay were still lacking in the lyrical, erotic, and intimate features that are needed to express an embodied life.

But McClung's story is not less useful in mapping women's auto-biographical accounts because of its limitations. If women like McClung can sometimes be counted on to defeat their own purposes through their need for connection, through their ability to be sen-sitive to others' opinions, others' knowledge, and through their own residual patriarchal definitions, then such a life story can offer us the darker side of the theories of Chodorow, Gilligan, and the authors of *Knowing* and serve as a cautionary tale for the academic researcher. Although Chodorow certainly recognizes the ambivalence of women's subject position (her Freudian precursors almost mandate this), texts like Gilligan's and *Knowing*, by mapping the positive aspects of female identity construction, may also expose women to a danger. Their mapping of these positive aspects is a necessary feminist pursuit given that these very characteristics are those that are denigrated by patriarchal standards and that women are often encouraged to rid themselves of before assuming public roles. However, by lauding them, they can fall into another epistemological trap, the one identified by Ann Douglas vis-à-vis the nineteenth century. If academic feminists take as their mandate only a positivist explication of women's gendering as social subjects, we may become the new moral mothers, allowed a modicum of influence in subsidiary worlds such as the academy, but thereby becoming the vehicles of the enforcement of a new version of the "angel in the house" or the "cult of true womanhood," one that will serve the function of keeping women in positions of limited power in the worlds of business, economics, and government.

Christie Farnum puts the problem succinctly in examining recent feminist research and the problem of falling into a prison of advocating either only sameness or difference: "There is no equality if the standards of the dominant class are the only ones applied and the positive attributes of the victims are ignored. Yet, the celebration of differences increases women's vulnerability to oppression by providing for its rationalization, even as the insistence upon equality obscures what has been forged in the crucible of adversity."[20] I hold that it is in the examination of women's own stories that we can find the nuances of the interrelationship of subjectivity and society that will allow us to avoid these two epistemological traps. Such stories can become revisionistic tools to add a sophisticated layering of personal insights onto sociological, psychological, educational, and scientific gender research; they can also offer a starting place for revising male-dominated literary canons and literary genres that favour the retelling of masculine experience of the world. In this regard, I wish to further illustrate my point by referring to the stories of women closer to our own time.

After the consciousness-raising experience of the 1960s and 1970s, one would expect to begin to see autobiographies that are more assertive in confronting society with its failures vis-à-vis women. This is not necessarily the case. Even the account of Florence Bird, who headed the Royal Commission on the Status of Women in the 1960s and recorded her life as media personality Anne Francis and as head of the commission in *Anne Francis, An Autobiography*, does not stray far from the traditional structure of the memoir or from a belief in a liberal humanist position that sees society's treatment of women as flawed but mendable.[21] Bird, like McClung, is basically an insider in society, a middle-class woman whose lifetime place of privilege leaves her protected from the worst situations society can inflict on women. Even when such women intellectually realize injustices, as Bird does when she sees the desperation of her house-maid, who is driven to a life-threatening, self-induced abortion by economic and moral imperatives implicit in patriarchy, even when such women devote a good part of their lives to the service of less fortunate women, as Bird and McClung do, their written accounts remain within the economies of the patriarchy. The memoir style they prefer allows them to reveal the interconnections between them-selves and the other, but at the same time implicates them in estab-lished societal structures. Novelistic conventions, while offering the opportunity to inscribe an alternate story, also impose certain plot conventions, such as the heroic archetype and happy, or at least optimistic, endings, closures that often lie about female life. And the essayistic techniques adopted so well by women such as Binnie-Clark and Florence Bird, while offering a chance to record feminist philosophy directly, also tend to make the self of the writer an observing self, one that sees the female life as object of study rather than as subject of intimate self-inscription. All these forms tend to silence the needed investigations of life lived in a female body.

When, however, we move outside the accounts of women who occupy privileged societal positions to those of women who have experienced great deprivation, some interesting phenomena can be observed, both in the ways in which these women's accounts differ from those of privileged women and, surprisingly, the ways in which they seek similar maps of subjectivity. Ann Henry suffered from just about every disadvantage a woman could suffer from in Canadian society. I say "just about" because Henry had the not-too-negligible advantages of being white and conventionally pretty. Her autobiog-raphy, *laugh, baby, laugh,* begins with an account of her mother being taken away to a mental hospital because she had tried to kill Ann and her older sister with a knife.[22] It continues to narrate (in fairly low-key language that ironically highlights the horrific nature of the events) the death of Ann's older sister in her late teens due to a dreadful medical error and Henry's own fate at the hands of a neglectful father, who allows his naive sixteen-year-old daughter to take a job as a high-diver in a circus, though she can neither dive nor swim, warning her only that she be careful to keep her virtue intact. Henry undertakes a too-early marriage to an abusive and undependable man whom she seems to marry largely because she admires his very domestic mother, a woman who compounds Henry's problems by always favouring her son and blaming his wife for situations while ignoring the impact of her son's immature and self-centred personality.

Henry is able to do what autobiographers such as Bird and McClung cannot: she figures her personal situation in psychological language. In fairness to McClung, this is partially a historical advantage, since discourse of the self became increasingly psychologized as the Freudian revolution permeated the twentieth century, but I think it is also the result of Henry's specific subject position. Hers is a desperately and dramatically deprived position, one that forces the person caught in her life to examine, as a means of survival, the effect on the self: if one probes the wound and cleanses it through an intense discourse of the self, it may heal. The personality Henry presents to the reader is in many ways like the part in a play she humorously describes herself as having played at seventeen: "Lil-Mim, half-savage, half-civilized, half-woman, half-animal" (1). Characterizing herself as never civilized (read privileged) enough to gain a proper toehold in society and always undermined (read taken advantage of) because of her savage (read instinctual) self, Henry offers us something like the divided self of the male confessional document. But this is a female rewriting of the confession style, for what saves Henry is not the God-love of an Augustine or the self-love of a Rousseau, but her children's need for mothering and her own determination to give them what they need. As well, Henry does not figure herself healed of a sinful self or saved from the forces of society, but made whole by the very act of survivorship. "Sweet are the uses of adversity" (187) is her motto.

Personal confession seems to be a luxury not many women can allow themselves to indulge in in their autobiographies. They shy away from its implied solipsism, its implied privileging of the singular self; the technique that allows Henry this indulgence is the "laugh" of her title, by which she always preserves an attitude of self-mocking humour, which tells us not to take the construction of a separate self too seriously. For example, in describing the time she and her children spent in life-threatening rural poverty, Henry typically calls up the image of movie star Joan Crawford: "In dirndl and kerchief, I would stand behind a gay stall at the market, selling my plump, dressed birds and bring home bagfuls of cash ... [this hope] was based on the assumption that the chicken-raiser knew something about chickens and also had plenty of food and other facilities" (106). Under the disguise of humour, Henry reveals the ridiculously romanticized images her society presented her with as a model of the independent woman.

The writing act, informed by humour, becomes the way in which Henry heals the division in her personality and maintains her sanity as her mother could not. It has the additional benefit of becoming, through her labours as a journalist, the way she earns her living and supports her family. But her psychological mapping and the humour she uses in her self-appraisal have a price. Because she has little or no feminist consciousness of her condition, despite her revelation of an inhuman social welfare system and the way the facts of her account tend to reveal the advantages men have in her society, she herself does not offer to overlay the psychological discourse with a map of a societal responsibility for her problems as a single mother. In some ways this allows for her reappropriation in the economy that so deprived and abused her. Henry ends her autobiography by contemplating not her own achievement but that of her son, the actor Donnelly Rhoades. While as mother she does have a right to be proud of having brought up successful children, it is ironic that she features Rhoades, who in his lifetime in film, television, and on the stage has played many typically patriarchal parts – as hero, as villain, and more recently as father figure – in a popular culture that in subtle ways still tells us "father knows best." In fact, Henry's story, that of a mother who painfully learned how to "know best," is easily subsumed by a culture that could never find a marketable story in such a life as hers, but could easily find one in her son's life. Henry, by featuring her son as symbol of her success, is complicit in her own reappropriation. Stylistically, the device of self-mocking humour is double-edged: it allows Henry the discourse to speak of the inner self, a self that needs humour or it could not bear to reveal its painful condition, but it also tends to trivialize that self, presenting another's story (a male story) as more important, more substantive, more serious.

This is not to say that Henry's autobiography is a failure. For a reader reading not only through informing feminist psychological theory, but through an informing feminist cultural position in which the personal psychology is seen always in its societal context, Henry's revelation of her life is an indictment of a cultural oppression that brings the autobiography close to the form of apologia. I use "apologia" in the sense that Cardinal Neuman used it in his autobiography: the indictment of society's insufficiency by a narration of the personal story, a narration that is also a defence of what society condemns as incorrect behaviour. In fact, one of the most outstanding autobiographies by achieving women, that of Maria Campbell, is so because it is able to combine many of the aspects of memoir, essay, confession, and apologia to reproduce a complex *métissage* of class, race, and gender factors in a proactive style, a mapping of self and other that voices not an individual alone, but a community.

Maria Campbell, in *Halfbreed*, tells of her struggle to achieve a womanhood complicated not only by poverty and the deprivation of maternal protection, but also by her position at the bottom of everyone's social scale, that of a Métis. As Campbell reveals, her people, "Road Allowance people," were not only despised and persecuted by white society, but often looked down on by registered Indians who felt that they at least had reserve benefits and the trace of a tradition.[23] However, it is because of the very difference in Campbell's story that the startling similarities between these women's accounts stand out. A large part of Campbell's psychological situation stems from that same disturbingly ambiguous early relationship with the mother and the later intense relationship with the father, or male surrogate, that seem both to present these achieving women with such difficult paths and to make possible such amazing accomplishments. What makes this similar formation so visible is the dramatically intensified suffering of this psychological paradigm when acted out in the kind of social and economic conditions that have often been the typical lot of native and Métis Canadians.

Like other achieving women, Campbell starts life as her father's favourite, a father who wanted a son. Until a younger brother is born, she is the one who accompanies her father hunting and engages in other father/son activities. Her identification with him would seem to be part of the cause of her later abuse of her female self. Her father, though often generous and loving, beats her mother as a consequence of his own frustrations as a Métis persecuted by white society. Campbell, unwilling to describe the abuse that her beloved "Daddy" inflicts on the mother, saying only that her father occasionally "hit" her mother, does, however, allow herself to describe the terrifying aftermath of "days in town" when the Métis men got drunk and an evening of "nightmare and fun" began:

Then Mom would call us and we would crawl out back of the tent, to hide in the bushes and watch until they all fell asleep. The men would get happy-drunk at first and as the evening progressed white men would come by. They all danced and sang together, then all too soon one of the white men would bother the women. Our men would become angry, but instead of fighting the white men they beat their wives. They ripped clothes off the women, hit them with fists or whips, knocked them down and kicked them until they were senseless.

When that was over, they fought each other in the same way. Meanwhile the white men stood together in a group, laughing and drinking, sometimes dragging a woman away. How I hated them. They would be gone when the sun came up. Our men would be sick and hung over and ugly-mean, the mothers black and blue and swollen. (38)

Speaking on a societal level, Campbell is able to describe accurately a scenario that illustrates an aspect of patriarchal control at least as important as that in McClung's depiction of the way patriarchy generalizes female blame and appropriates female accomplishment. One of the ways cycles of poverty and oppression are perpetuated is by encouraging the oppressed man to act out his anger on his female. I say "his" deliberately because a man within patriarchy is partly controlled by being given the impression that he, like the master, has property, a measure of control, and someone to blame for his misery. The victimization of females sets up an internal economy of victimization that allows the oppressor to continue his hegemony, a hegemony that is also rewarded by his "dragging a woman away" and knowing that it is the woman and not he who will be blamed.

But being able to make the telling slippage from the personal familial life indicated by "then Mom would call us" to the societal frame of "the men would get happy-drunk," speaking of all the Métis men and not directly of her own father, is the only way Campbell can allow herself to voice this important shaping fact of her life. When she finally comes to speak of this phenomenon in her own family's life, it is in quite a different key. She tells of the year her father becomes a political activist, finds new purpose in life, holds meetings, gives speeches that make her "tingly all over with excitement" because of her intense love for him. Then comes the inevitable betrayal by whites and natives, the ridicule that characterizes him as Saskatchewan's "new Riel" (74), the loss of income, the accusations of communism, the finale coming when his wife begs him to quit in order to save the family. As Campbell observes, "Something inside him died, and he became another defeated man" (75). Campbell states that "Daddy still trapped, but only because it was an escape for him. He would be gone for long periods at a time, then when he was home he drank and often brought white men home with him. Sometimes he'd hit Mom, and she would take the baby and run away until he was sober" (75). It is left to the reader to read this flat relatively veiled statement intertextually with the graphic description of violence quoted above. Campbell merely concludes that her mother "lost" three pregnancies in three years; she says nothing more about the cause of the lost pregnancies. Her own feelings as this man's child are painfully ambiguous: "I was full of bitterness over what had happened that year and was angry at my father, but above all I hated the men who had fought him ... I felt in a way she [her mother] had betrayed Dad by not understanding what he had to do. Her concerns were for her family. She didn't realize that what happened outside was important too" (76). In this passage Campbell reveals her divided loyalties. Encouraged by her mother to "keep loving" her father despite his problems, she does, and she also finds she can at least partially excuse him by blaming her mother, a person living under at least as much disadvantage as the beloved father. Thus, the psychological condition that will make it possible for her own female self to be victimized and blamed is reinforced. It is well to note at this point that the rather moderate, analytic, referential language of the personal essay/memoir style of this portion of the text has none of the drama and enacted horror of the description of the drunken orgy of the earlier example. As readers, we need to compensate for Campbell's displacement of feeling in her text by reading into this second low-key revelation the same intensity and importance as the first, since by doing so we may understand why Campbell enters a life of abuse of her own psyche and body through prostitution and drug addiction.

Her anger at her father makes her disobedient to his will, especially since after the mother's death in yet another pregnancy, she is, at thirteen, made completely responsible for the care of all the children while the father grieves his dead wife. Campbell does not give emphasis to the fact that while the father has time to grieve, the thirteen-year-old girl does not. Premature responsibility leads to premature assumption of adult roles, and Campbell becomes sexually active. Since she is angry at her father and at other Métis men for their weakness, but is still male defined in her identity connections, she chooses a white man as her rescuer. In her immaturity, in the lack of value she sets on femaleness, including her own, she chooses badly. Her husband, brought up in a society where native and Métis women are the ultimate victims, makes her a victim. Her slide towards tragedy is not aided by the fact that her father has no other way to deal with a recalcitrant daughter than to whip her. Furthermore, the social agencies of the larger white world offer her no advice regarding mothering and birth control (any help here would have had to come from the personal mother) and then take her brothers and sisters from her when the combination of her own pregnancy, the desertion of her husband, and her youthful ignorance combine to defeat her.

There are even more dire consequences to these events, events described in unemotional language, centring around her father's failure and her mother's death. All her life Campbell's mother tried hard to counteract the tomboy effects of the father's favouritism of his daughter by encouraging Maria to be more ladylike, less aggressive. The mother's desire for a ladylike daughter is at least partially the result of the mother having been raised by a mother who was considered "white" and who held middle-class values, including the belief that a woman should be dainty and decorative, an image that filters through to the granddaughter only in terms of its ill effects – that is, Maria's idea of what it is to be a woman is to be a sexual object. This, combined with the girl's intense identification with and worship of her father, leads not only to her blaming her mother's passive and conservative philosophy for part of her father's failure, but to her being deeply divided in her gender identification. Identifying with her father enough to refuse to be pretty, passive, and home identified like her mother, Campbell goes adventuring in the world. But she does not have enough of an identification with her father to have his self-preserving qualities, and of course she must adventure in the world in a female and not a male body, a native female body that gets none of the protections a white girl might expect. What she ends up doing is identifying the female in her as the victim figure her mother was, allowing it to be victimized not just by a husband, but by a whole society of men convinced that such a woman deserves, indeed invites, her own victimization. Campbell is caught in all the negative identification patterns of both of her parents, with none of the small advantages that either of them had.

Three things rescue Campbell from the fate of many other women in her cultural situation: her ability to change her anger at white society into social action, as her father very briefly did; her desire to be a loving mother to her children, as her own mother was despite all her disadvantages; and her ability to discover, in her life and her text, a permission-giving mythic female ancestress. Thus, even though her male identification serves her badly in many life situations, even though her mother was her model as female victim, it is her ability to map what was positive in these figures that allows her to change from a depressed and oppressed woman who would turn on the gas jet to destroy herself and her children, to a female leader who can even defy her male mentors, one who observes when they wish her to adopt a position of silent helpmate in their proactive community work; "I realize now that the system that fucked me up fucked up our men even worse. The missionaries had impressed upon us the feeling that women were a source of evil. This belief, combined with the ancient Indian recognition of the power of women, is still holding back the progress of our people today" (168).

The figure that allows Campbell to come to this succinct analysis of her situation as woman of colour is her crone-like great-grand-mother, Cheechum, a figure who weaves in and out of Campbell's story like a spirit from prehistory, what Mary Daly calls a "female-identified power," allowing Campbell to begin her own facilitating myth-making act, which we participate in through her autobiography. Cheechum, who is old even in Campbell's girlhood, is a niece of Gabriel Dumont, Riel's lieutenant, and having lived through the whole history of Métis persecution, she remembers something of the freedom of the plains they once enjoyed. At crucial moments in Campbell's life, she explains, forgives, chastises the girl as need requires, offering her a facilitating perspective on familial and societal history and a strong image of female as powerful and good. The re-creation of Cheechum in her life and the narrating of her story and teachings in the autobiography allow Campbell to break out of her destructive definitions of woman as evil, woman as responsible, blamable, punishable, but never powerful, never good. Thus, ironically, unlike the privileged women I have mapped here, she is able to reach past the degradation of the personal mother in our culture, past the figure of female in patriarchy, to that mythic figure Mary Daly speaks of in *Gyn/Ecology*, which is more a mode of telling than a figure: the making of stories that contain primary and archetypal mappings that act as the first tracings upon which the map of a positive subjectivity, one capable of having agency in the world, can be drawn.

I think Campbell achieves the degree of effective womanhood she does for both personal and discursive reasons. She begins with the same disadvantages of other women whose accounts I have mapped, as well as the special disadvantages of female aboriginal people. Like other women, she begins with the absent mother – that is, she is culturally impoverished as a female person because the mother is absent, first because of her powerlessness, her lack of supportive female net-works, her lack of a female story of her own. This lack, more intense for the girl-child because she can never define herself entirely by separation but must include some connection with the mother in her identity pattern, is compounded by the father's appropriation of his daughter as female son and the intense and continuing identity crisis this initiates. Later, for Campbell, the personal mother is also physically absent, at the time of adolescence when the girl-child most needs maternal identification to facilitate the entry into womanhood. This individual psychological situation constructs damaging patri-archal assumptions about the world, a world that reinforces these assumptions for the female and thus appropriates her femaleness for patriarchal purposes, just as the father appropriated his daughter's affection inside the family.

Part of the patriarchal nature of the world she enters as an adult is a set of generic imperatives in which language, itself patriarchally constructed, allows insufficient generic forms (such as confession, apologia, essay, memoir) for the inscription of a female subjectivity. Campbell is as much victim of this insufficiency in telling her story as are other women. The force of generic convention makes her nostalgic about a childhood that was anything but a good preparation for life as a female. Still, she adopts this nostalgic position because she wishes to express the positive in her heritage; however, our writing tradition offers her only the gloss of nostalgia, a gloss that hides the terrible economic and social conditions under which Campbell lived. In the same way, she falls into a confessional and romantic mode in which she is the sinner rather than the victim and too often seeks to be the maiden rescued by a hero. Ironically, Campbell sometimes gives credit for her "conversion" to her identification with a cause (like the spiritual autobiographer in the European tradition, identification with a religion), thus disguising the record of her own growth in womanhood through the help of female surrogate mothers and her own imaginative efforts. It is difficult to estimate the effect of the mandate a writer receives in the personal world where friends, relatives, and cultural allies wish her to represent only a portion of the reality of their shared past, but at the very beginning of the account she reproduces a conversation with a friend who asks her to make her book a "happy book" (13). This is perhaps our warning, and our permission, to read Campbell's account in the larger context of other women's accounts and through facilitating theories of female development, since sometimes the effort to make the book happy leads Campbell to elide important aspects of her identity as a woman.

However, these textual slants may not be entirely Campbell's doing, since she has admitted that *Halfbreed* was a much longer book before the editors at McClelland and Stewart began to shape it to marketable length and form.[24] Yet somewhere in the bridging of these male life-writing forms, and perhaps despite her editors, she is able to inscribe the trace of an alternate subjectivity, one rhythmed by her paradigm of Cheechum and her own place as mother and female community worker, one that can be maximized by a feminist reading for female subjectivity and genre transgression and bridging.

But even if Campbell's story is seen only as a very partial inscription of female subjectivity, it and other women's personal narratives reveal something important about theories of development and about the construction of subjectivity through language: the personal situation and the societal are always in a state of interconnection, nuancing and changing theoretical possibilities of development, and in terms of their inability to express their fullest sense of their lived lives, it is not so much that women are in a position of lack in entering language as it is that language and, by implication, generic formats, construed and limited by patriarchy, lack the ability to fully express female subjectivity. In other words women have not failed in language, but patriarchally limited language has failed women. However, women who write their stories show that by acts of imaginative use of language in mapping the individual life, we can begin to heal language, and thereby to heal our selves.

5 Literary Women: Finding "The Words to Say It"

> Mother approached – timid, almost frightened, holding out a box of chocolates. "Do you know me?" she asked. My sister's blurred gaze focused for a moment, her voice came clear with a feeling that would have blighted buds. "How should I not know *you*?" After that, there was nothing to say.
>
> Fredelle Bruser Maynard, *The Tree of Life*

> How, then, can one return into the cave, the den, the earth? Rediscover the darkness of all that has been left behind? Remember the forgotten mother?
>
> Luce Irigaray, *Speculum of the Other Woman*

The expression "the words to say it," which forms part of the title of this chapter, is taken from Marie Cardinal's *The Words to Say It (Les mots pour le dire)*, in which Cardinal describes how she overcame "debilitating sexual and racial stereotypes" and learned to write herself out of a subjugated position. What Cardinal has to free herself from is the debilitating form her female subjectivity has taken because of a dreadful mother/daughter relationship in which Cardinal is the object of her mother's "murderous contempt," a state of affairs that has existed between them since the mother tried to abort the pregnancy that would produce her daughter. The negative impact of this relationship has led to the daughter becoming physically ill with continuing uterine bleeding. Through the help of a Freudian male psychoanalyst and an imaginative comparison of her own condition to the colonial status of her homeland, Algeria, Cardinal becomes partially healed, but as Françoise Lionnet points out, it is "the death of her mother [that] frees this daughter, who can simultaneously terminate her analysis and end her narrative: writing *is* symbolic matricide. Writing is the act of self-emancipation which allows the narrator to reach autonomy, despite her painful bleeding," much as Algeria won independence from France through its own bloodbath.[1]

I am struck by the fact that a book about symbolic matricide in which the daughter is saved by a male rescuer, in which autonomy, freedom, and self-emancipation are achieved for the female writer by "killing" her mother, has become a book lauded around the world. I make no disguise of my conviction that if such a configuration of women's place in language is to become paradigmatic, I would consider it the most crippling acceptance of the Freudian and Lacanian theories of women's lack. To figure a female person's place in language as achieved at the price of her alienation from the maternal brings us full circle to the negative viewpoint concerning women's creativity expressed in the nineteenth century: "Women who wrote did so within a framework of dominant cultural myths in which writing contradicts motherhood."[2]

Ironically, if we look at Freud's own final word on the subject of women's identity, we may find more positive directions than indicated by Lionnet's exploration of Cardinal's text, a text greatly influenced by Freudianism.[3] Lucy Irigaray exposes the fact that Freud himself doubted his own theorization on female development late in his life and that in "Female Sexuality" he voiced this doubt rather strongly:

As for the mother-daughter relationship, Freud will admit in his old age ... "that the *duration* [Freud's italics] of this attachment had also been greatly underestimated," "that a number of women remain arrested in their original attachment to their mother and never achieve a true change-over toward men," that "the pre-Oedipus phase in women gains an importance which we have not attributed to it hitherto," and *"we must retract the universality of the thesis that the Oedipus complex is the nucleus of all neuroses."* Notably because he suspects that "this phase of attachment to the mother is especially intimately related to the aetiology of *hysteria."* But "everything in the sphere of this first attachment to the mother seemed to me so difficult to grasp in analysis – so grey with age and shadowy and almost impossible to revivify – that it was as if it had succumbed to an especially inexorable repression." "Our insight into this early, pre-Oedipus, phase in girls comes to [us] as a *surprise,* like the discovery, in another field [but is it really another] of the *Minoan-Myceanaean civilization behind the civilization of Greece."* It is as if, finally, so late on, – perhaps because he was close to *his* death – and with the wish for "scientific honesty" that is never to be doubted in him, Freud had an inkling that woman's sexuality was indeed foreign to all that history. To history in general? That it remained covered up – repressed? – by the shape of this Greek civilization and that it would take an archaeologist, such as Freud was also, to excavate deeper into the earth, to where the cultural vestiges lie concealed, and to rediscover there a more archaic arche behind that beginning represented by Greece, and the concept of origin which Greece set in place.

Whatever we make of these belated insights, Freud continues, elsewhere, to interpret and prescribe female development in terms of that history and, notably, its conceptual economy.[4]

I quote this rather long passage from *Speculum*, in which Irigaray interrogates Freud and makes her own theory by italicizing portions of the master's words, giving the emphasis added of a subversive feminist interpretation, to illustrate that our culture, to the degree it is influenced by psychoanalytic theory, or any male-centred theory of subjectivity, is operating under a male-defined view of female creativity, one inevitably announcing female lack, one that always names the *effect* of the problem, mother alienation, to be the *cause* of the problem. More importantly, Irigaray shows us that even when an intellectual leader like Freud doubts such a theory, he still interprets and prescribes by it, indicating that such theories, from Aristotle to Lacan, must be too valuable in the service of men for them to release them, despite doubt or outright disbelief. Such a position indicates that social constructions will not change for women just because theories are discredited, making me suspect that even Irigaray's theoretical conversation with the master and investigations that take Freudian theory as their starting-point, such as Chodorow's, while helpful, must ultimately seek another form if change is their aim, since disproving the fathers does not necessarily change their ways. (They disprove themselves everyday with theories of the post-Christian, post-humanist, post-colonial, and all the "post" positions that can be imagined, but like Freud before them, they continue, despite the implications for change in their theories, to operate in the world as if nothing had changed.)

Feminist investigation must therefore take a turn, a tactical swerve, to place itself outside of a constantly reappropriated position, to find the pre-text of the voice that sounds so hysterical, so inexpressible, to the patriarchy. Irigaray's metaphor of the archaeologist who will "excavate deeper into the earth" to discover the "more ancient arche" that lies under, before, the unknown supporting structure on which man has built his history, is indicative of the turn we must take, and the difference between history and archaeology indicates the nature of that swerve: history is a story, a story composed from documents and observations that give a credence and an order to events and men's participation in them; archaeology in a patient gathering of bits and pieces on the site of ancient dwelling places, and the patient mapping of each piece's place of discovery and its place in relation to every other piece, the accumulation of a "bricolage" of artifacts that together reposition us vis-à-vis the past and therefore the present. It is the thisness of archaeology that makes its story different from history's.

For me, an archaeological mapping, one done from a feminist theoretical position, one in which the accumulations of history are carefully peeled off, layer by layer, and grids of location are laid down for a careful excavation and remapping, is a necessary task for feminists if we are to avoid the reappropriation of our energies by patriarchy. This time-consuming and specific mapping of our lost and/or misread ground of female subjectivity is also the lost ground Freud felt was "almost impossible to revivify," concerned with a mother so "grey with age" that she was not open to man's Greek-defined history or psychoanalysis. This ground is also the subject of a literary search, a female search for appropriate modes of telling a female story. Christa Wolf, the German writer, speaks of finding this story by starting with the archaeological remains of Greece itself. She proposes we begin by examining the fate of the statues of the "korai" (maidens), which though once at the Erechtheum, once indeed the support of that structure, are now housed in a museum to protect them against pollution: "The korai, the maidens, once the fertility goddess Persephone and her daughter, later reduced to supporting beams, now infertile, placed out of bounds."[5] For Wolf these maidens represent females' increasingly tragic role in patriarchy, our distance from a world once closely connected to the sources of life:

The choral song of the priestesses, completely embedded in the unfolding seasons among a largely undifferentiated group of human beings, is a hymn; there is no narration. Only the advent of property, hierarchy, and patriarchy extracts a blood-red thread from the fabric of human life, which the three ancient crones, the Moirae, had in hand; and this thread is amplified at the expense of the web as a whole, at the expense of its uniformity. The blood-red thread is the narrative of the struggle and victory of the heroes, or their doom. The plot is born. The epic, born of the struggles for patriarchy, becomes *by its structure* an instrument by which to elaborate and fortify the patriarchy. The hero is made to serve as a model, and still does so down to the present day. The chorus of female speakers has vanished, swallowed up by the earth. The woman can now become the object of masculine narrative, in the role of heroine. (296–7)

What kind of archaeology of story will take us back to the "hymn," teach us to make our own hymn, the rhythmed and polyphonic-voiced song of female worship of the life source embodied in each woman? I think we cannot immediately abandon narrative and leap backward to the hymn, for its form and detail have been lost to us.

Rather we must take that "blood-red thread" in hand and, like the patient archaeologist of Irigaray's metaphor, use the thread of narrative as a path backward, picking up the lost threads as we go, joining them to make the whole cloth of the hymn. This kind of mapping has been one Canadian women writers have been involved in, even when they have not always had the theoretical language to articulate their mission.

In opening this chapter, I have strayed far from my home place of Canadian women's accounts, not only to illustrate the scope, the global nature of the search I am part of, but also to illustrate its profoundly specific nature. Each of us must begin with the archaeology of our own lives, our parents' lives, and those of our forebears in the places they made their homes, the places that have become our homes. This mapping will give each of us our voice, but only when it is gathered in the palimpsest of other mappings, other voices. We must begin with the effect that Freudianism tried to make into the cause. We must begin with our own bodies and those of our mothers, with our own embodied lives and those of our mothers. A surprising number of Canadian women professional writers have – some stumblingly, some repeating inscriptive gestures, seeking the truth of repetition, some keeping the search private, away from their public discourse, some surprisingly sure considering their cultural positions, all of them involved in the problem of form, the problem of reckoning with telling a female story out of a male generic tradition.

I begin my exploration of these women's work with a cautionary tale. Dorothy Livesay has been trying to write her autobiography for a good part of her life. In many ways her considerable accomplishment in poetry is her autobiography, but she has also tried to write prose narratives that represent themselves as autobiographical. One of them is *Right Hand Left Hand*, a collection of documents, poetry, fiction, and non-fiction by Livesay and others that illustrates the major social, political, and literary events important to Livesay's life in the thirties. Subtitled in the paper edition *A True Life of the Thirties*, the book contains items as contrasting as socialist handbills, social-realist art, photographs of the unemployed, Livesay's poetry, personal narratives of the times, excerpts from her letters, her associates' letters, and even a hazy picture of Livesay and her women friends in the nude.[6]

Such an archaeology of a life, a bricolage, so dependent on selection and arrangement, must necessarily owe as much to a shared vision between writer and editor as to the writer's ability. In an interview, Livesay's editor, David Arnason, revealed that his idea of the project was that it was an excellent opportunity to use some of Livesay's unpublished or forgotten work to give a portrait of an important cultural era.[7] It was his conception to make the book a collage of many kinds of items that would illustrate the texture of the times and the life of a poet whose political commitment was as great as her literary commitment. On Livesay's specific instruction, Arnason maintains, the book was not meant as a memoir or autobiography, for she was at that time (the mid-seventies) involved in writing her memoirs. Eventually, since she abandoned that project, Livesay agreed to the use of certain parts of the memoirs in the collage project. Arnason completed two-thirds of the work towards the book, choosing from the mass of material offered by Livesay, editing the poetry and fiction, gathering the external materials, and working out the chronology of the book and of Livesay's life during the period. Rather abruptly, according to Arnason, Livesay took the materials out of her editor's hands and completed the selection of photographs, the final selection of letters, and the final positioning of items with the help of the book's designer, Kim Todd. Arnason then suggested that Todd's name appear as editor as well as his own.

Arnason pointed out specific ways in which the order and selection of items changed after the book left him. In examining these changes, I find that they seem connected with Livesay's personal life and her feelings about being a woman. Such additions are several letters to "Dear Jinnie" (36–48), which Livesay wrote in Paris to Jinnie Morton in Canada and which describe her personal life as a student, including reference to the man with whom she lived. Arnason had intended to use only one of these letters. A projected section entitled "Toronto 1934" has items such as "Women Are Mugs" inserted and is headed by a quotation from Livesay: "Such were the dichotomies I found in male-female relationships in the thirties. In theory, we were free and equal as comrades of the left. In practice our right hand was tied to the kitchen sink!" (115). As well as giving the book its title, The new inclusions add a different overlay to the section. "Toronto 1934" at one level would seem to be about conditions of unemployment in Canadian cities in that year, but the new material and commentary add a feminist dimension and – with the nude picture – a quasi-erotic dimension that does not seem to be the intention of the original book.

Arnason's introduction helps to underline this in hindsight, since it ties the title of the collection to the divisions between the wealthy and the poor in Canada, whereas Livesay's reference to the right/left dichotomy in the kitchen sink comment, as well as some of her other additions, points to the hypocrisies of leftist males who preached equality as long as it did not apply to their women. Arnason's ideas about the "massive contradictions" of the thirties, which he describes in his introduction, do not propose such an exploration of male/female dichotomies.

Why did Livesay not simply tell her editor that her conception of the collage had changed and that she had not entirely abandoned her memoir, but rather intended to make the collage the vehicle of a more personal story? As a practised imagist in her poetry, with a fine sense of formal arrangement, Livesay must have become aware as they worked on the book of the possibilities of the form. I think the answer lies partly in Livesay's own male definitions and partly in the philosophy of her editor. When we examine the public and private collection of her work, we see that Livesay has been a woman obsessed with the effort to tell more of her life story in prose directly (in a form in which the name of the author and the name of the subject are the same), but never quite succeeded under one set of covers. Besides *Right Hand Left Hand*, Livesay has published a series of short stories, collected as *A Winnipeg Childhood*, which are, by her own testimony, autobiographical in all aspects except the names of characters. The archival collection of her private papers also includes the journals she kept over many years and in which reference is made to several autobiographical projects, including a proposal for an autobiography based on comparing her own experience of Africa with her mother's travels on that continent.[8] The fact that all these projects were not brought together within one book or series of books can be explained by her own traditional and patriarchal definition of the genre: "Autobiography ... concerns one self, one's inner life; whereas memoirs are recollections about other people."[9]

Livesay seems to have been trying to use her bricolage to create a woman's autobiography and thus counteract her own consciously maintained male definitions of the genre, without admitting this to herself perhaps, and certainly without admitting it to her editor, who confesses to not seeing the point of many of the enclosures Livesay wanted to add. Whatever David Arnason's achievements as distinguished fiction writer, as academic, and as editor, no one would accuse him of being a long-time feminist. I do not think that either writer or editor fully understood that in a woman's life the personal is the political. Livesay knew instinctively that "a true life of the thirties" could not be told without the inclusion of kitchen sinks and nude pictures, without the revelation of leftist male hypocrisies, or without violating the law of the secret nature of love affairs (especially the rule that one never reveals men's names), but neither she nor her editor had a consciously realized feminist position from which to voice this instinct.

Pamela Banting's explorations of Livesay's correspondence with her father, in which the daughter is often enlisted by the father in his campaign to denigrate and ridicule Livesay's mother, can act as one of the intertextual contexts, along with a large collection of Livesay archival material, for understanding Livesay's problem as an autobiographer.[10] Livesay's own admission of her jealousy of her younger sister in her childhood memoir and her anger at her mother for sending her teenage poems off to *Dial* (an act which, although characterized by Livesay as being done without her permission or desire, nevertheless did begin her lifetime career) and more recently Livesay's sometimes ungenerous remarks about Florence Livesay in her introduction to a book of her mother's translations of Ukrainian work are other contextual cues to the nature of Livesay's feelings about her personal mother.[11] Such a psychic situation would make it a difficult writing task to compose an autobiography about her own voyage to Africa as teacher and writer that involved a comparison with her mother's voyage as journalist. In writing the true story of a life, a woman may often have to face unpleasant and painful truths about her mother and herself. The revelation of these truths will leave neither mother nor daughter safe in their patriarchal stereotypes.

Livesay's own lifelong desire for justice for others and her honesty in her writing practice have led her to make one more autobiographical journey, one in which she begins to come to terms with her difficult relationship with her mother. In *Journey with My Selves: A Memoir 1909–1963*, Livesay explores her mother's imprisoned place as a woman in patriarchy with much more feminist political awareness than in the past, allowing her to admit that many of her mother's faults – her conservatism, her prudery, her disregard for personal appearance – were reactions to both the institution of marriage and to Livesay's father's abuse of that institution. Livesay's former hero worship of her father also seems mediated by her feminism in this text, and although she cannot quite forgive her mother, she does announce a measure of parity between her parents by saying: "Each parent sought to reign over me."[12]

I call my compilation of Livesay's life-writing a "cautionary tale," first, because I do not think that contemporary women writers are in any less danger of purchasing their creative space in a male-dominated tradition by blaming their personal mothers, and second, because I wish to remind myself and my readers of the importance of heeding Nancy Miller's advice regarding the necessity of reading an individual work by a woman intertextually with all that woman's work. In that regard we can gain a real insight about the maternal pre-text and the difficulty of incorporating it into the female life story by mapping a woman's writing over more than one autobiographical work and registering the changes in focus. Fredelle Bruser Maynard offers such a possibility. This registering of changes applies not only to Maynard as writer, but to myself as reader. When I first read Maynard's *Raisins and Almonds,* before the publication of her second autobiographical text, *The Tree of Life,* I was charmed by her portrayal of her relationship with her father, a poetic, artistic man who had to spend his life making a meagre living rather than in the scholarly and artistic pursuits to which he seemed suited. In the short stories of that first text, she re-creates the life of her family as Jewish shop-keepers in a series of prairie towns, weaving the personal life with the societal in a beautiful evocation of what it is to be an ethnic person in a culture that feels very different from the self, from the family. In this first book, Maynard credits her lack of conflict about being an achieving woman and a writer to her father's influence: "I was born a woman in a family where women were valued."[13] "In a quite innocent and unselfconscious way," she recalls, her father "treated us as sexual persons – future mothers, future brides. Being a woman, I knew, was a privilege. Women were *special"* (182). There is very little direct attention devoted to the mother in this text; she seems a figure always in the background, although Maynard does credit her own action-oriented practicality, good sense, and good health to her mother's example. Maynard's sister, her only sibling, is practically non-existent in the text. For Maynard it is the father who is centre stage in her psyche, whose example of "clear nobility" provides "a standard of value in my life" (185).

I have to admit that I did not, in my earlier reading, see the irony of a woman claiming that she gets her sense of self-worth as a writer and achiever from a father who "treated us as sexual persons – future mothers, future brides." In fact, I confess, I was drawn in by May-nard's father/daughter romance. I, like many of the achieving women studied in the last chapter, have believed, like a good daughter of this Freudian century, that getting one's self-definitions as an adult woman in the context of the father/daughter childhood relation was somehow natural. But exploring Maynard's second book in relation to her first and under the conditions set out in my own first chapter, I find quite a different reading.

Maynard's later autobiography, *The Tree of Life,* would seem most preoccupied with Maynard's marriage to academic and artist Max Maynard, a marriage marked by the unhappiness of both partners:

the husband forced to occupy academic positions for which his brilliant but flamboyant and undisciplined talents did not suit him; the wife, the equally brilliant and more disciplined academic, caught in a situation where she cannot work at what she does best because of the prejudice against faculty wives as intellectuals and yet she is always compelled to work at something in order to supplement her husband's income. Maynard's conclusion on the marriage is that "Max and I had a good divorce: we found, each of us, a new, freer life."[14] For the present-day reader, the wonder may be that she stayed in the marriage so long, especially when she claims such a positive relationship with her father, the relationship that is supposed to shape a woman's heterosexual commitments. But just beneath the surface of the marital text of *Tree*, is that alternative female story, partly told in the context of various female victims whom Maynard meets in the course of her work as a journalist, and partly told in four central chapters of the text's twelve chapters that are devoted to her life with her mother, her sister, and her own two daughters.

Tellingly, the writing and publication of the first book helped Maynard arrive at the different subjectivity position that allows her to write the second. To her amazement, "my mother accepted instantly my occasional elaborations and inventions; I would hear her telling friends, as her own experience, something that never happened; she read it in *Raisins and Almonds*" (135). She is also taken aback by the number of people who ask her why she did not include her sister in the book. The kind of personal and casual critique a writer gets when she has written an admittedly autobiographical work is much more challenging to her notions of self than are those received by a fiction writer who can deflect disturbing comments by the claim that, after all, she has written fiction, can leave anyone out, include who she wishes. The challenge offered to the autobiographical stance makes Maynard rethink her version of her family romance and realize that her mother is able to accept her daughter's written scripts because she herself has been scripting the family all her life: the husband was "the artist," the older daughter "the pretty one," Maynard "the bright one." This realization leads Maynard to investigate some of the politics of her family relationships and the tragic events of her mother's childhood that caused her to need the security of scripts. Although often a bitter remembering, Maynard's archaeology of her own life, her sister's life, her mother's life, allows her to forgive many things, to understand others, to accept that the painful closeness of her relationship with her mother had many elements of injustice and responsibility not under the control of either of them.

Coming to terms with her mother's rape as a child, her mother's persecution by her own mother, who only loved her sons, and understanding that the complex and terrible relationship of her sister and her mother is anchored in the death of a first baby, a son, a difficult labour (with the sister), and the coincidental death of her mother's mother allow Maynard to include her sister in the second book, while learning to forgive herself and her sister for all the rivalries between them. The irony of the sister's comment to the mother with which I began this chapter, a comment with a bitterness that would have "blighted buds," is that although the sister believed that she could not help but *know* her mother, neither daughter knew that the mother limited her daughters because of a mapping of self and other that emerged from her own suffering. But what is important for me as a mapper of autobiographies is that it is writing itself – the writing of the first book – that pushed Maynard to the position that allowed her to realize a more textured subjectivity. And in writing the most insightful chapter of her text, "A Mother and Two Daughters," she does not "kill" the mother or the sister, but rather gives them a real life in her psyche for the first time, an act that mediates her former patriarchal views of them.

As well, the narration of the history of the two women most important to her own formation of selfhood allows her to write a kind of hymn to her mother – the chapter entitled "Kaddish for My Mother." The use of the word "Kaddish" for this memorial chapter – in which Maynard lovingly places before us the details of her mother's old age, details that expose not only the old woman's tragic fragility, but also her enormous strength, talent, and determination – is ironic. The Kaddish is a kind of hymn commemorating in recitation the departed one, a hymn that helps the soul of the departed towards its journey into eternal life, but in orthodox Jewish tradition, it is a male relative who must recite the Kaddish, it being forbidden to women. Thus, there is an ironic taking on of the power of the male in language here, whereby language is transformed to matriarchal purposes as the daughter mourns and commemorates her mother. Maynard's title signals another irony of female appropriation of male tradition (more accurately reappropriation), one perhaps unrealized by Maynard, since she points out in her epigram page that her title is taken from the metaphorical name of the Torah, "the tree of life." However, long before the first of the great monotheistic patriarchal religions took the tree of life as the metaphor of its primary text, the tree was the symbol of a more ancient worship. As Erich Neumann points out in *The Great Mother*, the tree "as fruit-bearing tree of life … is female: it bears, transforms, nourishes; its leaves, branches, twigs are 'contained' in it and dependent on it."[15] Maynard's naming of her text *The Tree of Life* gives the feminist reader permission (either by the writer's conscious or unconscious act) to read the book as a new Torah, a woman's spiritual guide and moral law. Thus, just as the male tradition appropriated the mother's body as text, a new, hardly articulated, female tradition reappropriates text to inscribe the body of the mother.

But despite Maynard's considerable achievement in this second text, there is at its centre a silence, what Roy Pascal has called the "darkness" at the heart of every autobiography, an untouchable zone that makes Maynard leave her father out of the second text in the way she left her mother and sister out of the first.[16] Despite a long discussion of her marriage and its failure, a courageous move when one considers how many women autobiographers find it difficult to admit to anything unpleasant in their marriages, Maynard never connects any aspect of her relationship with this significant male other to her relationship with her first male other, her father. To do so would be to recognize that she and her sister were taught to worship the father, to accept his definitions of them, not just by a mother who had grown up thinking it was correct female behaviour to serve her indolent brothers, but by a father who accepted that service and that worship as his right as a male, and who took first place in his daughters' hearts not just because he was good and kindly and generous in his judgments, but because his wife's energy and service gave him the leisure, both physically and psychologically, to act as the beneficent *pater familias*. Perhaps Maynard's own service in her difficult marriage results from the need to serve the male that is incorporated into her identity as a woman defined by a patriarchal mother and father, as the patriarchy defines us all, to one degree or another, for its own needs. This, of course, is my feminist intertextual reading of both Maynard's texts and the silences recorded there. Maynard herself makes little negative comment on her father, beyond musing on why her mother married a poor man when she had been courted by so many rich and distinguished men. She gives no answer to that musing. However, a woman who has written two autobiographies may well write a third, and I may yet find my own speculations confirmed or confounded.

In fact, the serial autobiography seems to be a useful mode by which women overcome limitations in their identity patterns and facilitate their self growth. If Emily Carr is any example, certain darknesses in autobiographical writing can be mapped if the writer is persistent in the autobiographical pursuit and is not convinced that her life can be summed up with one integrated text undertaken at one moment in time. Emily Carr is a most amazing, though largely unrecognized, phenomenon in Canadian literature. She did not even seriously begin the writing part of her long artistic career until, in her late sixties, declining health limited her access to her beloved forests, which were the inspiration and subject of her best painting. In a burst of creativity in the few years before her death in 1945, she wrote several books, one of which, *Klee Wyck*, won the Governor General's Award for non-fiction. All her books were autobiographical in a time when "serious" Canadian writers generally avoided the genre, and taken together her writings offer us a guide to the stages of a creative woman's life unparalleled in our literature. Carr's unique sense of form, developed as a painter, were transferred to her writing choices, and the stylistic variations of her writing offer a rich ground for speculation about the generic locations of women's autobiography.

The chronology of publication begins with the archetypal *Klee Wyck*, a poetic exploration of her relationship with an Indian mother figure, Sophie. Carr's love for Indian culture, learned from this woman, and the artist's discovery of her own artistic directions through her paintings of the great totem poles of the Pacific Coast Indians constitute the subject matter of this text. Carr's friend and editor, Ira Dilworth, describes the text as giving an impression "almost of magic, of incantation."[17] Like Carr's painting, a series of seemingly swift, deceptively simple, sweeping sketches reveals her artistic maturation while telling the stories of her beloved maternal other. Carr, who lost her own mother as a child, shows in all her books a great need for female approval. Sophie is the first of a series of mother surrogates described by Carr in the context of her discovery of the D'Sonoqua, the Indian totem figure of the Great Mother. For Carr, the totem embodies the archetypal female: "Her head and trunk were carved out of, or rather into, the bole of a great red cedar. She seemed to be part of the tree itself, as if she had grown there at its heart, and the carver had only chipped away the outer wood so that you could see her."[18] An Indian child tells Carr that the totem is the "terrible" one, but for Carr "the whole figure expressed power, weight, and domination rather than ferocity" (35). Enquiring further, Carr finds that D'Sonoqua means "wild woman of the woods," that she is responsible for stealing children, carrying them off to her cave, that she is "sometimes bad ... sometimes good" (35). Examining her again, Carr is overwhelmed by the power, not of the totem itself, but of "some tremendous force behind it, that the carver had believed in" (36). This time, despite her fear, her "eye caught something that I had missed – a tabby cat asleep between her feet" (36). It is this image of female power that Carr takes away with her, that leads her to eventually seek the "tremendous force" and the protective care of the natural world in her art. I think immediately of paintings such as her rendering of a tiny white church enclosed by a womblike forest, expressing her vision of the feminine. *Klee Wyck* is a powerful act of "naming" for Carr, of naming herself as artist, for the title is the nickname Carr was known by as an art student in England. Naming oneself, consciously choosing and announcing adult identity, is for Carr, as it is for aboriginal people, a spiritual act of self-creation. The archetypal evocations, the qualities of incantation, of magic, in the style of the text, are well chosen.

The archetypal simplicity of *Klee Wyck* is replaced by the more memoir-based style of *The Book of Small*, in which Carr describes her early childhood. It is interesting to observe that while the wild natural world is associated with a female spirit, the garden world of her own upbringing is associated with her father, a very Victorian patriarch: "Father wanted his place to look exactly like England. He planted cowslips and primroses and hawthorn hedges and all the Englishy flowers. He had stiles and meadows and took away all the wild Canadian-ness and made it as meek and English as he could."[19] England is the place where Carr becomes sick with tuberculosis when living there as an art student. She must be sent home to her Canadian woods before she can become well.

The Book of Small has an interesting stylistic split. In the first section of the book, also entitled "The Book of Small," Carr represents herself in the third person and tells of her place inside a large and close family. In the second half of the text, "A Little Town and a Little Girl," she becomes "I" but draws further away from her "small" place. In chapters such as "Servants," "Christmas," "Schools," and "Saloons and Roadhouses," she relates a much more sociological and less personally located version of her early life in Victoria. Both the third-person narration of the first section and the more impersonal focus of the second allow Carr the distance she needs from her childhood, which though remembered nostalgically in this text was in fact marked by the traumatic event of her mother's death when Carr was twelve. There is no mention in the text of the death of her beloved and gentle mother except in a brief sentence in an early chapter, in which, following Carr's characteristic tendency to break the chronology of her chapters and range forward and backward in time, she announces that "years passed. Small's father and mother were dead" (54). We learn later in *Growing Pains* that the death of the mother was devastating for the family, but in *Small* it is as if Carr cannot allow her mother or her father to die, for after the announcement of her parents' death they keep reappearing in various sketches, still strong forces in her life. In fact, the history-based style of the memoir, like the evocative, archetypal style of *Klee Wyck*, represents the history of important stages in empowerment, the first a spiritual mothering, the second a historical placement that allows the child/mother/father configuration a life in the present of Carr's remembering, in a context that is not strictly chronological but rather breaks chronology to keep the mother as an important feature of the personal development. This is not an act of "killing" but rather one of revivification, of making an enabling mythology for the inscription of a female tradition of subjectivity.

In fact, the parents remain symbolic of certain aspects of Carr's subjectivity in adult life, the father representing all that is civilized and confining, but very powerful, for Carr, and the mother more closely associated with the female force Carr glimpsed in the Indian totem D'Sonoqua. However, it is the gentler side of nature – nature as mother – that her personal mother represents for her. In *Growing Pains*, in a memorial chapter devoted to her mother, Carr describes a picnic and walk she and her mother once took together: "I stepped with mother beyond the confines of our very fenced childhood. Pickets and snake fences had always separated us from the tremendous world."[20] It is after her mother's death that she realizes the power of this modest, self-effacing woman, a woman she had thought was only a reflecting water-surface for her father: "Her death broke Father," she reveals. The children seem little better off as they try to find their mother again through retreating to her room. They "creep up the stairs, turn the door handle, go into emptiness, get caught there and scolded for having red eyes and no bravery" (9). Never having fully mourned her mother and realizing that despite her father's seeming dominance he and their whole world had depended on the presence of this woman, Carr turns into a seeker of the mother and the "tremendous world" outside the fenced garden, the world she constructs in her work.

The House of All Sorts (1944, 1971), the book Carr published after the memoir of her childhood, covers the middle years of her life, when her artistic interests took a back seat to her attempts to earn a living. In *Growing Pains*, her official autobiography, she devotes only one short paragraph to this period of her life. In a chapter entitled "Rejection," she says: "I never painted now – had neither time nor wanting. For about fifteen years I did not paint" (232). *House* would not at first seem to be about the creativity of an artist, but in fact covers the years between youth and middle age, which in the life of a female body are the most creative years in terms of reproduction. But as in the nineteenth century, maternality and artistic creation do not always find a joining place in the world of living. *House* is mostly concerned with the tenants that occupied the modest apartments of a building Carr had built with the last of her inherited family money in an attempt to be self-sufficient and have a place for her studio. Unfortunately her tenants were as intrusive in her life as a horde of children might have been, and like a harried mother she writes of them with a grudging indulgence.

But at the centre of the various vignettes, which in style are like portraits on canvas, are two central chapters entitled "Studio" and "Art and the House," in which she describes her attempts at art during those years. The building, symbolically and actually, was built so that one could not enter Carr's life without coming through the studio. It was the entranceway to her own small apartment, and every complaining tenant, every city inspector, every frowning relative, even strangers, had access to Carr: "A tap on the door – I was caught at my easel; I felt exposed and embarrassed as if I had been discovered in my bathtub."[21] The studio had five doors and five windows. Exposed in this manner by an architect who had not understood the needs of the artist, Carr accomplished little in the way of painting.

Yet it was not just architecture that stood in Carr's way, for she herself in those years invited a life in which she was all things to all creatures. Several of the stories in *House* centre around Carr's rearing of bobtail sheepdogs, an energetic breed that took much of her time. Why she undertook this additional distraction from her art is revealed in the overwhelmingly maternal tone of her vignettes concerning these animals, culminating near the end of the book with the story of "Flirt," who very reluctantly became a mother. The dog was frightened at the birth of her first puppies, and Carr had to run around the yard digging up the puppies from the holes in which the mother had tried to bury them. Carr "restores them to life" and brought another dog to show the animal how to mother. Then she "sat an hour in Flirt's pen reasoning with her" and watched as the dog's "realization of motherhood came with a rush" (152).

It would seem that Flirt's maternality came with the same rush that Carr's renewed creativity arrived when she first saw the work of Lawren Harris and the Group of Seven and returned home to dig up her art from the psychic places she had buried it. The care with which Carr writes of her pets, indeed the care and delicacy that she shows in writing of her tenants, indicates that the barren period of her middle years was at least partially self-inflicted, despite her complaints of the world being too much with her. The eccentric woman who pushed her puppies in a baby pram down Simcoe Street in

Victoria to do her grocery shopping often seemed thoroughly to enjoy the life of the house-mother, living the completely interruptible existence in her studio/office/living room at the top of her own apartment building. I would suggest that the lean years, artistically speaking, were full years in terms of her personal development as a woman and as an artist able to see the way the spirit embodies itself in the flesh. The submergence of herself in life rather than art for this period must have been at least partially responsible for the artist's creed that Carr writes of in her journals: "We are still among material things. The material is holding the spiritual, wrapping it up till such time as we can bear its unfolding. Then we shall find what was closed up in material is the same as is closed up in our flesh, imperishable – life, God. Meantime bless the material, reverence the container as you reverence a church ... We cannot elude matter. It has got to be faced, not run away from. We have got to contact it with our five senses, to *grow* our way through it. We are not boring down into darkness but through into light."[22]

The years of her middle life were part of her instruction in this creed, years in which, to the degree she could as a single woman in the early twentieth century, she became a mother. Becoming a mother and practising any other creative endeavour remained for many women in the twentieth century, and especially for Carr, a problematic situation.

It is very difficult to speak of any of Carr's books in isolation, as each becomes an intertextual map for the others. Her official autobiography, written with her artistic career chronologically and topically centre stage, especially benefits if the other texts are used as maps of the private Carr. These other texts help mitigate the tone of the often defensive, assertive, sometimes bitter *Growing Pains: The Autobiography of Emily Carr*. Not that the anger that Carr shows is not justified. As an artist she had to suffer more than her share of rejection. Even when famous and lauded, she endured the loneliness that many women artists find so difficult. Despite the fact that she was greatly influenced by the Group of Seven, despite her long correspondence with Lawren Harris, and despite what was to eventually be her equal public acclaim, the Group of Seven did not become a co-educational Group of Eight to accommodate a female vision. The problem with the anger in *Growing* is that she doesn't seem to have a facilitating place for it, cannot find a full expression of it. It crops up in strange places, often making Carr appear ungenerous, insensitive, rather than justly and rightly angry at the discrimination she suffered. For example, *Growing* has as its penultimate chapter "Seventieth Birthday and a Kiss from Canada," in which Carr basks in the long-postponed fame and the implied pleasure of finally having all the people who jeered her applaud her as she accepts her due: "My voice rang out strong as a bull's and I was not scared" (274). Yet she confesses to being so frightened at the prospect of facing the public reception that she "wilted" when she entered. The movement between a near timidity and a sudden and sometimes ineffectual bravado is typical of Carr's representation of herself in all her books, and it betrays, I find, a discomfort with the conflicting roles of genteel female person and ambitious, confident, courageous artist. It is only by reading this book, her official autobiography, in the context of all her other autobiographical writing that we find the full person, in all her tenderness and talent as well as her courage and perseverance.

The expression of female anger, then, is a difficult proposition in the autobiographical format. A reading of *Hundreds and Thousands: The Journals of an Artist* reveals how difficult is the expression of many other aspects of female subjectivity, from the intimate desire for familial approval to the serious artistic philosophy. The selected diary entries tell the progress of the artist from 1927, when she first met the Group of Seven, to 1941, when she began her public writing career. The book reveals Carr's work during the years that produced the paintings that have made her reputation. The first notable thing about these years is that they fall between her fifty-seventh and her seventieth birthdays, which means her public writing career began at age seventy-one! These are not the typical periods we have been taught to associate with artistic production. Reading the diary, one realizes all the factors that made Carr postpone these years: the lack of sympathetic artist companions, both because of her place, but also her gender; the teachings of male mentors who impressed on her the second-rate nature of female work; the inhospitable domestic environment in which her beloved older sisters give approval to only the most conventional acts; and the problem of earning her living as a "lady" artist. In fact, reading the diary intertextually with the public accounts brings a realization that, from Carr's position as a woman, to be an artist was to forego all the praise and love of normal human contacts. I have become convinced that she delayed because every step meant further isolation, further ridicule from everyone who mattered to her. Sometimes her correspondence with Lawren Harris seems the only positive aspect in her life, but she eventually relinquished even this comfort when he became too much the patriarchal mentor, too little the friend.

Yet while finding a convincing case for this view of the woman artist as reluctant to achieve because of the fear of loss of connection, I also find that Carr may have, in part at least, delayed necessarily, delayed because there was no cultural expression of the grounds of subjectivity she needed and she had to find it slowly and painfully through her own lived, female life. It is only in her late years that she was able to fully express the philosophy of the "material holding the spiritual." Reading her books intertextually with the journals, I find that those years spent literally and figuratively in the *House* were an important part of that development. Thus, both the necessarily slow development of a fully female experience because of the special impoverishment of female-facilitating forms in our culture and the blocks put in the way of female creativity outside of childbearing acted to postpone those years of her creative surge.

Reading the selected journals also makes one aware that it is often only in them that Carr can speak openly of the fullness of her thought and feeling, as if many parts of herself are censured in the world. The conviction that the diary offers creative women an outlet not offered by public genres grows when we turn to the writing production of a woman such as Lucy Maud Montgomery. The editors, Mary Rubio and Elizabeth Waterston, as can be seen from the introductions to the texts, are aware that their task is a very special and demanding one, that the editing process is as important as the writing process, for they are the midwives who must bring Montgomery's personal voice into the world. When reading background material (editing and publishing history) on many of the women I have written of in this text, I have come to realize how important the editorial process is: writers from Livesay to Campbell, because they are attempting to articulate a subjectivity that has remained uninscribed, have a special need of editors with a firm grasp of how certain voices have not been mapped in our society.

Fortunate in the editors of her diaries, Montgomery was not so fortunate in her lifetime in articulating her self in her public autobiographical writing. To read her public autobiography, *The Alpine Path: The Story of My Career*, is to read of a person entirely different from the diaries.[23] This autobiography is the positivist expression of a straightforward climb to success, an "alpine path" to an uncomplicated literary stardom, one that must have confirmed the readers of the famous Anne books in the opinion that there is nothing so difficult in life that a girl of spunk and daring cannot overcome, given a fast-moving plot line and the lesser intelligence and imagination of all the powers that be. *The Selected Journals of L.M. Montgomery* tell a different story. Volume 1, covering the years 1889 to 1910, reveals a childhood often associated with the artistic temperament: fragile health, a supersensitive temperament, a lively imagination, and an early trauma (her mother died when she was just under two and her

father moved west, leaving her to be cared for by relatives). At fourteen she begins keeping her adult diary, and for the teenage years
the kind of girl that is revealed is highly motivated, a bright scholar,
a happy girl bent on academic success, a girl much like Anne and
the figure portrayed in *Alpine Path*. But the diary also reveals a darker
side, one she never really expressed in her public works. In her
twenties, after proving her ability to earn her living as a teacher and
after some success as a writer of poetry and stories for magazines,
at the time of life when the personality of the writer would be
expected to flourish, the shadow of her place as adult female begins
to interfere with her development.

The first and most spectacular occasion of this shadow's intrusion
is in 1898 when she breaks her marriage engagement to a young
man who must have been considered entirely suitable. She discovers
that if she is tied to one she does not love, "my haunting humiliation
and sense of bondage would never be lessened and would wear my
life out."[24] Yet she finds that the effect of the man to whom she is
really attracted is quite frightening: "like a *spell* [,] the mysterious,
irresistible *influence*" (209). The psychological effect of being pulled
between two impossibilities takes a tremendous toll on the young
romantic temperament. She can take no pleasure or feel no power in
the attraction the young men feel for her. Informing her psychological
division is an important economic fact that we realize when reading
from a feminist position: the first young man is suitable because he
is of the right economic class and would expect his wife, like any
Victorian gentleman would, to defer to him in all things and use her
creativity in creating babies and keeping a beautiful home. The
second young man is a farmer, and she would be expected, by him
and by society, to adopt his place in the world and become a good
farm wife. Neither position would be conducive to the needs of an
artist.

The private portrait of the artist as young woman, drawn for us in
Montgomery's journals, is an interesting contrast to all the public
portraits of the artist as young man published in our century. The
young man, confined by convention, leaves the home front to go
on a quest for self-discovery in foreign lands, usually accompanied
(or easily finding) a young female person willing to sacrifice her
reputation and her security to nurture his talent. What are the
options for a female talent? They are certainly not those of Stephen
Daedalus or his creator, James Joyce. Montgomery had two options,
both of them typical of her time: the life of an overworked teacher
(sixty students in eleven grades were typical for Montgomery)
boarding in other people's homes with no intimate relationship to

nurture the artistic self, or a return to the childhood home where she must live in a state of semi-childhood, bearing many responsibilities but with no independence, no power.

In addition to there being few other options, home is the necessary choice in other ways for Montgomery. As she is the last unmarried female relative, it is her duty to look after her grandmother who raised her. As well, as the years go by, she finds it harder and harder to write anywhere except in her native place. Even late in the second volume of her journals, when she has lived away from Prince Edward Island for many years, she expresses an incurable homesickness for the place. She attempts to work elsewhere but returns home, despite the fact that home becomes more and more imprisoning, a place where she feels her presence is essential and unappreciated at the same time. As she reaches her thirties and her personal opportunities narrow, even though she has begun to have considerable professional success with the publication of *Anne of Green Gables*, she begins to suffer bouts of depression and nervous illnesses, with an increase in the migraine headaches that she has had since youth. She writes: "I have had a month of nervous prostration – an utter breakdown of body, soul, and spirit." She finds that she must compel herself to do her simplest duties. She cannot eat, work, think, read, or talk. She is "possessed by a very fury of restlessness, only to be endured by walking the floor until my limbs failed from exhaustion" (392).

How would the father of psychoanalysis have diagnosed Montgomery if she had had the fortune to be born in Vienna instead of Prince Edward Island? Perhaps he would find her to be a case of melancholia in which the subject, having lost the primary love object, the mother, never is able to fully place identification elsewhere and becomes a site of emptiness expressed in symptoms of feeling "slighted, neglected or disappointed" and an exaggerated "fear of being poor." Freud (as quoted by Irigaray) might say that Montgomery has that typically female melancholia in which "the complex ... behaves like an open wound, drawing to itself cathetic energy – which in the transference neuroses we have called anti-cathexis – from all directions, and emptying the ego until it is totally impoverished" (70). Of course, if Freud could have treated Montgomery, he would have helped her to become a "normal" woman by encouraging her to overcome her wrath at the mother who did not give her a penis and fall in love with a man in order to get a penis by becoming the mother of a son. But perhaps melancholia would not have been the diagnosis, since it takes a considerable "capacity for narcissism" (71) to become a melancholic, a capacity of the sort women in their deprived state of female "castration" usually cannot muster. The most likely diagnosis would be hysteria, which allows no signification appropriate to self-representation, since after all she has no proper ego self to represent, and must find its substitute in bonding with a superior male who does have an ego. I summarize Irigaray's inter-rogation of Freud in order to put psychoanalytic theory in juxtapo-sition with Montgomery's historical and cultural position. What Freud diagnoses as a necessary lack, I diagnose as a lack caused by the societal and familial structures in which Montgomery lived. Not rage at her dead mother, but rather the lack of suitable surrogates for maternal nurturing was at the root of Montgomery's childhood lack (if the father had died and the mother had gone west, our society would certainly know whom to blame). Her emotional and physical exhaustion and the other symptoms she exhibited were not so much the symptoms of personal insufficiency caused by immature ego boundaries as they were the result of her never having been allowed a place of her own, literally and figuratively, as woman or as artist, in which she could have fully developed herself. Her inability to voice herself, and thus her possession "by a fury of restlessness," seems to me an artist's reaction to all the silencing mechanisms of the familial and societal world in which she lived.

During the years between twenty-three and thirty-six, "these long hard, lonely thirteen years," her only "comfort and refuge" is her diary. At a time when a young male artist would be beginning his challenge to the public world of literature, Montgomery writes care-fully conventional public stories and keeps her thoughts that come from her own subject position private, "writing them out" in her diary. Although intertextual readings of the fiction with the diaries can lead to a richer understanding of the fiction, such subtexts were not available to readers before the publication of the *Journals*. Like Emily Dickinson in an earlier time, she has to forego the public world in a "strategy of reticence" necessary to the maintenance of human connections. In her thirties, Montgomery seeks the solution that Freud would have advised: she marries. In exchange for getting a home of her own, something she devoutly desires (large sections of volume 2 show her decorating and caring for that home), she has to move to Ontario where her husband will be a clergyman, leaving the island which in her own conviction is the only place where she can really write. As the years unfold, she must sideline her own "hys-terical" symptoms, ones that might have – if understood and nur-tured into a positive expression of dissent – led to a greater public expression of her voice, and spend a great deal of her emotional energy and intelligence and time being a good preacher's wife, actively engaged in parish work, and the care giver for a husband who exhibits more and more symptoms of religious melancholia (his ego was intact enough, it seems, for this disease).

The second volume, in its early sections, shows Montgomery rather clear-eyed about what she has compromised and what she has achieved for that compromise:

I am pleased with my home ... Up to New Year's I was so busy all the time that I really had no time to *enjoy* my home – to realize it. But now I have more leisure and am beginning to realize the delight and comfort of many things that have been long absent from my life – or were never in it.

This doesn't mean that I do not even yet have agonizing hours of home-sickness – hours where nothing seems to make up for the loss of my old beloved haunts and the wild sweetness of solitary dreaming therein ... There is absolute happiness and comparative happiness. Mine is the latter. After the unhappiness and worry of the past thirteen years this existence of mine seems to me a very happy one. I am – for the most part – content.[25]

The doubled discourse of the passage speaks to the problem of female happiness, a condition that is happiness only when compared to the much more miserable existence of a former time. But Montgomery does receive many benefits from her position as wife. She delights in the birth and early childhoods of her two sons, and it is obvious that being able to offer them a secure and beautiful home that is theirs as a result of their father's profession and their mother's good book sales is very fulfilling. She enjoys welcoming old friends and relatives into her own home, and with her ability to "write it out" in her diary, the strait-jacket of the role of minister's wife is at least interesting. Even the death of a third child is bearable, made to seem part of a rich life experience, because it is shared by a loving husband and wife and set in the context of a supportive world of relationships. In fact, for a number of years at least, Montgomery achieves the combination of "money and a room of her own" in the context of a rich texture of relationships that Virginia Woolf felt was necessary to women writers.

Why was Montgomery not able to produce the public writing that would have allowed her to achieve something like the stature of a Woolf? Part of the answer lies in the literary establishment's lack of respect for the fine body of literature produced for non-adult readers. But as well, important factors in both the familial world and the societal world played crucial roles in making the different reputations of the two women. Virginia Woolf had a husband who knew a writerly talent when he saw it and who helped establish an in-house publishing firm so that Woolf would always be able to afford her stylistic adventures even when they were not welcomed by the public. Montgomery had a husband who, if the diaries are any indication, saw his wife's talent, when he noticed it at all in his increasing self-absorption in his illness, as secondary, as adjunct, to their real lives as clergyman and wife. Of course, every societal factor around him would encourage him in that view, even his wife when she was behaving as wife and not writer. As well, there was no supportive literary culture in Canada, and the problems of publication of writers in this corner of the empire were debilitating at the best. Montgomery's record of dealings with American and Canadian publishers affords the student of Canadian literature the opinion that little had changed since the books of Richardson and Moodie were pirated by American publishers, edited of their Canadian content, and sold in numbers not reflected in the minute (or absent) recompenses offered the writers. Publishing in Canada, without American distribution rights, meant accepting even more miniscule returns and a very limited reading audience. One of the reasons Canadians noticed Montgomery at all was because of the persistent Canadian belief that she must be good if she was published outside of Canada. Today she is a high-profile Canadian writer not only because of her accomplished fiction or these splendid diaries, but also because of the Poles and Japanese who come halfway around the world to visit her island home. Canadians reap great profits by homogenizing Anne (even more than Montgomery had to) and selling the films based on her for hard cash abroad.

In fact, Anne became a bit of a burden for Montgomery even in her lifetime. She records her exasperation with the project:

On September first I began work on a third "Anne" book. I did not want to do it – I have fought against it. But Page [her publisher] gave me no peace and every week brought a letter from some reader pleading for "another Anne book." So I have yielded for peace sake. It's like marrying a man to get rid of him!

I don't see how I can possibly do anything worth while with it. *Anne* is grown-up and can't be made as interesting as when a child. My forte is in writing humor. Only childhood and elderly people can be treated humorously in books. Young women in the bloom of youth and romance should be sacred from humor. It is the time of sentiment and I am not good at depicting sentiment .... I might be doing something so much more worthwhile. Perhaps when I get fairly underway I shall warm up to the task but at present I feel very coldly towards it. (133–4)

She is held captive not only by Anne but also by both her own and her society's attitudes towards female subjects. She probably would have been very good at humour based on romantic young women's illusions, humour about "marrying a man to get rid of him," but by setting the subject of young women apart from treatment as a subject of humour, an attitude encouraged by a society that sentimentalized nubile females (in much the same way as our popular culture defines them through a humourless pornography), she leaves herself without a ground, since her life as wife and mother, even if she could have found a permitted public format in which to write, are for her increasingly not funny at all.

By 1919, her husband is completely dependent on her care. She ends a ten-page account of his illness with his doctor's instruction *"not to let him out of my sight* [her italics]" (330). She confesses:

My heart sank like lead at this hint – it seemed to voice a fear I had not dared to face though I knew it had been lurking in my mind from the very first ... I felt very wretched ... After I had sobbed myself calm I rose up, grimly determined to renew the fight, made Ewan take a drink and a dose of chloral and went to bed myself.

It was the next day that I began to write notes for my journal, partly by entries I will copy here. They reflect with tolerable accuracy my summer that I had hoped would be "quiet and restful!" (330–1)

The passage shows not only that her personal situation would leave little time for the mature writing career she might have wanted, but also a growing admission on her part that the journal has more than the therapeutic purpose of "writing it out," but also serves the needs of accuracy, which will be achieved by including all her notes, that is, her full testimony of female subjectivity, which she could only do in this private document. By this time in her life, as indicated by the fact that she is recopying her earlier Cavendish diary (405), the private diary is becoming her principal literary tool. My first reaction to her decision vis-à-vis diary writing is to wonder at the effect on a writer of knowing that an important part of her work is only for posterity, can never speak to her own generation. My second reaction is the doubled one of regret that a document like this has not been a public part of our tradition since Montgomery's time and gratitude that it is ours now, and to wonder if young women a generation from now will be brought up in a literary tradition that prizes such an art as it is practised by women.

The literary woman whose art is most praised in *The Literary History of Canada* is Laura Salverson. In *The Literary History*, the document often responsible for shaping the reading expectations of students of Canadian literature, Jay Macpherson applauds Salverson's *Confessions of an Immigrant's Daughter* for being "rounded, intelligent, and attractive" in its ability to create "wonderful characters" and "illuminate the qualities of independence and imagination developing in the sickly little girl" that was Salverson.[26] Macpherson notes that it is Salverson's humour and "sense of proportion" that allow Salverson to do a better job than some others in portraying the difficulties for Canadians in an era when migration, poverty, and class inequality mitigated against personal success. I find, however, that Salverson's autobiography, of all the accounts of this century the seemingly most artfully shaped to fit into a male-defined tradition (even in its use of Augustine's title "confessions"), speaks most loudly in the doubled discourse of female autobiography in which the maternal pre-text erupts through the gaps in the patriarchally defined surface text. The degree to which a reader must learn a consciously feminist reading subjectivity is indicated by the fact that Jay Macpherson, who is a very good reader, a sophisticated, well-educated reader, one with the sensitivity to the connotative qualities of language of an excellent poet, finds no disruption in the "rounded" nature of Salverson's autobiography, no unattractive shrillness in this "attractive" account that might indicate the hysteria of the silenced woman, no disturbing ambiguities in the "wonderful characters" that might reveal the painful split in Salverson's sense of herself as a woman and a writer – all of which I find speak so loudly from every page.

I do not compare myself as reader to Macpherson in order to congratulate myself on being able to see more than she can. Indeed, for several years I read Salverson's text as she did. Except that I was always disappointed in the last chapters, which comprised a rather skimpy coverage of the years of her marriage and her publishing success, I was pleased (and as a woman proud) that Laura Salverson had produced an autobiography that could be compared favourably with any male autobiographer's product, from Rousseau to Malcolm X. Indeed, when comparing her with Canadian males, I, like Macpherson, rated Salverson superior. But this research has made me a different kind of reader, one who reads not for literary product, but for the attempt to inscribe subjectivity. I read not as one interested in the way in which women are as good as, or the same as, men, but as one interested in female difference and the many possible modes of the expression of that difference, given that the formal arrangements of genre, language, and social structure forbid that difference (except in the way that "difference" may be defined as "lack" or by its service to male needs).

Now as I read Salverson's autobiography, I find her difference and her problems with that difference announced even in her foreword, in which she hopes "to make of a personal chronicle a more subjective therefore more sensitive record of an age."[27] The title of the text indicates a confession, the spiritual development of an individual; the foreword indicates a desire to write a memoir, the form that interweaves the "personal chronicle" with the "record of an age." If there is a generic ambivalence at the very outset of this text, there is also an identity ambivalence. Augustine and Rousseau had no need to qualify the word "confessions" in their titles – their names as men identify whose confessions we will read. Even Roland Barthes, in this age of multiple, sliding, slippery, and defaced identities, still need only name his self-construction in language by his own name. No matter how obsessed all three are with their mothers (and for each the mother is an important factor in identity), there are no subtitles like "A Christian Woman's Son," "A Motherless Child," or "Mrs Barthes' Little Boy" to indicate that any of these men feel themselves inevitably defined by their significant others. But in her *Confessions*, Salverson's very first confession is that she is "an immigrant's daughter." She inscribes herself by the significant other of a parent and makes that parent's life story an integral part of her own identity. This has an immediate effect on the form of the autobiography in that for a large part of the first one hundred pages Salverson does not "exist"; it is the parents' Icelandic origins and their immigration that are the subject of this section of the book. Thus, although the text begins with her evocation of her first moments of consciousness of herself as a human being, this consciousness is immediately subsumed in the telling of the parents' story. An additional ambivalence is first found in the title. The title should more accurately (but perhaps not sonorously) read "Confessions of the Daughter of Immigrants," since both Salverson's parents were immigrants. By announcing only one parent, she begins to inscribe a subjectivity that wishes to locate itself in an unambivalent relationship, as being like one parent, and yet she is unable to name herself "daughter of an immigrant father" or "daughter of an immigrant mother." This allows for a text expressing a different complexity of subjectivity than in other confessions.

The next indication of Salverson's ambiguous identity situation is contained in the description of her first awareness of independent consciousness: "Far ahead, in the midst of an ocean of darkness, two jets of light stood out like candle flames braving the night. Why it should be so, I cannot say, but those wavering jets of yellow light marked a division of time for the little girl at her father's feet. From that moment her little thought and starry impressions were distinctly individual, and she herself no longer just the little girl who existed as a small obedient extension of her mother" (12). The moment of independence is not one illuminated by singularity, but by *two* lights. Significantly the child's location of herself is at "her father's feet" and she senses that she is no longer just an "extension" of her mother. In the very next lines, which describe their arrival at the house that is the end of their dark prairie journey, the child Laura announces to her parents her first resolve as an individual: "'Even if it's a troll's house I WON'T eat an EGG [emphasis hers].'" In this ironic emphasis added, it is not an act of self-definition that Salverson voices, but an act of rebellion against the mother who is intent on feeding her sickly child what she considers proper nourishment. In refusing this nourishment, symbolically, in terms of identity formation, the child is caught in a definition of self that will always refuse a certain kind of self nourishment, that offered by the mother. Since the child is female, the statement has further implications. Salverson writes, and I read, the word "egg" in capital letters, both of us therefore investing it with more than ordinary meaning. It is be Salverson's refusal of the "egg" of womanhood, as that word connotes the reproductive role of female, that is central to her identity for the rest of the narration of her life story. Laura Salverson's life story equipped her with all sorts of splits, that of Icelandic/Canadian, Canadian/American, romantic/realist, but none so powerful as the split she finds herself caught in between her parents. She describes it this way:

Temperamentally, they were poles apart. He was impetuous, warm-hearted, and, like every romanticist, superficial in his emotions; quick to forget both pleasure and pain. On the other hand, she was deeply reserved, somewhat cold in deportment, and, although far too sensible for neurotic brooding, seldom forgot either an injury or a kindness. Father, whose emotions were colored by the passing moment, found it easy to express himself; whereas mother, whose sentiments were fixed, was always helplessly inarticulate where her innermost sensibilities were concerned. She had the keenest wit, in latter years often devastatingly caustic, but in those early years of growing disillusionment I think she must have suffered mental agonies for which she found no words, and pride drove deeper and deeper into her heart. (69)

The description of the father is comparable with how Salverson sees herself as separate ego-consciousness and romantic writerly talent, one with a "dreaming heart" that "cries out against the swift eclipse of beauty, and mourns with a mist of tears the golden leaves of a thousand yesterdays," one that sees a nature sympathetic in its mentoring, offering her "the purple shadows that veil in mystery the sailing horn of the young moon and the little winds that run before the night on softly whispering feet," a sensibility that believes in the reality of "the innermost senses which life has stirred to passion by its flaming sword" (95–6). The self that she sees as independent, imaginative, and writerly is the same romantic temperament she sees in her father. On the other hand, the Salverson I find later in the text, who is "helplessly inarticulate where her innermost sensibilities were concerned," who uses a "devastatingly caustic" wit to disguise how difficult her life as a woman often is, the woman who can find almost no words to say the life of a wife and mother who is also a writer, is very much like her mother.

Salverson does not admit this kinship, finds that her inability to be more fully like her admired father was "my mother's fault. In the end, she weaned me completely away, made an alien of the parent whose vagaries I shared, and, as I now know, diverted my normal instincts into channels of activity for which I had no natural talents" (108). The word "weaned" tells the saddest of Freudian identity stories: the girl-child has symbolically reversed the functions of male and female parents, defining herself as her father's offspring, nurtured and nursed by him, blaming the mother for any lack in herself. As Irigaray puts it in her characterization of Freud's theory of female development, "The girl turns toward her father ... because she turns away from her mother in disillusion, and transfers, transports to her father her disappointed maternal cathexes" (62). Am I thus verifying Freud's theory of female lack in mapping Salverson's identity? No. What I wish to demonstrate is quite different. On the one hand, Salverson's personal confession may reflect a Freudian identity pattern in which she, like our culture, mistakes effect for cause and attributes her mother's inability in language and her own discomfort with maternality to some lack in the personal mother, to the female condition, and to her own body. On the other hand, her personal chronicle, or memoir, documents a cultural oppression, a cultural lack, a linguistic censorship that keeps women, including Salverson, from the fullness of their female subjectivity. Thus, the memoir contradicts the identity formation of the confessional form.

She seems aware of this dichotomy on the level of the style of the written text if not on the level of its consequences in her own life: "In a really smart chronicle, any struggle ends at a prescribed climax, preferably with a happy recompense for all concerned, save the willful sinner. But unfortunately for the artistry of this tale, life is not smart. Life is a colossus too great for smart declensions, and as indifferent to human vanities as the individual destiny. It cares nothing for the canons of art, and pursues its ironic rhythms, piling up anticlimaxes as a tidal wave piles up the wreckage it has made of some once seaworthy ship" (34). It is noteworthy that she uses the word "anticlimaxes" to describe the effect of life on art and by implication the effect of autobiography on prose generic forms. Life does change the rhythm of art, and any honesty in the attempt to tell the personal story will interfere with art's rules. The facts of a female life, when pushed into the familiar forms of male-shaped genres, will indeed, like a tidal wave, pile up an alternate story. To someone as hostile to the female as Salverson is in her autobiography, that piling up will certainly seem like the wreckage of a once-seaworthy patriarchal ship. In particular, the tidal wave of her documentation of the personal, familial, and societal conditions of women at the turn of the century contradicts her tendency to blame her personal mother for her own condition as female and writer.

In many ways, however, Salverson does manage to stay within her format, to achieve both the unified ending of her story as immigrant's daughter and her ambitions to be a North American success. Whatever the criticisms of her own ethnic group vis-à-vis the authenticity of the Icelandic elements of her novels, whatever present-day critics might say of her style, Salverson really does fulfil the import of her confessional moment, which is Augustinian in its tone and structure, when in the Duluth public library the adolescent girl looks around at the hundreds of books and vows "in a blinding flash of terrifying impertinence ... I too, will write a book, to stand on the shelves of a place like this – and I will write it in English, for that is the greatest language in the world!" (237–8). The child who did not learn English until she was ten, who came from an economically deprived background, who lived under the disadvantages of being female and of an ethnic minority, went on to become that most rare of types, a successful Canadian writer in the 1930s. Not only that, but she did it by writing about her own ethnic group, the Icelanders.

If, considering the odds against it, she was able to make that kind of achievement, then I must conclude that her inability to explore the female side of her life story sufficiently is due, not to any lack in this amazingly determined and very insightful writer, but to a lack in the social structures, the discourses, and the generic forms in which she had to map her identity. She is honest, however, in mapping the origins of her problem with femaleness as much as she can, and the memoir style of her confessions facilitates this. She admits that the beginning of her dislike of the female function of baby making came from her early years when her life was marked by the deaths of her mother's infant children, the effect of which "was a kind of fearful distaste for all babies. They were such unstable entities, predictable in nothing save the certainty of their sure departure" (138–9). Later, when she was a teenager, her mother's pregnancy alienates her: "My cognizance of her condition had erected a wall of inhibiting reserve between us ... Mamma was my unquestioned voice of authority, my inspiration and source of wisdom. I had not thought of her in terms of human weakness, nor expected from her the kind of easy sympathy I had found in Papa. Consequently, I was completely dazed by the shocking realization that even Mamma was not exempt from the arbitrary fates. For the same intuition which had quickened my first understanding left me in no doubt as to my mother's own secret resentment. She had had enough of babies" (211). This dawning awareness that the maternal function can enslave otherwise powerful beings leads Salverson into an alienation from her own body. She shows little interest in the grooming and fashion obsessions of young girls, never describes her youthful physical self (except that she cannot resist telling the reader, in a self-mocking humour that safely distances the writer, that she was once offered a job in a chorus line because of her "perfect" legs). Her experiences as a female worker does nothing to mitigate her sense of the disadvantage of being female: "Whirling the old [sewing] machine, I thought of the millions of women committed to this sort of thing, world without end. To drudgery, and pinching, and those niggardly economies that stifle the spirit and slay all hope" (291).

But her experience does not radicalize her politically or philosophically, giving her a facilitating feminist stance – nor does her experience as an apprentice in her Aunt Haldora's midwifery establishment, a training she took up at the urging of her mother. She describes her first experience of a birthing: "My impulse was to flee, but my feet refused to move. What followed was so hideous, I felt as though my own flesh were riddled and torn with a battery of javelins. The sudden assault upon the nerves was nothing compared with the subsequent shock of horror when the significance of those ghastly cries flashed upon me. Everything in me revolted, every quivering sense rebelling hotly against this obscene anguish at the roots of life ... A shambles of suffering, senseless and cruel. And, I thought with fierce loathing, no life was worth such a trial of suffering" (259). Words such as "hideous," "horror," "ghastly," and especially "obscene" indicate the extent of her problem. She feels not only terror at the thought of how much women must suffer, but also that such suffering is obscene. The word calls up not just its denotative meanings of loathsome, filthy, disgusting, but also connotes that which should not be represented in communication, a banned content. Salverson's is a cultural and generic problem and not just a problem of personal psychology. In writing of "Autobiography and the Construction of the Feminine Body," Shirley Neuman makes the point that "bodies rarely figure in autobiography"[28] because autobiography is "synonymous with spiritual quest and has consequently repressed representations of bodies within the genre" (2). Neuman finds, however, that in some women's accounts there are "moments when self-representations of a feminine body rupture and exceed the spiritual discourse of autobiography" (3). I find this to be one of these occasions. Salverson's documentation of her own disgust with birthing coincidentally gives us an unusually detailed picture of a bodily activity and its social context that are banned from the genre. I hold that it is the doubled generic imperative that Salverson has set herself – both to make a personal confession and to write a chronicle of the age – that allows this rupture of form. It is especially forceful for the feminist reader because Salverson, as memoir writer, as one concerned with her self-formation in a world of others, gives us a detailed picture of her Aunt Haldora's establishment, which allows us to realize the social plight of young women who were unwed and unwanted, the courage of women like Haldora who made a place for them, tried to teach them about their bodies, about mothering, and tried to find them a way to survive after their birthings. Salverson herself realizes the courage of such a woman, for she observes that although "those awful moments were often to infest my dreams, awake and asleep … the sturdy figure of my aunt came to the rescue. Life was full of terrors, that I perceived, but courage, plain human courage, was a force that worked miracles." She sees her aunt as having such courage, so much in fact that when she meets St Peter she "will wave [her] forceps under his nose" to silence him" (260).

But even this statement, pregnant with feminist possibility (in that the male world, as represented by one of its great saints, can be silenced by the challenge of female competence in a female activity), does not allow the confessional Salverson a conversion from seeing the femaleness as at fault to finding the conditions of female life in patriarchy at fault. She remains unreconciled to the maternal world: "a world I frantically sought to dodge by burying myself in books more deeply than ever" (260). Language, then, saves her from the fate of femaleness. Unfortunately, that same language leaves her without a means to properly communicate her own life as wife, mother and woman writer. The whole final section of the autobiography, from the time she marries onward, is in opposition to the open, detailed, and authentic voice to which we have become accustomed. She says little of her relationship with George Salverson, recording almost as an aside, the important fact that he typed her first manuscripts, indicating to a feminist reader that at least George's definitions of male/female roles were open to change. Her comment on her marriage is that it was "a good way to end all my foolish fancies, and assume a time-honored business of commonplace existence" (374). Her dismissal of her "foolish fancies" – the material of selfhood she has been asking the reader to take seriously for almost four hundred pages – is a serious compromise of her autobiographical endeavour. As a result, Salverson deals with the important years of her adult life, as she struggles with home, family, and writing, in a short forty pages. In taking on the maternal role she takes on all the disadvantages her mother lived under, including being "inarticulate where her innermost sensibilities were concerned." These are the pages that Jay Macpherson describes as the "happier days that followed her marriage" (132).

These years, despite what would seem to be a sympathetic and supportive husband, were anything but happy; they show that societal and linguistic constructions of female subjectivity, when fully internalized, are hard to mitigate even when one's intimate love relationships would seem to encourage change. Salverson cannot join the housewife's world to the loftier world of the writer. When her husband urges her to come to a bookstore and bask in the pleasure of seeing her first published book, she wishes to take "an hour to cut myself off in spirit from pots and pans and the four enclosing walls of a jealous house" (412–13). She confesses that she did not experience "any of that marvellous elation that embryo authors are supposed to feel on such an occasion." She is too busy remembering "all the hundred things that have stood in the road of this simple ambition" (413). Since in this short last section of the autobiography Salverson's wonderful ability to give us the detailed historicity of the memoir writer's stance seems to leave her, I find I have not enough evidence for the fullest of alternate reading. She has silenced much of the doubled discourse. But even with that silencing, a feminist reading for the inscription of female subjectivity can read many of Salverson's silences as informed by the openness of expression she allows herself earlier in the text. For example, she avoids any detail regarding the having and raising of her son by indicating that mothering, like other nasty aspects of life, such as faulty plumbing or cold winters, can be coped with in a competent, no-nonsense manner. Of the birth of her son she says: "There is nothing to say of my baby, except that the prospect bored me, and to give it an enterprising turn, I decided to travel fifteen hundred miles two weeks before he was born, to test the 'twilight sleep'" (375). Having read her reactions to other women's labours and deliveries, we can read "enterprising turn" as a terrified woman's effort to avoid the worst thing she can imagine, consciousness during the embodied experience of labouring.

In fact, the whole last portion of her autobiography, from her marriage onwards, seems to be under a twilight sleep of its own, as Salverson, normally so articulate, is reduced to a forced and often inappropriate tone of self-mocking humour. The text loses its intimacy, the humour its healthy cathartic effect, and the narrative voice moves away from us into self-defensive pride and protective aphorism. The account ends with a philosophical tone in which Salverson states her belief that life can become what we "earnestly believe and relentlessly strive to make it" (415). These words are too simplistic a closure for an artistic rendering of a complex selfhood that attempts to join the dichotomies of ethnic, national, sexual, and personal identities.

Salverson's autobiography is a continuingly important document of our literature not only for the writer's ability to articulate through a personal chronicle a "more sensitive record of an era" than other writers, male and female, have been able to make, but also because of what Salverson cannot articulate for her own subjectivity, yet which we can read in shaping our own: the tremendous restrictions that women suffer from in language and culture and the imperative need to unearth and remap our linguistic formation and our generic tradition to find the parts of ourselves patriarchy has suppressed, disallowed, so that we may address – in a self-constructive and healing manner – the maternal pre-text on a personal and cultural level.

PART THREE

Finding a Counter-discourse

In writing of the dialogic nature of language, Mikhail Bakhtin observed that "Understanding [an 'active' process] is in search of a counter-discourse to the discourse of the utterer,"[1] and as I read my own "utterance," my introduction to Part 2, entitled "Becoming a Twentieth-Century Woman," I immediately find a new understanding of myself in dialogue with that self-script written only a few months ago. In the time since I wrote those words, I have written two chapters on Canadian women autobiographers of my own century and tried to map their negotiations of selfhood in language. In doing so I have found that it was very difficult for them to resist the dominant life scripts of their culture, life scripts that often coerced the female self into male-defined scripts, and realized that for many of them this coercion was located in the nature of the relationship with the personal mother, in which some enabling process was hampered, absent. This hampering of female-ness was then compounded by patriarchal generic modes that culture and language offered these women. It is with a wry surprise that I now see my own autobiographical attempt caught in the same restrictions. Indeed, I find my own story very much that of a twentieth-century woman who, constructed by dominant male identity patterns, sees the self informed by the orality of the mother, only to find that orality, like Lacan's pre-symbolic language, superseded by the father's written language, to which, in my cozy conversation with my father as an adult, I portray myself as successor, the new son, the inheritor of patriarchal power! And where is my mother in all of this? Is she, like Binnie-Clark's mother, displaced in my adult identity by my father? Is she, like Salverson's mother, left behind in childhood, along with all the limitations of being female?

My questions make me attend to the details with which I have figured my mother. I have not told untruths about her, but neither has my story told the whole truth. How does a writer tell the whole truth? Life is so filled with a multiplicity of detail, selection becomes inevitable. Must selection inevitably distort, lie? For example, I have figured my mother as censoring my grandmother's story, and indeed she, like all mothers, often acted to protect me from what she considered beyond my ken. But as I re-remember the past, I cannot now decide whether it was my grandmother or my mother who told me the story of the midwife's other role at the birthing bed. In fact, since my mother was always the best story-teller in our family, the chances are she did tell me the birthing-bed story. This "disremembering" makes me want to examine my narrative strategy. Why did I figure a conversation between the three generations of females? Why did it end in a censoring? Perhaps it was so that I could more easily construct the figure of the child as silent listener and thus allow myself to build a selfhood suitable to an interpreter of others' texts? My purpose in the present stream-lines my story of my past.[2]

Now, as other memories rush into the place I have opened with these questions, I realize that if I asked either of my parents (and I often do) how they would figure my childhood self, they might well represent a very noisy child, the one in five who always had an observation to make, often an embarrassing one for parents, the one in five who could be counted on to become hysterical, filled with babble at any loss: an imaginary friend left behind in the rush for a tram, a brother moving too fast for her on his bicycle, a father going to war. They might well portray a confrontational child who would, at fifteen, tell the women assembled at her mother's tea table that she hoped she would have more than kids and plumbing to talk about when she was their age!

Now that I have lived many years of a woman's life and search for a way to include the kids and plumbing in my own story, I find myself as bereft of a language to tell a maternal story as Laura Salverson was. This is a puzzling irony to me, since my life from its beginnings – in the oral traditions of Newfoundland, in my own family's loquacity, in my formal education, in my own roles of daughter, sister, student, wife, mother, teacher, writer, critic – seems bathed in language. Friends have called me everything from articulate to impossibly verbose. Yet at the centre of all this speaking and writing there is a silence, a lack, one that often excites my speech and even sometimes my writing with an edge of hysteria, a flight into babble, a speaking in strange tongues that affects me when I cannot make myself understood, when I want terribly to touch another woman's consciousness and find that my words cannot.

I have come to believe that it is not myself as woman that is lacking, but language as it works through me, constructs me. What I lack is a fully embodied female tradition in language, a language that would rescue the vivid imaginations of those women at my mother's tea table, without censoring them, a language that would put all that I have learned about language as symbol, language as sign, in the service of my experience of life in this female body. The need I find in Salverson's beautiful and painful autobiography is a need I find in my own body, my own hand writing, my own voice speaking from the same body that made my children, that made me. But although Salverson has the advantage over me in imagery, in her talents as storyteller, I have one advantage she did not have. I, as reader, have her story. I have her story and all the other women's stories that I have gathered to make this map, to begin this archaeology of women's subjectivity. These stories are my intertexts, my *métissage*, from which I can begin to braid my inquiry into my own history, my own self-construction in language. I can begin, as woman, as writer, as scholar, to conceive of a subjectivity that Shirley Neuman calls a "matrix of differences from others," a subjectivity "conceived of with a specificity that resists appropriation to a hegemonic poetics and resists the demand for 'planned authenticity.'" If, as autobiographer and as theorist, I can find in the stories of other woman a rich enough intertext, then I need be bound neither to "the unified subject of traditional theory of autobiography nor the discursively produced and dispensed subject of poststructuralist theory." I can become a human being that Neuman describes as a "complex, multiple, layered subject with agency" in the world and its discourses. I can become "a self capable of choosing, inscribing and making a difference."[3]

So, in this last chapter, I want to compile and comment on several surveys of selfhood, written by Canadian women from a variety of writing positions, voices that braid themselves in dialogue with one another, offering me a theory and a practice of autobiography. This theory will offer the radical critique that de Lauretis calls for and will allow me to undertake a "re-reading of the sacred texts," the dominant life scripts of my culture, from a subject position motivated by "the passionate urging of a different question, a different practice, and a different desire."[4]

6 Gestures towards an Embodied Tradition

Perhaps what we wake up to in autobiography is a beginning realization of the whole cloth of ourselves in connection with so many others. Particularly as women analyzing our lives, putting the pieces together, the repressed, suppressed, putting our finger on the power dynamics at play. It is exactly in the confluence of fiction (the self or selves we might be) and analysis (of the roles we have found ourselves in, defined in a complex socio-familial weave), it is in the confluence of the two that autobiography occurs, the self writing its way to life, whole life. This is the practice of the imaginary in its largest sense, for without vision we can't see where we're going or even where we are. Autobiography is not separable from poetry for me on this ground i would call fictionalysis: a self-analysis that plays fictively with the primary images of one's life, a fiction that uncovers analytically that territory where fact and fiction coincide.

Daphne Marlatt, "Self-Representation and Fictionalysis,"
"Auto-graph(e)," *Tessera*

Every word smells of the context and contexts in which it has lived its intense social life.

Mikhail Bakhtin, *The Dialogic Imagination*

In 1987, Patricia Claxton's translation of Gabrielle Roy's autobiography, *La Détresse et l'enchantement* (*Enchantment and Sorrow*), was published; in 1989 *Dance on the Earth*, Margaret Laurence's memoir, was released. The books, like the women who wrote them, offer great differences. Roy's autobiography, constructed as a narrative of her early years as a Franco-Manitoban, her youthful adventures in North America and Europe, her decision to move to Quebec and begin her long-time French-language writing career, is preoccupied with personal development, the angst of the outsider, the problems of a French-language writer in a North American English milieu. Laurence's book, less chronologically structured, is a series of personal essays, each with a woman as its subject, but ranging widely over the causes, issues, and beliefs of a writer who is very aware of her privileged place in

English Canadian culture. But despite their differences, these two Manitobans leave us in their last works – both published posthumously, both written by women who knew their time was short – inscriptions of the personal mother that are moving, eloquent, and enabling. It would seem ironic that these two writers, two of the first women in Canada to have a successful full-time writing career that centred around the subject of the difficulties women encounter in our culture, should at their death leave such testimony to the positive and pervasive influence of their own personal mother. In fact, I find these accounts unprecedented in Canadian women's autobiography; they offer high-profile mainstream texts that illustrate an important feature of my mapping.

Roy's text is particularly intriguing in the way it ties the figures of maternal language and personal mother. The narrative with which she begins her text becomes a metaphor for her life as a writer. She describes her childhood shopping trips with her mother when they would leave francophone St Boniface for neighbouring anglophone Winnipeg. She finds that she "was one of those people destined to be treated as inferiors in their own country," yet the experience is one that "opened my eyes, trained me to observe things and stimulated my imagination."[1] The reason the negative experience of prejudice can be turned to positive results in life is that these expeditions are undertaken in the company of a mother whose courage and resourcefulness are a continuing subject of Roy's text. Throughout Roy's life, it is the comfort of writing in her mother's language that will sustain her as she was sustained when she and her mother survived downtown Winnipeg to return home to hear "other French voices in harmony with ours" (7), to feel once more enclosed by maternal language, maternal love. Much of the autobiography returns again and again to the enabling relationship with her mother, even to crediting "Maman" with offering her the beginnings of her poetics of writing. When the young Gabrielle refuses to tell her mother a story she has told too often, the mother muses:

"After all ... it's only natural for stories about life to wear a little thin. Just like life."

That exasperated me.

"Stories wearing thin! What am I supposed to do about it?"

She smiled at me soothingly.

"Make up new stories or combine old ones. Or keep telling an old one but made over so it's new."

I think that was the first time I began to see – fortunately still far away and very vaguely – that the road I'd taken in life wouldn't lead tidily to what writers, when they reach the bottoms of certain pages, naively or in self-delusion call "The End." (120–1)

It is in such "homely" dialogues that Roy expresses her poetics. At first the method seems deceptively simple, unplanned: an old-fashioned realist telling a mimetic life story. But the technique of using small scraps of conversations with the mother – at her work, during her shopping, at arrivals and departures of the daughter, finally at her bedside as the mother ages and illness comes – has a gathering force of words that "smell" of their contexts, as Bakhtin would have it. In an incremental verbal music, Roy offers the subjectivity of one who understands that it is by entering, as Bakhtin says, into "the memory of languages, genres, rituals" that a writer enters "into people's discourses and dreams" and creates "the hybrid construction" of an art that "actually contains intermingled within it two utterances, two manners of speaking, two styles, two 'languages,' two semantic and axiological horizons."[2]

This sense of a dialogic mother/daughter utterance is very strong in the Laurence memoir, not only because each of the first three autobiographical essays is devoted to a mother figure important to Laurence's development, but because knowing that she would not live to participate in the final editing of the text, she left it in the hands of her daughter Jocelyn to see the book through to publication. Explaining that Laurence worked – for the first time in her life and because of her increasing physical frailty – with tape-recorded drafts, Jocelyn Laurence observes in her introduction that this is the book that most speaks in her mother's voice, and she makes a succinct observation on how her mother discovered her structure for this text: "She'd written pages and pages merely to get to the point where she turned eighteen, and was bored silly ... She conceived of a new structure, one in which she could not only incorporate the facts of her own life but also touch upon the lives of her three mothers, as she called them – her biological mother, her aunt, who became her stepmother, and her mother-in-law. This new approach allowed her momentary digressions too, into the issues that most concerned her: nuclear disarmament, pollution and the environment, pro-choice abortion legislation."[3] In fact, Laurence discovered a mode suitable to her own subject position as a feminist writer who sincerely believed she had moral agency in the world. As Graham Good observes, the essay form offers "a focus of individual resistance to 'systems' of various kinds, political, intellectual, and cultural. This form of individualism lies between the elite and scholastic 'high' styles of academia and the manipulated and sensationalized 'low' styles of the media, both of which tend to approach their content through 'systems' of analysis and 'models' of presentation which determine its construction in advance."[4] For Laurence, who did not write a novel in the last decade of her life, the novelistic form she first tried gave her only "pages and pages" of chronological narrative without any feeling that she was telling her life. Instinctively turning away from something that left her "bored silly," she turned towards a construction that neither trapped her in male autobiographical models, where indeed the emphasis is often on the kind of ego-based growth typical of late male adolescence – a growth pattern that heroic and anti-heroic modes tend to prolong well into late adulthood for males by emphasizing personal and separate self-development over communal and relational self-development – and chose a style that allowed her to speak of her own growth as a female writer while making the digressions into the larger communal and global issues that were so much a part of Laurence's public commitment.

Some time before her death, Margaret Laurence was interviewed on the radio show "Morningside," and the interviewer humorously scolded her with a question about why a talented writer was devoting so much of her time to public causes such as nuclear disarmament when she should be home producing great novels. Laurence replied that she was not just a writer, but a mother too! This humorous moment illustrates better than many that for Laurence her subjectivity lay as much in the digressions from a writerly life as in the male-defined boundaries exposed in the kunstlerromans and writers' autobiographies of this century. In fact, her daughter's use of the word "digressions" is theoretically salutary, for what Laurence effects in her unassuming and very readable text is what Teresa de Lauretis argues for in her theoretical consideration of "Desire in Narrative": "an interruption of the triple track by which narrative, meaning and pleasure are constructed from his [male, Oedipal] point of view. The most exciting work in ... feminism today is not anti-narrative or anti-Oedipal; quite the opposite. It is narrative and Oedipal with a vengeance, for it seeks to stress the duplicity of that scenario and the specific contradiction of the female subject in it, the contradiction by which historical women must work with and against Oedipus."[5]

This is exactly what Laurence does, for inside her essay style she is very concerned not only with creating a narrative of her life, but with origins, in the sense of showing which early family romance had constructed her as social subject. But while narratively returning to the childhood family setting, she disrupts and destabilizes traditional family romances based on Freudian Oedipal models. By devoting each of four chapters to four mothers – her biological mother, who died when she was four; her aunt, who became her stepmother (her father's second wife and the mother of Laurence's only sibling); her mother-in-law, a writer who remained her loyal friend even after Laurence was divorced from the woman's son; and herself as mother of David and Jocelyn Laurence – Laurence is able to explore that misnamed pre-Oedipal relationship, the mother/child cathexis and its effect on subjectivity, and by doing so to illustrate that, for women at least, the relationship with the mother is not "pre" anything, but rather, through its continuing and surrogate expressions, is the shaping relationship that engenders and sustains productive adult females. At the same time, Laurence's digressive essayistic style avoids any sense that the continuing presence of the maternal influence creates an infantile dependence, since every mature communal and political effort, including her writing, is seen as a communal extension of maternal or maternal-surrogate influence and example. Nor does her style force her into any Oedipal gesture of separation from male figures such as fathers and sons, since digressively their lives are seen as interwoven with the beloved maternal figures, and more importantly, their suffering as males in a patriarchal system is part of the motivation for the female moral agency that Laurence sought to express in the world.

Teresa de Lauretis is concerned, in her theoretical study, that given that we are all constructed by the "mythical mechanism" that "produces the human being as man and everything else as, not even 'woman,' but non-man ... what forms of identification are possible, what positions are available to female readers, viewers, and listeners."[6] For her the positions available are largely ones of contestation, of subversion, of questioning. And much female cultural production in our time confirms her position. But I find artists such as Laurence reaching for alternate mythical mechanisms. Like de Lauretis, they do not seek a utopian past or future mythical place, but rather, in a concreteness true in spirit to mythic searching, they seek alternatives as embodied in our culture in those very physical places implied by de Lauretis's own metaphor of the "*margins* of hegemonic discourses, social *spaces* carved in the interstices of institutions and the *chinks and cracks* of the power-knowledge apparati [emphasis mine]."[7] In seeking these concrete rather than abstract places, women writing autobiographically find them, often to their surprise, not on the margins or the "chinks and cracks" of the culture, rather they find these spaces for female growth at the very ignored centre of our culture, their own bodies and their lives lived in female and maternal bodies.

As Neuman's exploration of bodies in autobiography indicates, finding a suitable expressive form (or forms) for the intimate experience of living in a female body is not easy. Neither Laurence nor Roy, despite the ways in which they rescue their mothers in their texts, can quite approach directly the subject of living in their own female bodies. One writer who throughout her career has sought to enter more fully and articulately into the life of female bodies is Daphne Marlatt, who in a compilation of some of her personal journals, poems, and her long poem *Rings*, in the form of *What Matters*, works at the realization in words of her maternality through her pregnancy and birthing of her son. Marlatt's title for the book and the very fact that this autobiographical text is a compilation of various surveys of selfhood indicate some important features of my mapping of women's autobiography. "What," in this context, is as concrete as the historicity of memoir and plays on two different meanings of "matters": the subjectivity "matters" to be emphasized and "matter," material, maternal material, *Mater*/matter, the bodiliness of female experience, which Marlatt maps. As she charts the progress of her pregnancy, she recognizes her "need to feel at home here at Impenetrable skin" and yet knows she has to confront all the patriarchally inspired fears that tell us that "Mother is inarticulate dark?/smothering?"[8] An answer to her question is essential for women whose work is with language, for if to become mother is to become inarticulate, smothering, in our own work with words, then we fall back into the old taboos about combining maternal creativity and artistic creativity. By making her maternal experience metonymic with all creative activity, one in which, like the artist creating, the labouring of her body is both a conscious and unconscious activity, Marlatt conflates maternality and artistic production. The breathing rhythms of her own labouring are like creating poetry, making "a familiar place to work" (97), the birth both a loss and an erotic fulfilment: "something like a loss, like the end of a sigh" (100). Marlatt continually makes connections between acts of the female maternal body and acts of language. Also, "Rings," or the creative act, is seen as a continuum of female body, female creativity, female communal relationship, as the poet finds that in "those first days how, with every suck, I could feel the walls of the uterus contract. You, isolate now, & born, healing my body for me" (105). This is not the expression of the phallic mother who sees her male child as healing the wound of her female castration as in Freudian definitions of female subjectivity, but rather a celebration of female plenitude whereby the dialogic act of nursing not only sustains the child, but heals the mother's own body: "I felt reborn with him, that clear, pure feeling, childlike, & in my emotions ... a tremendous sympathy with *his* tears, his hunger or miserableness ... never felt so plentiful, never been so delighted with my body, that it was more than adequate" (115–16). There is no sense that the italics of "his" is meant to indicate that the child's sex has anything to do with the poet's plenitude, but rather indicates the quality of surprise that new mothers often feel at the degree to which one can gain self-affirmation and intense bodily pleasure from the physicality of (m)othering. This quality of surprise is engendered by life in a cultural milieu that prizes acts of self-separation as self-affirming and casts nurturing as self-sacrificial. Marlatt makes the point that it is the sense of one's service to the other that constructs the woman as poet as well as the woman as mother when she speaks of a "sense of being *in the service of* (poetry, language)" (121) in the same way as she speaks of her body's delight in its service to the child. Marlatt's work, always characterized by her etymological creativity, here moves the word "serve" away from its connections with slavery and hierarchical servantry and towards its connotations of a female sufficiency for creative tasks, the pre-*serving* and con*serving* acts of reproduction: pregnancy, birthing, caring, and nurturing.

Marlatt's writing history is an exemplary history of a woman's autobiographical experimentation. Not only has she always claimed that "[my] work has been extremely autobiographical" in the face of a literary establishment that still associates the autobiographical with the amateur effort, the unliterary text, but she sees her choice of autobiographical writing as a cultural and political necessity for women: "I think that most women's lives have been so fictionalized that to present life as a reality is a strange thing. It's as strange as fiction. It's as new as fiction. I'm not interested in inventing because what actually happens is so huge ... what's the necessity of inventing? Whatever it is that writing gets at, it's precisely that remarkable quality of being alive at this point in time. I don't see any way of honoring that quality except by writing directly out of your own life. It's the real I want to get at, in all its facets, in all its multiplicities."[9] Marlatt's writings, from her exploration of the physical and spiritual territory of lesbian love in the poetic and essayistic *Touch to My Tongue*[10] to her "novel" and archival engagement with women's search for female precursors in *Ana Historic*, indicate the breadth of what Marlatt considers the "whole cloth" of women's autobiography.[11]

Marlatt's implied proposal in *Ana Historic* that women must seek the lost and obscure texts of the lives of forgotten women, women whose utterances would never be valued by "literary" standards, is especially affirming for a researcher like myself who spends a great deal of time seeking the alternate female history available in archival collections and in the obscure, "unliterary" texts of women who have never been included in any great tradition, whether that be the tradition as set by the values of past schools of literary value or the present increasingly hegemonic dominance of postmodernist values. In the spirit of Marlatt's own search in *Ana Historic*, I would like to use her enabling theory of the "whole cloth" of women's autobiography to examine the text of a woman who has no literary pretensions, a poor woman named Marge B. Clement, who in *My First Thirty Years (1920–1950)*,[12] tells her story of "sexual abuse by her family, alcoholic abuse by her husband, medical and economic abuse by her society."[13] But this "abuse" is the word that Shirley Neuman uses to name the revelations in Clement's account in *Literary History of Canada*. Clement does not "name" her life in any literary, historical, sociological, or psychological context. Hers is as close as we can come to an "authentically naive" text in which a "virtual illiteracy" keeps the writer from making "causal connections" or "narrative links" that would give us the "editorializing of experience which is part of the hidden agenda of every literary convention." Clement is only capable of a style "in which climaxes, sensationalism and analysis all appear equally unavailable to the author" (339). But while noting the "unusual integrity" offered by Clement's account in "a genre known for its manipulations of 'truth,'" Neuman does not comment on the special benefit such an account can have for a reader seeking the inscription of female selfhood.

A sophisticated writer such as Marlatt offers the whole cloth of herself in connection with so many others by consciously putting the pieces together, the repressed, suppressed, by guiding my reading through "putting our fingers on the dynamics of power," by offering me a well-realized and literary "self analysis that plays fictively, with the primary images of one's life." And I am happy to be informed and changed by her literary art. But Clement makes me the mother of her text by her inability to name the primary images, the shards and pieces of the life she records for me. I must perform the maternal archaeology of her text, putting my fingers on the dynamics of it as I reconstruct her life. But in doing so I point to my own primary images, as Neuman points to issues important to her in naming Clement's abuse. Indeed, from a position that underlines an ethical feminism with an unspoken but activist political agenda, Neuman finds that Clement's life is one of great abuse. While that naming brings Clement's text into the whole cloth of life-writing for

Neuman, in doing so she becomes sister and daughter of the text in that she gives emphasis to the way in which as critic she reconstructs the evidence of this text's archaeological site. I might find that my analysis "plays fictively" quite differently with Clement's text. As one who has a great admiration for women who survive difficult economic and cultural positions (perhaps because of my own subject position of economic and cultural privilege in contrast to that of my foremothers), I have in my past readings emphasized Clement's good-humoured fairness in dealing with her parents, her siblings, her neighbours, her community, for she seems (to me) to recognize that although many people abused her, they too were all disadvantaged in similar ways to herself. As one with a tendency to feminist romances (perhaps because of the impact of my Newfoundland childhood), I have emphasized the amazing strength and courage of a woman who after the horrendous life experience of a Marge B. Clement, one in which she seems seldom to be valued for herself, she can speak with loving pride of her decision to keep a baby she conceived by a man other than her abusive husband (though not one necessarily better): *"He is my mistake. I'll have him, love him and I did* [her emphasis]" (32).

In choosing to emphasize the way in which Clement, in this statement, constructs agency, or at least seems to believe she does, or perhaps only seems to appear by my reading of the text that she does, I, like Neuman, become a particular kind of sister and daughter of the text. As sister, I take in the detail of her experience as a woman like me, although one more vulnerable to particular patriarchal forces than I; I realize all the possible implications of her experience that my experience can allow me; and through my own attitudes, experiences, skills, and agendas, I then read her experience in one way or another. Neuman reads it in terms of its societal and political implications as well as in terms of the ways in which it exposes life-writing's manipulations by its contrast to more literate texts. I read her experience through my agenda of the therapeutic inscription of female selfhood. Both Neuman and I, by reading this text, having to construct it in ways it cannot construct itself, thereby realize the construction of our own positions and priorities as literary critics and as feminists, thus participating as reading mothers, sisters, and daughters in the inscription of this text. We read through it, to paraphrase my own words in my introduction, "arteries of our own actions and the veins of our own response."

When I speak of being in these familial relationships to a text, I speak metaphorically, but in regard to at least one particular work of women's autobiography I speak more literally. The kind of intercourse with the mother's text that Marlatt undertakes fictively in *Ana Historic*, which I as researcher undertake vicariously when I read in archives, becomes quite literally possible for Mary Meigs in *The Box Closet*. Meigs, a Montreal-based visual artist, wrote an autobiographical account of her own development as an artist entitled *Lily Briscoe: A Self-Portrait*, in which she describes her upbringing as the privileged daughter of a prominent American family whose emphasis on correctness in social behaviour, whose conservative and self-preserving class values, necessarily lead their daughter, who constructs herself as artist and lesbian, to flee parental domination and seek an alternate lifestyle. Meigs's first book is a literate and often insightful account of her life, her friendships, especially her love for Québécois writer Marie Claire Blais, which leads Meigs to settle in Canada. Early in *Lily*, Meigs writes of her female relatives: "My sister, married, with four children, her life a reflection in some ways of our mother's, of course could talk to her [their mother], could feel that anything she said would be understood. But I am thankful that I lived those last years of her life in a dishonest shadowland and am convinced that its air was the only air she could breathe. It was not only to protect myself, but also to protect her from the killing force of the word or words: homosexuality, Lesbian, that could not be said or attached to a person without triggering a sort of moral madness."[14] The autobiographer seems regretful but certain of the rightness of her concealment, perhaps also unknowingly angry beneath her confessed shame, when she remembers her relationship with her mother.

One of the great and terrifying aspects of writing acknowledgedly autobiographical texts, as Fredelle Maynard discovered, is that persons such as real sisters read them. Meigs's sister did and sent Meigs their mother's letters, which she had kept and put "in order, turned them over to me."[15] Perhaps Sarah Meigs, Mary Meigs's twin sister, wanted her to stop "filter[ing] out the good times" she had with her mother, as Meigs put it in the earlier book, to cease being ashamed, to re-create a mother in whom she could take pleasure. Perhaps she wanted Meigs to understand the life of a more conventional woman, a wife and mother like herself. Perhaps she wanted to write her own identity into existence. Whatever her motivation, the gift of the letters allowed Meigs to enter into a dialogue with her mother's text that inscribes a female indentity of the most interconnected kind, a mapping Meigs dedicates "To Arthur, Wister, and Sarah, and our parents whom we still share." This is a literally embodied life, embodied in the text of the mother, the parents, the family, speaking so compellingly of the personal and the familial as it traces these forces acting themselves out over time that it speaks a whole society into existence in the way no conventional history can.

This is possible because Meigs writes very good memoir, has a real grasp of American history and politics, of the changes in that society over a full century of national life, a perspective perhaps aided by her Canadian experience. As well, since the memoir has the doubled task of public and private record, Meigs's painstaking inquiry into her own family's history and connections, as well as her lengthy, painful, and loving readings of her mother's letters, offers special insights. Her researched account demonstrates dramatically a twentieth century of enormous change in which the constructions of class privilege, of familial relationship, and of female selfhood changed drastically and in ways that reveal the poignant gaps and silences between mothers and daughters, and expose many of the causes of the tragic alienation that exists in the late twentieth century between mothers and daughters, between sisters, between women. In doing so, Meigs gently indicates how many of the alienating situations that fathers, husbands, brothers, and sons find themselves suffering from are part of a larger discord between women. The mother's letters, and Meigs's musings on them and on the history of her times, reveal that the discords between women begin in the male need to construct women's lives and identities for the needs of a patriarchal and militaristic society. *The Box Closet* becomes the memoir of an era as well as the autobiography of a mother's daughter.

Two of the most famous established Canadian women writers of our century, Laurence and Roy, choose to honour the mother as primary element in their identity as women and writers, and find styles that express that conviction; Marlatt and Clement, at the two extremes of literary sophistication and naivety, offer us examples of the way in which female selfhood, especially maternality, is actually constructed in the process of making texts; and Mary Meigs, a visual artist who became a writer, fortuitously discovers, through the existence of her mother's letters and her sister's gift, the autobiographical route to self-construction offered by an intercourse with the mother's text. Each text differs widely from the others, offering, from traditional literary grounds, seemingly no generic comparison. Laurence's text is so different from Marlatt's it would seem reckless to group them. Clement's text's lack of conscious connecting devices is so far away from Meigs's sophisticated historical and psychological consciousness that it would seem an insult to one to group it with the other. And yet I do group them together, not so much because of their styles but because of their common purposes, to bring into existence the articulation of femaleness, of many female persons, as inscribed by females for female needs. And that common purpose does give them a similar stylistic imperative: no matter what traditional literary devices of narrative, poetry, essay, or braiding of forms these accounts use, their one common point is the dialogic nature of their texts, their continuing intercourse with the significant others of their lives and their identities. This involves them in styles that often come close to the traditional memoir and yet experiment with all the ways in which lives can be made matter, through the others of place, history, culture, family, and, not least, the text of the other. These are texts that smell of their contexts.

To extend my generic description to the present moment of writing and to emphasize that maternality need not be the direct subject of a text in order for it to work as a process of (m)othering, I would like to name two recent texts, one that calls itself a novel, Kristjana Gunnars's *The Prowler*, and another that names itself a "geografictione," Aritha van Herk's, *Places Far from Ellesmere*, as Canadian women's autobiographies. Why would I want to contradict the writers of these two texts, who seem to have taken some pains to avoid the label autobiography? I do so because the naming of generic locations is a necessary literary/political act. It is the method by which we locate ourselves in relation to our pasts and provision ourselves for the future. Women have been given a raw deal in the naming of genres, always marginalized, always subsidiary, never quite pure enough. Ironically, one of the reasons given in the past for women's exclusion from mainstream generic contracts has been that they write too autobiographically. And now that autobiographical reference is becoming popular with postmodern poets and prose writers, women are often accused of concentrating too much on the facts of their actual lived lives, being unable to realize that the purpose of the new, more playful autobiography is to deface the idea of referential existence of the self. I think that women need to name what is important to them, to name themselves outside of male generic contracts, or else they will be judged lacking by those contracts. I believe this naming will be a liberating act. It can be an act that does not reject our fathers, brothers, lovers, or sons, but that refuses to be named by our places in their stories. It is an act that can finally name us our mothers' daughters, our sisters' sisters, our daughters' mothers. It is for these reasons that even though Gunnars may feel it necessary to name her personal memoir of a twentieth-century international citizen's life a "novel," to protect it and herself from all the baggage the word "autobiography" carries in traditional definitions, and van Herk may need to make playful spoof of the need to name genre at all by her invention of the word "geografictione," as feminist critic I also need to name their texts with the other accounts I survey and compile in this text. I do so in order that the fullness of these texts can impact upon readers, I do so as a permission-giving gesture for other women writers who may need such critical sanction in order to experiment with autobiographical materials, I do so for reviewers and critics who may need an enabling rubric for the consideration of these texts, and I do so for myself in order to facilitate my construction of my female identity as reader and writer.

Like Salverson and Meigs before her, Gunnars shows a great ability to do what her literary foremother, Laura Salverson wanted to do, to "make of a personal chronicle a more subjective and therefore more sensitive record of an age." But whereas Salverson uses a combination of personal confession and history-based memoir and Meigs uses the mother's text as part of a dialogic utterance, Gunnars writes a memoir that displaces historical chronology, conflating places and times, and engages not one personal mother's text, but the whole century of personal stories as text of her own living. She is in a good position to carry out both acts. She has lived through what culturally amounts to several centuries of change in a life of less than fifty years and has lived a life of such international proportions that the lives of many seemingly diverse others are intimate texts of her own living. Born in Iceland in 1948, when that country existed in almost Third World and very isolated conditions, in a culture whose history and its reasons for existence were tied to colonial conditions, Gunnars has experienced the full force of post-colonial change living in Denmark, the United States, Canada, has experienced life as an academic's daughter, an Oriental's daughter-in-law, an art student, a linguist, a writerly refugee, to name only a few of her guises. No wonder she names her text and her self-construction in her text *The Prowler*. She prowls, as writer, as subversive, as outsider, as female, as seeker for identity, just as Meigs prowled her mother's letters, as Salverson prowled the public libraries of a foreign language. Interestingly, Salverson's autobiography is an unstated intertext of Gunnars's book, since Gunnars has written about Salverson.[16]

Despite its connotations of secrecy, of illegality, the prowler that Gunnars constructs is a loving one. This identity prowls because it wishes to escape the identities mapped out in romances. Gunnars declares in her section numbered 53 in this book without page numbers: "All stories are romances. Detective stories, spy thrillers, horror tales are all romances. They are not real. The romance of the threat. The male romance."[17] There is no more satisfaction for this prowler in female romances: "Sentimentality. Emotion. Feelings of love. Fears of rejection." She rejects this entrapment along with all romances: "I imagine a story that is not a romance." In order to do so she keeps moving from story to memoir, to essay, to literary comment, to political analysis, to manifesto, to namings. At one point she names herself and her sister "two white Inuit girls," for this is what they seemed to others when they lived in their mother's homeland, Denmark. In her article "The White Inuit Speaks," Diana Bryden calls Gunnars's literary strategy "contamination," that is, the breaking down of pure notions of identity by multiplying languages, citizenships, roles.[18] I prefer the term "braiding" of identities which I borrowed from Lionnet, for there is no sense in Gunnars's text that she feels the negative sense of contamination from any of her multiplicity of selves, rather, as she says in H.D's words, "You are contained in the things you love" (section 54). And Gunnars loves much, but especially she loves textual prowling, moving in a now-you-see-me-now-you-don't meandering, her suit of disguise blending in with her milieu, then suddenly standing out in the brilliant light of one swift image, one glimpse of memory, before the text catches itself falling into some romance and dances quickly out of sight, climbing a new wall of memory, leaping from national rooftop to national rooftop, coming to rest for a moment in a place and a role we hardly recognize as our prowler.

I use the word "our" deliberately, for this text allows a fine sense of reader identification. Just as Gunnars confesses that "the text has been prowling in the reader's domain" (section 164), the reader has the sense of prowling in the writer's domain. In a way far different than the Clement text, but with a very similar readerly effect, one has the sense of building the identity of this text's person, an identity who may well be oneself. As the identity that calls itself "text" observes: "'The text is relieved that there are no borders in these matters" (section 164).

Constructing a text, which allows for difference, allows for a variety of ways of embracing it, both intellectual and emotional, yet puts no border between reader, writer, and textual activity, a text which is its writer, which is its reader, which contains itself in its otherness: to mother such texts into being is part of the inscription of female identity that is the activity of women's autobiographical writing and reading. What better way to construct the identity of a Canadian feminist writer and reader of texts than to represent her reconstructing the figure of a woman found in a patriarchal text while reading herself into the landscape of one of our countries unknown islands, Ellesmere? Elles/Mere. "Ellesmere," the play on the foreign language's "elles," a female "they," and "Mere," the mother contained in the island's name, is a suitably playful title for the special kind of feminist play that Aritha van Herk constructs in her autobiographical text. For just because the inscription of female identity may seem often a very earnest and difficult task, it especially needs this feminist playfulness, what Patricia Yaeger calls a "poetics of play," a strategy of playfulness that is "the place where the opposition between a reality which is 'objectively perceptible and objectively knowable' and a delirious inner reality breaks down," a way of "unburdening oneself of the dominant tradition, of lightening the weight of custom and making it open to change."[19] Such a place, such an unburdening, is *Ellesmere* for van Herk.

However, it takes the writer the process of three autobiographical essays to get to Ellesmere. "Edberg," the childhood place, is a "coppice of desire and return," a metaphorical small wooded place that one cuts down periodically to glean its harvest, but that is left in a state where regrowth is possible and one can return again and again to be renewed by its sustenance.[20] Thus, for this writer the childhood is not a place to be frozen in reified myth, but a continuing source-place of life-writing: "Invented: textual: un/read: the hieroglyphic secrets of the past. Come home" (40). The cities of Edmonton and Calgary make up two of the four portions of this writer's textual mandala of identity. Edmonton, the place that makes the rural girl into the urban writing woman, is a site of "seduction and rage" where identity is "an eternal long division of the self" (53) as the childhood is distanced, divided from, the necessary growth of youth. The working place of the adult life, Calgary, is figured as this "growing graveyard" (57) in which the writer excavates, explores, maps her "acrostic of place" (72), a mapping of the thisness of a twentieth-century materialist existence, textually folded, refolded, patterned, tracing the cluttered complexity of an identity living in a "Jericho" of a city where names like Shaganappi, Marquis de Lorne, Langevin, and Louise jangle the individual out of any foolish assumptions of streamlined, pure, unity of identity.

Ellesmere, "woman as island" with its treeless, clean horizon as beautiful as a body's lines, its long summer daylight unfettering the reader, the writer, from artificial light, its primal balance of vegetation, rock, animal, is a hospitable setting where woman and text can invent each other. The interface used by van Herk to aid her self-construction through this "Elles/Mere" is Tolstoy's Anna Karenina, the other "elle" of Ellesmere, the "mere" that will liberate the woman reader's desire, and with that desire the woman writer rewrites her "mere." Anna Karenina, like Marlatt's Ana, becomes van Herk's textual other as she bonds with her as suffering sister, mothers her into a new existence by reading her out of her limited existence in a male literary tradition and into a new life where she is joined to "Reader and Anna and Ellesmere. She sits on a large stone, turning pages in the slow-moving sun that rotates the sky beyond its own cycle ... where Anna is free to read Ellesmere" (139). In freeing her textual Anna, the writer becomes the liberated daughter of the textual tradition, an Anna who "trusts her reading and her body" (142). This new woman is nevertheless an "islanded woman waiting to be read a justice or a future" (143), figured as in a state of "glacial narcolepsy" (143) at the end of the text, when the writer's last words "Oh Anna" could sign any gesture from pity through yearning for an act of the imagination that could actually gain Anna's material existence, to a loving declaration of the solidarity of the "elles." The necessarily ambivalent ending signs for me the state of female autobiographical inscription at this moment in time. Van Herk's text recognizes both the inescapability of the literary tradition and the culture it is part of, and the necessary and terrible work of revision that women must undertake through their critical and imaginative reading and writing acts of self-inscription.

However, I do not wish to leave my reader with the impression that I have, in my attention to chronology, constructed a progressive tradition in which twentieth-century texts succeed nineteenth-century texts and respectably postmodern texts stand like stars at the top of a heap of less sophisticated texts. I reject a definition of tradition in which each literary school builds its foundations on the cultural murder of the literary school that precedes it. I deliberately take a feminist swerve at this point to the consideration of three texts which well may not become academically privileged texts as Gunnars's and van Herk's almost surely will. I choose two of them because they are so autobiographically close to my own life that they allow me to understand, in a quite intimate and personal way, how women's autobiographical texts work more directly and consciously in my self-construction, and I in theirs, than fiction, poetry, or male-centred autobiographical accounts. I choose the third because in its different experience of the place I now make my home, it offers me an unlooked-for layer in the palimpsest of prairie history and culture.

When I moved with my family to Winnipeg, Manitoba, at the age of fourteen, I was suddenly introduced to television, supermarkets, co-education, and all the cultural marvels of the twentieth century that were still a future dream in the the Newfoundland I had known. It seemed to me then that although much older people – parents, grandparents – had been at the centre of culture in that more oral, more connected place, here teenagers were the cultural centre. The music-filled airwaves, the fashions, the booming education budgets of the mid-fifties all sent the message that if you could live a certain kind of materialistic, youthful existence, you too were the centre of the world. I wanted that world terribly, but when I opened my mouth to communicate with it, the slack jaws and amazed eyes of my teenage peers told me that my broad, fast-moving, Irish-tinged St John's English marked me as an outsider. I vowed not to speak until I could speak exactly like these other people. For a year I was silent, until my language could let me pass. But an outsider gets marked in some way that insiders always recognize, so I stayed outside. Despite valiant and sometimes demeaning efforts, I never did fully know what that world of teenage culture at the centre of North America was like, never fully lived it. I do not regret this. Outsiderhood has stood me in good stead. The lives of insiders had almost stopped being interesting or significant to me, that is, until I read Melinda McCracken's *Memories Are Made of This*, a Winnipeg-born writer's account of growing up as an insider in the fifties, an account that offers me an entry into that world and allows me to understand myself as one on its fringes, as one shaped by but not being truly of it, and the difference that makes.[21] McCracken's book gives me an opportunity to reconstruct a certain version of the past that informs my subjectivity, not so much by contrast (in many ways our experiences are remarkably similar, as one would expect of middle-class girls growing up in the same city at the same time) as by the degrees of difference that her account measures for me, allowing a subtle and finely tuned sense of my teenage self, re-lived, re-made in the reading of her text.

McCracken's title is apt for her project, as it concerns a problem of "memory" and a problem of "this." McCracken found it hard to remember her childhood when she began to write the text, found that her childhood had been so secure, so unfilled with trauma, suffering, or adventure, that making a story of it proved difficult.[22] Therefore, she opted for the device of following a friendship group, herself and three friends, as a way into a past that is a collage of security: home, school, music festivals, and speed-skating, and later, television, rec-room parties, and teenage proms, all conspiring to keep her and her friends convinced that the world of the late twentieth century was a pleasant place to live in. McCracken does not blame parents who went through the Depression and war for trying to insulate their children, but rather she dissects the "thisness" of her world to find the nature of those shaping influences she feels left her generation so unfit for the challenges they were to face in the decade of the 1960s and on into adult life. Thus, the title of the popular song she chooses as her title is appropriate. It confirms the woman autobiographer's desire to connect with the historicity, the "thisness," of her life as a way of achieving connection of self with the broader community. Memories are made of "this." In her ability to concentrate on her own small neighbourhood, the real significant other of her text, and to bring to that neighbourhood the new "Toronto eyes" of her adult life and in her careful, loving reconstruction of the "thisness" of her place, she allows me as allied reader to do my sisterly reconstruction of my own teenage neighbourhood, a similar but different place; she allows me to reconstruct my daily habits, the oblique place of parents in my busy youthful life, the power of the media, the school, our peers, in the shaping of ourselves. All of "this," forgotten because it was so ordinary, comes alive in reading McCracken's text, allows me enough points of similarity and difference to see to what a great extent I have been fashioned by that world I felt left me outside. This text made me realize the truth and significance for women in my own time of Elizabeth Hampsten's conviction that for the nineteenth-century woman, location was a great deal more textured than the simple facts of historical time and place.

The neighbourhood as the structural device for a woman's personal narrative became even more clearly significant for me when I recently read Helen Porter's *Below the Bridge: Memories of the South Side of St. John's* and had the sudden shocks of recognition, the surging up of memories I did not know I had, which come to me now in middle age whenever a text relocates me in the city of my birth. I say "relocates" deliberately because it is Porter's ability to select the detail that so tangibly evokes a part of St John's that is now gone, the fringe community across the harbour from the larger city, that makes this such a powerful text. I did not live there, and I am too young to have Porter's prewar memories, but she and I did go to the same schools, had the same religious affiliation, both lived in the large extended families that were the norm in Newfoundland in those days, and most importantly we both grew up in a world-view that seems to have disappeared in the late capitalism of the "First World" economy we live in now. Both Porter and I remember when women were the central figures of strong, close-knit communities. It is not that men were not strong, or not terribly patriarchal on occasion; we can both tell roaringly funny stories of the antics of our favourite male relatives, and we both understand the power some of the less beloved males held over our lives. It is just that the females we knew personally cannot be rejected out of hand merely as the "moral mothers" described by historians and sociologists, who see them as pawns of the patriarchy. Porter and I have a peculiar advantage given to people raised in communities in which, for whatever reason – poverty, religion, location – the nineteenth century (perhaps in the case of Newfoundland, the eighteenth century) seemed to extend well into the twentieth. We knew in our personal lives a kind of construction of female subjectivity that most women our age can only read about.

Porter's memorialization of her maternal grandmother – a midwife like mine – and of her own mother allows me to reconsider my feminist revision of the place of women in the past. I do not intend to re-romanticize my foremothers, and I stand by the configurations of patriarchal power I have discussed, but Porter's book makes me realize once more how important it is for my personal empowerment that I re-create in language the subtle detail of those women (and their men) in the places where they lived so that I do not lose the strength that is mine as their girl-child. One small example from the cultural location of my and Porter's childhood will suffice. She complains that in the present time the differences between the sexes is emphasized too much: "Boys are encouraged to be active, girls passive, we're told. Boys exclude girls from their baseball games and leave them to bounce balls of sponge rubber on the sidelines. Boys have the best play areas, the finest equipment and, perhaps most important of all, the confidence in themselves that is necessary for success in any sport. It's supposed to have been much worse in the forties and the fifties than it is now. Here, then, is another way in which the South Side did not conform to the North American standard."[23] Reading this I was reminded of three facts of my childhood: I had a separate education from males, yet I played with males in every neighbourhood game, and my mother did not think it unusual that I played baseball, hide and seek, Simon says, and "Hoist Your Sails" on integrated teams. The difference between my childhood and my daughter's is that she was educated with boys and played almost exclusively with girls. This was considered normal in the middle-class neighbourhoods we have lived in. Although I easily remember separate classrooms, I had to be reminded by Porter's text that gender-integrated play, play that was not organized or supervised by adults, was the norm of my childhood. When I put the two facts of my education and my play together all sorts of maps begin to retrace themselves in my head, including pioneer women's accounts of their childhoods in remote Canadian communities, on the prairie or in the North. So many speak directly or indirectly of the rough equality pioneering created between the sexes. If we now marvel when we come across accounts of women skilled with canoes or horses or threshing machines, we can explain these phenomena by the necessarily integrated nature of their pioneer world.

Perhaps that is why I like reading their stories so much. They remind me of my own story. In my own adult life I have often been seen as an odd bird because of my ease in conversation with males. Sometimes my assumption of equal time in a conversation, along with my lack of modesty in presenting my ideas, has offended men (and made women avoid me). In my younger days, much to my chagrin, my intentions were sometimes mistaken by males used to the contrasting careful reticence and self-effacement of most white middle-class women. Reading Porter's account makes me aware that my separate education, whatever its drawbacks, had one important benefit for those of us who had it: we know how to speak up in a group, to express our ideas with confidence and effectiveness. We do so because there were no boys in our classes to defer to. This was aided by the absence of television as a shaping influence in our lives. There was no "Father Knows Best" or "Leave It to Beaver" to educate us girls to our subsidiary place. Somehow the church, the distant working world, and the texts of the school system were not quite enough to cancel out those women whose speech and actions energized our real lives. I agree with Porter that we may have had our separate life scripts defined early, but we never doubted the power of those women who ran our lives, and if we did, their very loud and very sure voices were around us all the time to let us know they believed in their own existence as effective adults. As well, in the world that was most real to us, the world of play, one's place depended not so much on one's gender, but on individual talents: on how well you could hide, how fast you could run, or how well you stole second base and talked back to the umpire. I cannot remember St John's girls ever having any trouble talking back. In fact, reading my childhood through Porter's text made me realize that although such common measurements of gender equality as work opportunities may be improving in certain respects for my daughter, in more subtle ways, through such shaping devices as the media, pornography, and the demands of a now universalized world of fashion, the younger generation may well be oppressed by a "cult of true womanhood" at least as intense as that of Victorian times, and I may have grown up in a culture just remote enough in time and place to have muted many of these pressures and to allow the construction of a kind of "gap" in (some aspects of) patriarchal culture.

Reading Porter's text was, for me, a continuing experience in remembering in the most therapeutic sense of that word; the carefully selected detail of her place "below the bridge" offered me a ground on which, using both our similarities and our differences, I could begin to map features of my adult self, features my present male-shaped world often views as offensive for my gender. I shaped them in a childhood that gave me advantages not all women I know possess. I am sure there are other parts of myself, perhaps ones more negative than the ones Porter offers me, to be uncovered by reading other women's personal narratives. But knowledge is always better than ignorance, and I welcome the very special literary and cultural consciousness-raising these women's stories will give me.

One of these occasions of consciousness-raising has occurred since I took up residence in Calgary, the place where I came to do the research and reading that has gone into completing this book. Making an effort to read autobiographical works by local women writers, I found Cheryl Foggo's *Pourin' Down Rain*, the autobiography of a young black woman who grew up on the Canadian prairies.[24] In my thirty-eight years of exile from my birthplace I have almost become a prairie person; I have studied here, lived in small towns and cities, married here, birthed children here; I have absorbed this place's sense of ethnic diversity, written about its early women, touched the very places where women writing as early as Isabel Finlayson lived. Finlayson, whom I mentioned at the beginning of this study, remains unpublished. Her words, like many others, wait in the archives for the future. It is cheering, therefore, to find that in our time Cheryl Foggo's words find a place in our culture. Foggo's careful documentation of her family and her people's contribution to this place offers me an unexpected and richly textured part of the prairie place. Her account revises my historical and cultural maps of this place, and her attention to personal, familial, racial, national, and cultural selves is a verification of the markers of women's work that I have mapped in this book.

I welcome texts such as Foggo's, and I think women have the right to insist that their culture nurture and encourage such works. I believe as well, that women have the right to insist that the academy, in its new recognition of women's texts, not construct a new exclusionary canon by embracing in its critical practice only texts that exhibit markers of a sophistication pre-established by unwritten agreement among academics. I believe we have a right to demand a tradition of our own, one that allows us to live and grow within its enabling embrace, one that does not disallow strategies of writing and reading that make the "dear domestic circle" an inscription of the whole world. And that is, in the long run, why I map these women's accounts; to locate them for myself and other women who need a reading space of their own, a tradition of their own, selves they can have agency in constructing because they have a voice in the culture, in the language. We need to name this tradition if it is to be ours. The irony of the classifications the publishing information pages give these last three books points to my conclusion. McCracken's book is classed as "social life and customs," Breakwater Press places Porter's book in their Canada's Atlantic Folklore-Folklife series. Foggo's text names "Black Canadians," "Alberta," and "Biography," as well as Foggo's own name in its description. All these discriptors are correct: social customs, social life, and the life of their different "folk" in their home places are what matters for these women, what constructs the connected knower to the world. Therefore, in an act that has a political, literary, and personal imperative, I choose to name them "Canadian women's autobiographies."

Notes

INTRODUCTION

1 Finlayson, "Notebook," 55
2 Gusdorf, "Conditions and Limits of Autobiography," 29.
3 Gusdorf, "Scripture of the Self," 114.
4 de Man, "Autobiography as De-facement," 919–30.
5 Paul Jay, "What's the Use?" 45.
6 For a reading of Jacques Lacan's *Ecrits* that facilitates feminist consideration of a number of Freudian/Lacanian theories, see Gallop's *Reading
   Lacan* and Groetz's *Jacques Lacan*.
7 Smith, *Poetics*, 27.
8 Benstock, "Authorizing the Autobiographical," 29.
9 Friedman, "Women's Autobiographical Selves," 42.
10 Eakin, "Narrative and Chronology," 33.
11 Brodzki and Schenck, "Introduction," 7.
12 "Mapping" is a frequently used literary and critical metaphor, certainly
   in Canadian literary criticism (see, for example, Godard's "Mapmaking"
   and van Herk's "Mapping as Metaphor"), but its most prominent use by
   a critic of autobiography is in Shapiro's "The Dark Continent of Literature: Autobiography." Shapiro sets out to give an overview of the history of autobiography and "to reveal the submerged mountain chains
   that link the continent of autobiography with the literary mainland and
   to help map this dark Africa of the genres" (425). Shapiro's overview,
   although using Freud's metaphor for women's psyches (the "dark continent") in its title, ironically refers to no accounts by women.

13 The problem of women's relationship to language is an ongoing debate. In her 1981 survey of "Feminist Criticism in the Wilderness," Elaine Showalter puts forward a theory that presents women as in an advantaged position, since they have access to the dominant zone of male public language and the muted zone of women's language use, an area that excludes men or from which men exclude themselves. This "wild" zone of women's language is figured as a place of revolutionary possibility. However, although this theory may be empowering in a metaphorical sense, I find the spatial metaphor insufficient to describe the ways in which men and women do not so much live in separate language areas, but use the same language differently. Margaret Homans in *Bearing the Word* (1986) describes a situation in which women speak two languages at once, the presymbolic language of the mother and the symbolic language of the father. But this Lacanian approach suffers, like the mirror metaphor, from dualism. Since men and women live in the same world and their discourses leak into one another language cannot always be so sharply figured as presymbolic and symbolic. Therefore, the cultural situation must be constantly referenced: the actual experience of real people at any given moment in history, and the generic modes available to them for self-expression.

14 Neuman, "Do I know this body?"

15 Kadar, "Whose Life Is It Anyway?" 13.

16 See Neuman's "Do I know this body?"; Hoffman and Culley, *Women's Personal Narratives*; Domna C. Stanton, "Autogynographies"; and Kadar, "Whose Life Is It Anyway?"

17 For the documentation of the history and theory of male autobiography see Georg Misch, *A History of Autobiography in Antiquity*; Olney, *Metaphors of Self*; Mehlman; *A Structural Study of Autobiography*; and Jay, *Being in the Text*.

18 Olney, "Autobiography and the Cultural Moment," 19–22.

19 Jelinek, "Introduction: Women's Autobiography and the Male Tradition," 1–20.

20 See Buss, "Reading for the Doubled Discourse."

21 Lionnet, *Autobiographical Voices*, 4.

22 Myers, "Significant Fictivity" 112–13.

23 See Mason, "The Other Voice"; Sommer, "Not Just a Personal Story"; and Watson, "Shadowed Presence."

24 Brodzki, "Mothers, Displacement, and Language in the Autobiographies of Nathalie Sarraute and Christa Wolf," 245–6.

25 Hinz, "Mimesis: The Dramatic Lineage of Auto/Biography," 195–6.

26 See, for example, Franklin, "Diaries of Forgotten Women," and Buss, "Pioneer Women's Memoirs."

27 Cully, " Introduction," *A Day at a Time*.

28 Nussbaum, "Eighteenth Century Women's Autobiographical Commonplaces," 148.

29 Peterson, "Gender and Autobiographical Form," 215.

30 Spacks, "Reflecting Women," 27.

31 Spacks, *The Female Imagination* 88–9.

32 See Spacks, "Selves in Hiding," 112–32.

33 See Spacks, "Female Rhetorics," 177–91.

34 Adams, *Telling Lies in Modern American Autobiography*, ix.

35 Neuman, "Life-Writing," 333.

36 Olney, "Autobiography and the Cultural Moment," 24.

37 Stanton, "Autogynography," 15–16.

38 Poulet, "Phenomenology of Reading," 1213.

39 Mandel, "Full of Life Now," 69.

40 Barthes, *The Pleasure of the Text*, 38

41 Schweickart, "Reading Ourselves," 135.

42 Myerhoff and Ruby, "Introduction," 4.

43 Godard, "Mapmaking," 3.

44 Myerhoff and Ruby, "Introduction," 6.

45 Myers, "Significant Fictivity," 115.

46 Bloom, "Frontier Feminists."

47 Carr, "In Other Words," 136.

48 Miller, *Subject to Change*, 47

49 LeJeune, *On Autobiography*, 19.

50 Personal Narratives Group, *Interpreting Women's Lives*, 263–4.

51 Stanton, "Autogynography," 16.

52 Eagleton, *Literary Theory*, 117.

53 Brodzki and Schenck, "Introduction," 14.

54 Brodzki and Schenck, "Introduction," 15

PART ONE

1 Kristeva, "Oscillation between Power and Denial," 166.

2 Yaeger, *Honey-Mad Women*, 16.

3 Homans, *Bearing the Word*, 1–16.

4 Hirsch, *The Mother/Daughter Plot:*, 3.

5 Miller, *Subject to Change*, 59.

CHAPTER ONE

1 Blodgett, *Centuries of Female Days*, 23.

2 Stewart, *Our Forest Home*, 294.

3 Leveridge, *Your Loving Anna*, 86.

4 Hopkins, *Letters from a Lady Rancher*, 89.

5 Fothergill, *Private Chronicles*, 154.
6 Fryer, *Elizabeth Postuma Simcoe*, 33.
7 Fowler, *The Embroidered Tent*, 10.
8 There are two editions of Elizabeth Simcoe's diary, one edited by Innis, the other by Robertson. I quote from the Innis edition unless otherwise noted.
9 Kostelnick, "From Picturesque View to Picturesque Vision," 36.
10 Quoted in Simcoe, *The Diary of Mrs. John Graves Simcoe*, ed. Robertson, 151.
11 Quoted in Fryer, *Elizabeth Postuma Simcoe*, 93.
12 Bunkers, "Midwestern Diaries and Journals," 199.
13 Hampsten, *Read This Only to Yourself*, 4.
14 Jeffrey, *Frontier Women*, 106.
15 Langton, *A Gentlewoman in Upper Canada*, 127–8.
16 O'Brien, *The Journals of Mary O'Brien*, 22.
17 Godard, "Theorizing Feminist Discourse/Translation," 50.
18 Roberts, *Alberta Homestead*, 264.
19 See Welter, "The Cult of True Womanhood," 152, and Buss "'The Dear Domestic Circle,'" 1–17.
20 Faragher, *Women and Men on the Overland Trail*, 130.
21 I argue for the ways in which women's accounts present a different view from Northrop Frye's "garrison mentality" in my article "Women and the Garrison Mentality," 123–36.
22 Miller, *Subject to Change*, 50.

CHAPTER TWO

1 Billson, "The Memoir," 269.
2 Dobson, *Dickinson and the Strategies of Reticence*, xi.
3 Johnston, *Recollections of a Georgia Loyalist*.
4 Lerner, *The Female Experience*, xxi.
5 Spengemann, *The Forms of Autobiography*.
6 Lionnet, *Autobiographical Voices*, 66.
7 Hoggart, "A Question of Tone," 80.
8 Sibbald, *The Memoirs of Susan Sibbald*, xi.
9 Davis, *Resisting Novels*, 45–7.
10 Smith, *Discerning the Subject*, 159.
11 Hiemstra, *Gully Farm*, 2.
12 Raber, *Pioneering in Alberta*.
13 Van Kleek, *Our Trail North*.
14 Allison, *A Pioneer Gentlewoman in British Columbia*.
15 Hirsch, *The Mother/Daughter Plot*, 197.

16 Hart, "History Talking to Itself," 209.

CHAPTER THREE

1 de Lauretis, *Technologies of Gender*, 109.
2 Foucault, "What Is an Author?" 137.
3 Miller, *Subject to Change*, 16.
4 Moodie, *Roughing It*. I use the CEECT edition.
5 Lucas, "The Function of the Sketches," 146.
6 Freiwald, "'The Tongue of Woman,'" 155.
7 Thurston, "Rewriting *Roughing It*," 201. Moodie's text fares no better by this postmodern consideration than by the formalist estimations that found *Roughing It* lacking in coherence. Once again, the gender blindness of the assessment works against a facilitating reading.
8 Ballstadt, "The Embryo Blossom," 137–45.
9 See Clark's foreword and notes in Bird, *The Englishwoman in North America*, for a discussion of the typical tone and attitude that the travel writer took to her material.
10 Freiwald, "'The Tongue of Woman,'" 159.
11 McClelland and Stewart's 1989 NCL edition of the text restores "The Walk to Dummer" after having excluded it in editions since 1923.
12 Myers, *Significant Fictivity*, 113
13 de Lauretis, "Introduction," *Alice Doesn't*, 7.
14 Jameson, *Studies and Rambles*.
15 Ballstadt, "Introduction," *Roughing It*, xx.
16 Thomas, *Life and Work Enough*, is my source for information on Jameson's life.
17 Thomas, "Afterword," *Studies and Rambles*, 543–4.
18 See Bina Freiwald's "Speaking Femininely" for the ways in which the epistolary style affects female self-construction, and my article "Anna Jameson's *Winter Studies and Summer Rambles in Canada* as Epistolary Dijournal" for some generic considerations.
19 Good, *The Observing Self*, 22

PART TWO

1 Jameson, *Studies and Rambles*, 494.
2 Gilman, *Women and Economics*.
3 Douglas, *The Feminization of American Culture*.
4 Chodorow, *The Reproduction of Mothering*, 92.
5 Belenky et al., *Women's Ways of Knowing*, 113.
6 Gilligan, *In a Different Voice*, 156.

CHAPTER FOUR

1 Misch, *History of Autobiography in Antiquity*, vol. 2, 356.
2 Kazin, "Autobiography as Narrative," 216.
3 Frieden, "Women Coming to Consciousness," 103.
4 Binnie-Clark, *A Summer on the Canadian Prairie*, 278.
5 Binnie-Clark, *Wheat and Woman*, 300.
6 Black, *My Seventy Years*, 17.
7 Reimer, "Revisions of Labor in Margaret Oliphant's Autobiography," 205.
8 Munday, *A Mounty's Wife*.
9 Hubbard, *A Woman's Way through Unknown Labrador*.
10 Chown, *The Stairway*.
11 Eaton, *Memory's Wall*.
12 McClung, *Clearing in the West*.
13 McClung, *The Stream Runs Fast, My Own Story*, vi.
14 Misao Dean comments in "Voicing the Voiceless: Language and Genre in Nellie McClung's Fiction and her Autobiography" that McClung cultivated a "studied ordinariness as a didactic stance to further the cause of feminism" (73).
15 Dean points out that McClung had to contend not only with the criticisms of public men, but with comments in the public press ridiculing her and calling her "Windy Nellie" (71).
16 Dean notes that McClung often subverts the form of the domestic novel by bringing the politics of power relationships involved in sexuality and the domestic economy back into the format (66).
17 Wendy Lill puts these very words in McClung's mouth in *The Fighting Days*, 110.
18 Savage, *Our Nell*, 115.
19 See Cooley's *Bloody Jack* (168), in which Cooley prints a letter by McClung in a context that satirizes her along with that portion of conventional society that censures the anti-hero whom Cooley is inscribing as part of the postmodern male tradition of the rebellious sons of the patriarchy.
20 Farnham, "Introduction: The Same or Different?" 5.
21 Bird, *Anne Francis*.
22 Henry, *laugh, baby, laugh*, 1.
23 Campbell, *Halfbreed*, 13. Road allowances in Canada are the strips of crown land (government owned) reserved by government for roads, including footage on either side of the roads; Métis people who had lost their land rights were forced to settle on these.
24 Neuman, in "Life-Writing," quotes Campbell as saying that her "non-Métis editor had insisted on [the excision of] 'the kind of material most people are not interested in'" (351).

CHAPTER FIVE

1 Lionnet, "Métissage, Emancipation, and Textuality," 270.
2 Homans, *Bearing the Word*. 22.
3 Here Freudianism is used to indicate the use of Freud's psychological theories reductively, without appropriate attention to individual and social contexts. V.N. Volosinov's *Freudianism: A Critical Sketch* is helpful in establishing the need to shift "from a psychologistic to a social framework" (ix) while realizing the interconnection between the personal and social level of human behaviour.
4 Irigaray, *Speculum of the Other Woman*, 63–4.
5 Wolf, *Cassandra*, 159. Wolf incorrectly identifies the goddess as Persephone rather than Demetra.
6 Livesay, *Right Hand Left Hand*.
7 Buss, interview with David Arnason, 14 March 1986.
8 Livesay, "Dorothy Livesay Papers," Box 1, Fd. 4, 5, 6; Box 2, Fd. 1, 2, 3.
9 Livesay, "Behind the Lines (an answer to my critics)," Box 100, Fd. 1.
10 Banting, "Daddy's Girl."
11 See Livesay's introduction to Florence Livesay's *Down Singing Centuries*.
12 Livesay, *Journey with My Selves*, 55.
13 Maynard, *Raisins and Almonds*, 181
14 Maynard, *The Tree of Life*, 213.
15 Neumann, *The Great Mother*, 48–9.
16 Pascal, *Design and Truth in Autobiography*.
17 Dilworth, "Introduction," *Klee Wyck*, n.p.
18 Carr, *Klee Wyck*, 33
19 Carr, *The Book of Small* 11.
20 Carr, *Growing Pains*, 8
21 Carr, *The House of All Sorts*, 91.
22 Carr, *Hundreds and Thousands*, 197.
23 Montgomery, *The Alpine Path*.
24 Montgomery, *The Selected Journals of L.M. Montgomery*, vol. 1: *1889–1910*, 207.
25 Montgomery, *The Selected Journals of L.M. Montgomery*, vol. 2: *1910–1921*, 87.
26 Macpherson, "Autobiography," *The Literary History of Canada*, 131.
27 Salverson, *Confessions of an Immigrant's Daughter*, 5.
28 Neuman, "'An appearance walking in a forest the sexes burn': Autobiography and the Construction of the Feminine Body," 1.

PART THREE

1 Todorov, *Mikhail Baktin*, 22.
2 This moment in my text is what Patrocinio Schweickart would call the "deconstructive moment" (137) in which my text leaves itself open to

an unravelling by deconstructors who will prove the futility of my text, of all texts, by demonstrating how all my positions are self-serving to my self-construction in the present. However, that is exactly my "constructive" point. I, like many other women, very much need to construct myself in the present through revisioning the past. Let deconstructors beware.

3 Neuman, "Autobiography: From a different poetics to a poetics of differences."

4 de Lauretis, *Alice*, 107.

CHAPTER SIX

1 Roy, *Enchantment and Sorrow*, 3. Roy's is the only account originally written in the French language that I will discuss. One of the great gaps in this text is the growing tradition of women's autobiographical works in Canada's other official language. I consider Roy's text alongside Laurence because, quite apart from her linguistic community, Roy grew up in the same province and shares many aspects of local and female culture with her English-Manitoban contemporary.

2 Todorov, *Mikhail Bakhtin*, 73.

3 J. Laurence, "Preface," *Dance on the Earth: A Memoir*, xi.

4 Good, *The Observing Self*, 185–6.

5 de Lauretis, *Alice Doesn't*, 157.

6 de Lauretis, *Alice, Doesn't*, 121.

7 de Lauretis, *Technologies*, 25.

8 Marlatt, *What Matters*, 83.

9 Williamson, "Speaking In and Of Each Other," Fuse, 26.

10 Marlatt, *Touch to My Tongue*.

11 Marlatt, *Ana Historic*.

12 Clement, *My First Thirty Years*, 32.

13 Neuman, "Life-Writing," 339.

14 Meigs, *Lily Briscoe*, 70.

15 Meigs, *The Box-Closet*, 13

16 See Gunnars, "Laura Goodman Salverson's Confessions of a Divided Self," 148–53.

17 Gunnars, *The Prowler*, 53.

18 Bryden, "The White Inuit Speaks."

19 Yaeger, *Honey-mad Women*, 231.

20 van Herk, *Places Far from Ellesmere*, 13.

21 McCracken, *Memories Are Made of This*.

22 Buss, interview with Melinda McCracken, 22 March 1986.

23 Porter, *Below the Bridge*, 77.

24 Foggo, *Pourin' Down Rain*.

Bibliography

Adams, Timothy Dow. *Telling Lies in Modern American Autobiography*. Chapel Hill and London: University of North Carolina Press, 1990.

Allison, Susan. *A Pioneer Gentlewoman in British Columbia: The Recollections of Susan Allison*. Ed. Margaret A. Ormsby. Vancouver: University of British Columbia Press, 1976.

Ballstadt, Carl. "Editor's Introduction." In Susanna Moodie, *Roughing It in the Bush or Life in Canada*. Ottawa: Carleton University Press, 1988.

–. "'The Embryo Blossom': Susanna Moodie's Letters to Her Husband in Relation to *Roughing It in the Bush*." In *Re(Dis)covering Our Foremothers: Nineteenth-Century Canadian Women Writers*, ed. Lorraine McMullen, 137–45. Ottawa, London, and Paris: University of Ottawa Press, 1990.

Banting, Pamela. "Daddy's Girl: Dorothy Livesay's Correspondence with Her Father." *Journal of Canadian Poetry: Studies, Documents, Reviews* 22 (Spring–Summer 1988): 10–21.

Barthes, Roland. *The Pleasure of the Text*. Trans. Richard Miller. New York: Farrar, Straus and Giroux, 1975.

Belenky, Mary Field; Blythe McVicker Clinchy, Nancy Rule Goldberger; and Jill Mattuck Tarule. *Women's Ways of Knowing: The Development of Self, Voice, and Mind*. New York: Basic Books, 1986.

Benstock, Shari. "Authorizing the Autobiographical." In *The Private Self: Theory and Practice of Women's Autobiographical Writings*, ed. Shari Benstock, 10–33. Chapel Hill and London: University of North Carolina Press, 1988.

Billson, Marcus. "The Memoir: New Perspectives on a Forgotten Genre." *Genre* 10, no. 2 (Summer 1977): 259–82.

Binnie-Clark, Georgina. *A Summer on the Canadian Prairie*. London: Edward Arnold, 1910.

–. *Wheat and Woman*. 1914. Intro. Susan Jackel. Toronto, Buffalo, and London: University of Toronto Press, 1979.

Bird, Florence. *Anne Francis: An Autobiography*. Toronto: Clarke Irwin, 1974.

Black, Mrs George, FRGS, MP for the Yukon. *My Seventy Years*. As told to Elizabeth Bailey Price. London: Thomas Nelson and Sons, 1938.

Blodgett, Harriet. *Centuries of Female Days: Englishwomen's Private Diaries*. New Brunswick, NJ: Rutgers University Press, 1988.

Bloom, Lynn Z. "Utopia and Anti-Utopia in Twentieth-Century Women's Frontier Autobiographies." In *American Women's Autobiography: Fea(s)ts of Memory*, ed. Margo Culley. Studies in American Autobiography. Forthcoming. Madison: University of Wisconsin Press, 1993.

Brodzki, Bella. "Mothers, Displacement, and Language in the Autobiographies of Nathalie Sarraute and Christa Wolf." In *Life/Lines: Theorizing Women's Autobiography*, ed. Bella Brodzki and Celeste Schenck, 243–59. Ithaca and London: Cornell University Press, 1988.

Brodzki, Bella, and Celeste Schenck. "Introduction." In *Life/Lines: Theorizing Women's Autobiography*, ed. Bella Brodzki and Celeste Schenck, 1–18. Ithaca and London: Cornell University Press, 1988.

Bryden, Diana. "The White Inuit Speaks: Contamination as Literary Strategy." In *Past the Last Post: Theorizing Post Colonialism and Post Modernism*, ed. Ian Adam and Helen Tiffin, 191–205. Calgary: University of Calgary Press, 1991.

Bunkers, Suzanne L. "Midwestern Diaries and Journals: What Women Were (Not) Saying in the Late 1800s." In *Studies in Autobiography*, ed. James Olney. 190–210. New York and Oxford: Oxford University Press, 1988.

Buss, Helen M. "Anna Jameson's Winter Studies and Summer Rambles in Canada as Epistolary Dijournal." *Essays on Life-Writing: From Genre to Critical Practice*, ed. Marlene Kadar, 42–60. Toronto: University of Toronto Press, 1992.

–. "'The Dear Domestic Circle': Frameworks for the Literary Study of Women's Personal Narratives in Archival Collections." *Studies in Canadian Literature* 14, no. 1 (1989): 1–17.

–. Interview with David Arnason. 14 March 1986.

–. Interview with Melinda McCracken. 22 March 1986.

–. "Pioneer Women's Memoirs: Preserving the Past/Rescuing the Self." In *Reflections: Autobiography and Canadian Literature*, ed. K.P. Stich, 45–60. Ottawa: University of Ottawa Press, 1988.

–. "Reading for the Doubled Discourse of American Women's Autobiography." *a/b Auto/Biography Studies* 6, no. 1 (Spring 1991): 95–108.

–. "Women and the Garrison Mentality: Pioneer Women Autobiographers and Their Relation to the Land." In *Re(Dis)covering Our Foremothers: Nineteenth-Century Canadian Women Writers*, ed. Lorraine McMullen, 123–36. Ottawa, London, and Paris: University of Ottawa Press, 1990.

Campbell, Maria. *Halfbreed*. 1973. Halifax: Formac, 1983.

Cardinal, Marie. *The Words to Say It, An Autobiographical Novel*. Trans. Pat Goodheart; preface and afterword by Bruno Bettelhein. Cambridge, Mass: Van Vactor of Goodheart, 1983.

Carr, Emily. *The Book of Small*. 1942. Toronto: Clarke Irwin, 1966.

–. *Growing Pains: The Autobiography of Emily Carr*. 1946. Toronto: Clarke Irwin, 1966.

–. *The House of All Sorts*. 1944. Toronto: Clarke Irwin, 1967.

–. *Hundreds and Thousands: The Journals of an Artist*. Toronto: Irwin Publishing, 1966.

–. *Klee Wyck*. Foreword, Ira Dilworth. 1941. Toronto: Clarke, Irwin and Co. Ltd., 1962.

Carr, Helen. "In Other Words: Native American Women's Autobiography." In *Life/Lines: Theorizing Women's Autobiography*, ed. Bella Brodzki and Celeste Schenck, 131–53. Ithaca and London: Cornell University Press, 1988.

Chodorow, Nancy. *The Reproduction of Mothering: Psychoanalysis and the Sociology of Gender*. Berkeley, Los Angeles, and London: University of California Press, 1978.

Chown, Alice A. *The Stairway*. Intro. Diana Chown. Toronto, Buffalo, and London: University of Toronto Press, 1988.

Clark, Andrew Hill. "Foreword." In Isabella Lucy Bird, *The Englishwoman in North America*. Toronto: University of Toronto Press, 1966.

Clement, Marge B. *My First Thirty Years (1920–1950)*. Markham, Ont.: Initiative Publishing House, 1980.

Cooley, Dennis. *Bloody Jack*. Winnipeg: Turnstone Press, 1984.

Culley, Margo. "Introduction." In *A Day at a Time: The Diary Literature of American Women From 1764 to the Present*, ed. Margo Culley, 3–28. New York: Feminist Press, 1985.

Davis, Lennard J. *Resisting Novels: Ideology and Fiction*. New York and London: Methuen, 1987.

Dean, Misao. "Voicing the Voiceless: Language and Genre in Nellie McClung's Fiction and Her Autobiography." *Atlantis* 15, no. 1 (Fall 1989): 65–75.

de Lauretis, Teresa. *Alice Doesn't: Feminism, Semiotics, Cinema*. Bloomington: Indiana University Press, 1984.

–. *Technologies of Gender: Essays on Theory, Film, and Fiction*. Bloomington and Indianapolis: Indiana University Press, 1987.

de Man, Paul. "Autobiography as De-facement." *MLN* 94, no. 5 (December 1979): 919–30.

Demetrakopoulos, Stephanie A. "The Metaphysics of Matrilinearism in Women's Autobiography: Studies of Mead's *Blackberry Winter*, Hellman's *Pentimento*, Angelou's *I Know Why the Caged Bird Sings*, and Kingston's *The Women Warrior*." In *Women's Autobiography: Essays in Criticism*, ed. Estelle

C. Jelinek, 180–205. Bloomington and London: Indiana University Press, 1980.

Dilworth, Ira. "Introduction." In Emily Carr, *KleeWyck*. Toronto: Clarke Irwin, 1966.

Dobson, Joanne. *Dickinson and the Strategies of Reticence: The Woman Writer in Nineteenth-Century America*. Bloomington and Indianapolis: Indiana University Press, 1989.

Douglas, Ann. *The Feminization of American Culture*. New York: Knopf, 1977.

Eagleton, Terry. *Literary Theory, an Introduction*. Minneapolis: University of Minnesota Press, 1983.

Eakin, Paul John. "Narrative and Chronology as Structures of Reference and the New Model Autobiographer." In *Studies in Autobiography*, ed. James Olney, 32–41. New York: Oxford Uuniversity Press, 1988.

Eaton, Flora McCrea. *Memory's Wall, the Autobiography of Flora McCrea Eaton*. Toronto: Clarke Irwin, 1956.

Faragher, John Mack. *Women and Men on the Overland Trail*. New Haven and London: Yale University Press, 1979.

Farnham, Christie. "Introduction: The Same or Different?", In *The Impact of Feminist Research in the Academy*, ed. Christie Farnham, 1–10. Bloomington and Indianapolis: Indiana University Press, 1987.

Finlayson, Isabel G. "Notebook 1840–43." Public Archives of Manitoba. Hudson's Bay Archives, E 6 (copy), E 12/5 (original).

Foggo, Cheryl. *Pourin' Down Rain*. Calgary: Detselig Enterprises, 1990.

Fothergill, Robert. *Private Chronicles: A Study of English Diaries*. London: Oxford University Press, 1974.

Foucault, Michel. "What Is an Author?" In *Language, Counter-Memory, Practice: Selected Essays and Interviews*, ed. Donald F. Bouchard, trans. Donald F. Bouchard and Sherry Simon. Ithaca, NY: Cornell University Press, 1977.

Fowler, Marian. *The Embroidered Tent: Five Gentlewomen in Early Canada*. Toronto: House of Anansi, 1982.

Franklin, Penelope. "Diaries of Forgotten Women." *Book Forum* 4, no. 3 (1979): 467–74.

Freiwald, Bina. "Femininely Speaking: Anna Jameson's *Winter Studies and Summer Rambles in Canada*." In *A Mazing Space: Writing Canadian Women Writing*, ed. Shirley Neuman and Smaro Kamboureli, 61–73. Edmonton: Longspoon-NeWest, 1988.

–. "'The Tongue of Woman': The Language of the Self in Moodie's *Roughing It in the Bush*." In *Re(Dis)covering Our Foremothers: Nineteenth-Century Canadian Women Writers*, ed. Lorraine McMullen, 147–55. Ottawa, London, and Paris: University of Ottawa Press, 1990.

Frieden, Sandra. "Women Coming to Conciousness." In *Autobiography: Self into Form, German-Language Autobiographical Writing of the 1970's*. Frankfurt am Min: Verlag Peter Lang GmbH, 1983.

Friedman, Susan Stanford. "Women's Autobiographical Selves: Theory and Practice." In *The Private Self: Theory and Practice of Women's Autobiographical Writing*, ed. Shari Benstock, 34–62. Chapel Hill, NC: University of North Carolina Press, 1988.

Fryer, Mary Beacock. *Elizabeth Postuma Simcoe 1762–1850: A Biography*. Toronto and Oxford: Dundurn Press, 1989.

Gallop, Jane. *Reading Lacan*. Ithaca and London: Cornell University Press, 1985.

Gilligan, Carol. *In a Different Voice: Psychological Theory and Women's Development*. Cambridge and London: Harvard University Press, 1982.

Gilman, Charlotte Perkins. *Women and Economics: A Study of the Economic Relation between Men and Women as a Factor in Social Evolution*. 4th ed. London: G.P. Putnam; Boston: Small, Maynard, 1905.

Godard, Barbara. "'Mapmaking: A Survey of Feminist Criticism." In *Gynocritics: Feminist Approaches to Canadian and Quebec Women's Writing*, ed. Barbara Godard, 1–22. Toronto: ECW Press, 1987.

–. "Theorizing Feminist Discourse/Translation." *Tessera* 6 (Spring 1989): 42–53.

Good, Graham. *The Observing Self, Rediscovering the Essay*. London and New York: Routledge, 1988.

Groetz, Elizabeth. *Jacques Lacan. A Feminist Introduction*. London and New York: Routledge, 1990.

Gunnars, Kristjana. "Laura Goodman Salverson's Confessions of a Divided Self." In *A Mazing Space: Writing Canadian Women Writing*, ed. Shirley Neuman and Smaro Kamboureli, 148–53. Edmonton: Longspoon/NeWest, 1986.

–. *The Prowler: A Novel*. Red Deer, Alta.: Red Deer College Press, 1989.

Gusdorf, Georges. "Conditions and Limits of Autobiography." In *Autobiography: Essays Theoretical and Critical*, ed. James Olney, 28–48. Princeton: Princeton University Press, 1980.

–. "Scripture of the Self: 'Prologue in Heaven.'" In *Studies in Autobiography*, ed. James Olney, 112–27. New York and Oxford: Oxford University Press, 1988.

Hampsten, Elizabeth. *Read This Only to Yourself: The Private Writings of MidWestern Women, 1880–1910*. Bloomington: Indiana University Press, 1982.

Hart, Francis Russell. "History Talking to Itself: Public Personality in Recent Memoir." *New Literary History* 11, no. 1 (Autumn 1979): 193–210.

Henry, Ann. *laugh, baby, laugh*. Toronto: McClelland and Stewart, 1970.

Hiemstra, Mary. *Gully Farm*. Toronto: McClelland and Stewart, 1955.

Hinz, Evelyn. "Mimesis: Drama as the Touchstone for a 'Poetics' of Life-Writing." In *Essays on Life-Writing: From Genre to Critical Practice*, ed. Marlene Kadar, 195–212. Toronto: University of Toronto Press, 1992.

Hirsch, Marianne. *The Mother/Daughter Plot: Narrative, Psychoanalysis, Feminism*. Bloomington and Indianapolis: Indiana University Press, 1989.

Hoffman, Lenore, and Margo Culley, eds. *Women's Personal Narratives: Essays in Criticism and Pedagogy*. New York: MLA, 1985.

Hoggart, Richard. "A Question of Tone: Some Problems in Autobiographical Writing." *Critical Quarterly* 5 (1963): 73–90.

Homans, Margaret. *Bearing the Word: Language and Female Experience in Nineteenth-Century Women's Writing*. Chicago and London: University of Chicago Press, 1989.

Hopkins, Monica. *Letters from a Lady Rancher*. Goodread Biographies. Halifax: Formac Publishing Co., 1982.

Hubbard, Mina. *A Woman's Way through Unknown Labrador*. 1908. Foreword by Pierre Berton. St John's: Breakwater Press, 1981.

Irigaray, Luce. *Speculum of the Other Woman*. Trans. Gillian C. Gill. Ithaca, NY: Cornell University Press, 1989.

Jameson, Anna Brownell. *Winter Studies and Summer Rambles in Canada*. 1838. Toronto: McClelland and Stewart, 1990.

Jay, Paul. *Being in the Text: Self-Representation from Wordsworth to Roland Barthes*. Ithaca and London: Cornell University Press, 1984.

–. "What's the Use? Critical Theory and the Study of Autobiography." *Biography* 10, no. 1(1987): 45.

Jeffrey, Julie Joy. *Frontier Women: The Trans-Mississippi West 1840–80*. Consulting ed. Eric Foner. New York: Hill and Wang, 1979.

Jelinek, Estelle C. "Introduction: Women's Autobiography and the Male Tradition." In *Women's Autobiography, Essays in Criticism*, ed. Estelle C. Jelinek, 1–20. Bloomington and London: Indiana University Press, 1980.

Johnston, Elizabeth Lichtenstein. *Recollections of a Georgia Loyalist*. Ed. Rev. Arthur Wentworth Eaton, BA. New York and London: Bankside Press, 1901.

Kadar, Marlene. "Whose Life Is It Anyway? Some Preliminary Remarks on Life-Writing." In *Essays in Life-Writing: From Genre to Critical Practice*, ed. Marlene Kadar, 5–21. North York, Ont: Robarts Centre for Canadian Studies, 1989.

Kazin, Alfred. "Autobiography as Narrative." *Michigan Quarterly Review* 3 (1964): 210–16.

Kostelnick, Charles. "From Picturesque View to Picturesque Vision: William Gilpin and Ann Radcliffe." *Mosaic* 17, no. 3 (Summer 1985): 31–48.

Kristeva, Julia. "Oscillation between Power and Denial." In *New French Feminisms*, ed. Elaine Marks and Isabel de Courtivron, 165–7. New York: Schocken Books, 1981.

Langton, Anne. *A Gentlewoman in Upper Canada: The Journals of Anne Langton*. Ed. H.H. Langton. Toronto and Vancouver: Clarke Irwin, 1964.

Laurence, Jocelyn. "Preface." In Margaret Laurence, *Dance on the Earth: A Memoir*, xi–xv. Toronto: McClelland and Stewart, 1989.

Laurence, Margaret. *Dance on the Earth: A Memoir*. Toronto: McClelland and Stewart, 1989.

Lejeune, Philippe. *On Autobiography*. Ed. Paul John Eakin; trans. Katherine Leary. Minneapolis: University of Minnesota Press, 1989.

Lerner, Gerda. "Introduction." In *The Female Experience: An American Documentary*, ed. Gerda Lerner. Indianapolis: Bobbs-Merrill Educational Publications, 1977.

Leveridge, Anne. *Your Loving Anna: Letters from the Ontario Frontier*. Ed. Louis Tivy. Toronto: University of Toronto Press, 1972.

Lill, Wendy. "The Fighting Days." *Canadian Theatre Review* 42 (Spring 1985): 73–179.

Lionnet, Françoise. *Autobiographical Voices: Race, Gender, Self-Portraiture*. Ithaca and London: Cornell University Press, 1989.

Livesay, Dorothy. "Behind the Lines (an answer to my critics)." Livesay Papers, Box 100, Fd 1, 1978.

–. The Dorothy Livesay Papers. University of Manitoba Archives and Special Collections, Box 1, Fd 4, 5, and 6; Box 2, Fd 1, 2, and 3.

–. "Introduction." In Florence Livesay, *Down Singing Centuries: Folk Literature of the Ukraine*. Ed. Louisa Loeb; trans. Florence Livesay. Winnipeg: Hyperion Press, 1981.

–. *Journey with My Selves, A Memoir 1909–1963*. Vancouver: Douglas and McIntyre, 1991.

–. *Right Hand Left Hand*. Ed. David Arnason and Kim Todd. Erin, Ont.: Press Porcepic, 1977.

Lucas, Alec. "The Function of the Sketches in Susanna Moodie's *Roughing It in the Bush*." In *Re(Dis)covering Our Foremothers: Nineteenth-Century Canadian Women Writers*, ed. Lorraine McMullen, 146–54. Ottawa, London, and Paris: University of Ottawa Press, 1990.

McClung, Nellie. *Clearing in the West, My Own Story*. Toronto: Thomas Allen and Son, 1935, 1965.

–. *The Stream Runs Fast, My Own Story*. Toronto: Thomas Allen and Son, 1945, 1965.

McCracken, Melinda. *Memories are Made of This*. Toronto: James Lorimer, 1975.

Macpherson, Jay. "Autobiography." In *The Literary History of Canada*. Vol. 2, ed. Carl F. Klinck, 126–33. 2d ed. Toronto: Toronto University Press, 1976.

Mandel, Barrett J. "Full of Life Now." In *Autobiography: Essays Theoretical and Critical*, ed. James Olney, 49–72. Princeton: Princeton University Press, 1980.

Marlatt, Daphne. *Ana Historic*. Toronto: Coach House Press, 1988.

–. *Touch to My Tongue*. Edmonton: Longspoon Press, 1984.

–. *What Matters: Writing 1968–70*. Toronto: Coach House Press, 1980.

Mason, Mary G. "The Other Voice: Autobiographies of Women Writers." In *Autobiography: Essays Theoretical and Critical*, ed. James Olney, 207–35.

Princeton: Princeton University Press, 1980. Reprinted in *Life/Lines: Theorizing Women's Autobiography*, ed. Bella Brodzki and Celeste Schenck, 19–44. Ithaca and London: Cornell University Press, 1988.

Maynard, Fredelle Bruser. *Raisins and Almonds*. Toronto: Doubleday Canada, 1972.

–. *The Tree of Life*. Markham, Ont., and London: Penguin Books, 1989.

Mehlman, Jeffrey. *A Structural Study of Autobiography: Proust, Leiris, Sartre, Levi-Strauss*. Ithaca and London: Cornell University Press, 1971.

Meigs, Mary. *The Box Closet*. Vancouver: Talonbooks, 1987.

–. *Lily Briscoe: A Self-Portrait, An Autobiography*. Vancouver: Talonbooks, 1981.

Miller, Nancy K. *Subject to Change: Reading Feminist Writing*. New York: Columbia University Press, 1988.

–. "Writing Fictions: Women's Autobiography in France." In *Life/Lines: Theorizing Women's Autobiography*, ed. Bella Brodzki and Celeste Schenck, 45–61. Ithaca and London: Cornell University Press. 1988.

Misch, Georg. *History of Autobiography in Antiquity*. Vol. 2. Trans. E.W. Dickes. Cambridge: Harvard University Press, 1951.

Montgomery, Lucy Maud. *The Alpine Path: The Story of My Career*. Don Mills, Ont.: Fitzhenry and Whiteside, 1917.

–. *The Selected Journals of L.M. Montgomery*. Vol. 1, 1889–1910. Toronto: Oxford University Press, 1985.

–. *The Selected Journals of L. M. Montgomery*. Vol. 2, 1910–1921. Toronto: Oxford University Press, 1987.

Moodie, Susanna. *Roughing It in the Bush or Life in Canada*. Ed. Carl Ballstadt. CEECT ed. Ottawa: Carleton University Press, 1988.

Munday, Luta. *A Mounty's Wife, Being the Life Story of One Attached to the Force But Not of It*. Toronto: Macmillan, 1930.

Myerhoff, Barbara, and Jay Ruby. "Introduction." In *A Crack in the Mirror*, ed. Barbara Myerhoff and Jay Ruby, 1–38. Philadelphia: University of Pennsylvania Press, 1982.

Myers, Victoria. "The Significant Fictivity of Maxine Hong Kingston's *The Woman Warrior*." *Biography* 9, no. 2 (Spring 1986): 112–25.

Neuman, Shirley. "'An appearance walking in a forest the sexes burn': Autobiography and the Construction of the Feminine Body." *Signature* 2 (Winter 1989): 1–26.

–. "Autobiography: From a Different Poetics to a Poetics of Differences." In *Essays on Life-Writing: From Genre to Critical Practice*, ed. Marlene Kadar, 213–30. Toronto: University of Toronto Press, 1992.

–. "Do I know this body? Remembering, imagining, inventing women's bodies in life-writing." Paper presented at the Conference on Re-imagining Women, Edmonton, April 1990.

–. "Life-Writing." In *Literary History of Canada: Canadian Literature in English*. Vol. 4, gen. ed. W.H. New, 333–70. 2d ed. Toronto, Buffalo, and London: University of Toronto Press, 1990.

Neumann, Erich. *The Great Mother: An Analysis of the Archetype*. Trans. Ralph Manheim. Bollingen series 47. Princeton: Princeton University Press, 1963.

Nussbaum, Felicity A. "Eighteenth-Century Women's Autobiographical Commonplaces." In *The Private Self: Theory and Practice of Women's Autobiographical Writings*, ed. Shari Benstock, 147–72. Chapel Hill and London: University of North Carolina Press, 1988.

O'Brien, Mary. *The Journals of Mary O'Brien 1828–1838*. Ed. Audrey Saunders Miller. Toronto: Macmillan, 1968.

Olney, James. "Autobiography and the Cultural Moment: A Thematic, Historical, and Bibliographical Introduction." In *Autobiography: Essays Theoretical and Critical*, ed. James Olney, 3–27. Princeton: Princeton University Press, 1980.

–. *Metaphors of Self: The Meaning of Autobiography*. Princeton: Princeton University Press, 1981.

Pascal, Roy. *Design and Truth in Autobiography*. London: Routledge and Kegan Paul, 1960.

Personal Narratives Group, eds. *Interpreting Women's Lives: Feminist Theory and Personal Narratives*. Bloomington and Indianapolis: Indiana University Press, 1989.

Peterson, Linda H. "Gender and Autobiographical Form: The Case of the Spiritual Autobiography." In *Studies in Autobiography*, ed. James Olney, 211–22. New York and Oxford: Oxford University Press, 1988.

Porter, Helen. *Below the Bridge: Memories of the South Side of St. John's*. St John's: Breakwater Press, 1979.

Poulet, Georges. "Phenomenology of Reading." In *Critical Theory Since Plato*, ed. Hazard Adams, 1213–22. New York: Harcourt Brace Jovanovich, 1971.

Raber, Jessie Browne. *Pioneering in Alberta*. New York: Exposition Press, 1951.

Reimer, Gail Twersky. "Revisions of Labor in Margaret Oliphant's Autobiography." In *Life/Lines: Theorizing Women's Autobiography*, ed. Bella Brodzki and Celeste Schenck, 203–20. Ithaca and London: Cornell University Press, 1988.

Roberts, Sarah Ellen. *Alberta Homestead: Chronicle of a Pioneer Family*. Ed. Lathrop E. Roberts. Austin and London: University of Texas Press, 1968, 1971.

Roy, Gabrielle. *Enchantment and Sorrow: The Autobiography of Gabrielle Roy*. Trans. Patricia Claxton. Toronto: Lester & Orpen Dennys, 1987.

Salverson, Laura Goodman. *Confessions of an Immigrant's Daughter*. 1939. Intro. K.P. Stich. Toronto: University of Toronto Press, 1981.

Savage, Candace. *Our Nell, A Scrapbook Biography of Nellie L. McClung*. Halifax: Formac, 1985.

Schweickart, Patrocinio. "Reading Ourselves: Toward a Feminist Theory of Reading." In *Contemporary Literary Criticism: Literary and Cultural Studies*, ed. Robert Con Davis and Ronald Schleifer, 118–42. 2d ed. New York and London: Longman, 1989.

Shapiro, Stephen A. "The Dark Continent of Literature: Autobiography." *Comparative Literature Studies* 5, no. 4 (December 1968): 421–54.

Showalter, Elaine. "Feminist Criticism in the Wilderness." *Critical Inquiry* 8, no. 2 (Winter 1981): 179–206.

Sibbald, Susan. *Memoirs of Susan Sibbald*. Ed. Francis Paget Hett. London: John Lane and Bodley Head, 1926.

Simcoe, Elizabeth. *The Diary of Mrs. John Graves Simcoe: Wife of the First Lieutenant-Governor of the Province of Upper Canada, 1792–6*. Ed. J. Ross Robertson. Toronto: William Briggs, 1911; Coles facsimile edition, 1973.

–. *Mrs. Simcoe's Diary*. Ed. Mary Quale Innis. Toronto: Macmillan, 1965.

Smith, Paul. *Discerning the Subject*. Foreword by John Mowitt. Minneapolis: University of Minnesota Press, 1988.

Smith, Sidonie. *A Poetics of Women's Autobiography: Marginalities and the Fictions of Self-Representation*. Bloomington and Indianapolis: Indiana University Press, 1987.

Sommer, Doris. "'Not Just a Personal Story': Women's *Testimonios* and the Plural Self." In *Life/Lines: Theorizing Women's Autobiography*, ed. Bella Brodzki and Celeste Schenck, 107–30. Ithaca and London: Cornell University Press, 1988.

Spacks, Patricia Meyer. *The Female Imagination*. New York: Knopf, 1972.

–. "Female Rhetorics." In *The Private Self: Theory and Practice of Women's Autobiography*, ed. Shari Benstock, 177–91. Chapel Hill and London: University of North Carolina Press, 1988.

–. "Reflecting Women." *Yale Review* 8, no. 63 (1973): 26–42.

–. "Selves in Hiding." In *Women's Autobiography: Essays in Criticism*, ed. Estelle Jelinek, 112–32. Bloomington and London: Indiana University Press, 1980

Spengemann, William. *The Forms of Autobiography: Episodes in the History of a Literary Genre*. New Haven and London: Yale University Press, 1980.

Stanton, Domna C. "Autogynography: Is the Subject Different?" In *The Female Autograph: Theory and Practice of Autobiography from the Tenth to the Twentieth Century*, ed. Domna C. Stanton, 3–20. Chicago: Chicago University Press, 1987.

Stewart, Frances. *Our Forest Home: Being Extracts from the Correspondence of the Late Frances Stewart*. Ed. E.S. Dunlap. Montreal: Gazette Printing and Publishing Co., 1902.

Thomas, Clara. "Afterword." In Anna Jameson, *Winter Studies and Summer Rambles in Canada*, 543–49. Toronto: McClelland and Stewart, 1990.

–. *Life and Work Enough: The Life of Anna Jameson*. Toronto: University of Toronto Press, 1967, 1978.

Thurston, John. "Rewriting *Roughing It*." In *Future Indicative: Literary Theory and Canadian Literature*, ed. John Moss, 195–204. Ottawa: University of Ottawa Press, 1987.

Todorov, Tzvetan. *Mikhail Bakhtin: The Dialogic Principle*. Trans. Wald Godzich. Minneapolis: University of Minnesota Press, 1984.

van Herk, Aritha. "Mapping as Metaphor." *Zeitschriftder Gesellschaft für Kanada-Studien*, ed. Kurt Jürgensen and Josef Niederehe.

– *Places Far from Ellesmere, A Geografictione: Explorations on Site*. Red Deer: Red Deer College Press, 1990.

Van Kleek, Edith Leona. *Our Trail North: A True Story of Pioneering in the Peace River Country of Northern Alberta*. Edmonton: Co-op Press, 1980.

Volosinov, V.N. *Freudianism: A Critical Sketch*. Ed. I.R. Titunik and Neal H. Bruss; trans. I.R. Titunik. Bloomington and Indianapolis: Indiana University Press, 1987.   ·

Watson, Julia. "Shadowed Presence: Modern Women's Writers' Autobiographies and the Other." In *Studies in Autobiography*, ed. James Olney, 180–9. New York and Oxford: Oxford University Press, 1988.

Welter, Barbara. "The Cult of True Womanhood: 1820–1860." *American Quarterly* 18 (1966): 151–74.

Williamson, Janice. "Speaking In and Of Each Other" (an interview with Marlatt, Daphne, and Betsy Warland). *Fuse* 8, no. 5 (February–March 1985): 25–9.

Wolf, Christa. *Cassandra, A Novel and Four Essays*. New York: Farrar, Straus & Giroux, 1984.

Yaeger, Patricia. *Honey-Mad Women: Emancipatory Strategies in Women's Writing*. New York: Columbia University Press, 1988.

Index

Adams, Henry, 37, 46
Adams, Timothy Dow: telling lies in autobiography, 20
Allison, Susan: the autobiographer as historian, poet, and fiction writer, 76–80
Anger, expression of: in autobiography, 163
Appropriation, of women's creative energy, 149; by fathers, 144
Arachne, 35. *See also* Arachnology
Arachnology, female, 60. *See also* Miller; Black
Archaeology: and history, 148; and mapping, 149; Maynard, 155; of women's subjectivity, 185
Archives, as a source for alternate female history and "unliterary" texts, 193
Arnason, David: as editor of Livesay, 150–1
Augustine, Saint: as autobiographer in compar-

ison with Johnston, 64, 65, 69, 137; and Salverson, 171–2
Autobiography: alternate feminist terms for, 14–15; as alternative to traditional genres, 70; the ambivalent ending of, in contemporary accounts, 201; and "apologia," as used by women, 138; the avoidance of, as a term, 197; Canadian women's, 207; the comparative excellence of Salverson's, 171; and the contrast between "being" and "becoming," 62–3; and the contrast between experiential "truth" and cultural roles, 116–17; definition of, 14–15; as different from memoir, 24; and the effect of critiques of, on writer's stance, 155; and the effect of, on prose genres, 175; and figure and ground, 24;

humanist view of, 4; male-centred theory of, 14; and matriarchal world-view, 120; as a necessary political and cultural act for women, 192; pioneer, 33; post-structuralist view of, 14; serial, 157; silence at the centre of, 157; Spengemann's types of, 64; the stigma of amateurism in, 27, 192; strategies of inscription in, 103; as synonymous with spiritual quest and repression of body, 177; therapeutic nature of, 25; as translation of environment through self, 49; as vignettes/portraits, in Carr, 161; women's use of, in eighteenth and nineteenth centuries, 19–20; and writing the self, 7
Autograph, 14
Autogynography, 14